Dinosaur Safari Guide
Tracking North America's Prehistoric Past

Dinosaur Safari Guide
Tracking North America's Prehistoric Past

*Complete descriptions and directions for over 170
dinosaur (and other prehistoric creature) sites,
museums, fossil exhibits, tracksites, and parks
in the United States and Canada*

Vincenzo Costa

Voyageur Press

A NOTE TO READERS:

All the information contained in *The Dinosaur Safari Guide: Tracking North America's Prehistoric Past* was verified just prior to publication. However, because museums, sites, and exhibits control their own fees, hours, features, and all the other data listed herein, neither the author nor the publisher is responsible for the complete accuracy of the information in this guide. All dinosaur hunters should contact the museums, sites, and exhibits before they finalize plans for their visits. Maps contained in this book are meant to be general locators; please consult a highway or city map for complete road details.

Readers are also advised to *visit* the museums, sites, and exhibits mentioned in *The Dinosaur Safari Guide: Tracking North America's Prehistoric Past!* And, if you wish to inform the publisher of any corrections, please write to Voyageur Press at the address below.

Printed in Canada
94 95 96 97 98 5 4 3 2 1

Library of Congress Cataloging-in-Publication Data
Costa, Vincenzo. 1956–
    Dinosaur safari guide : tracking North America's prehistoric past / by Vincenzo Costa.
        p. cm.
    Includes bibliographical references, index.
    ISBN 0-89658-231-0
    1. Dinosaurs—United States—Guidebooks. 2. Dinosaurs—Canada—Guidebooks.
    3. Geological museums—United States—Guidebooks. 4. Geological museums—
    Canada—Guidebooks. I. Title.
    QE862.D5C73 1994
    567.9'1'097—dc20   93–21362
                                        CIP

Published by **Voyageur Press, Inc.**
P.O. Box 338, 123 North Second Street, Stillwater, MN 55082 U.S.A.
From Minnesota and Canada 612-430-2210 • Toll-free 800-888-9653

Distributed in Canada by **Raincoast Books**
112 East Third Avenue, Vancouver, B.C. V5T 1C8

Voyageur Press books are also available at discounts for quantities for educational, fundraising, premium, or sales-promotion use. For details contact our marketing department. Please write or call for our free catalog of natural history publications.

Dedication
To Juliette Delrieu Henrie

Acknowledgments

I would like to thank Kacie Balfe, Claudette Bradley, Terri Davis, Hillary Gillanders, Randy Louge, Linda Stoffer, and Cynthia Xaiz for coming with me on my dinosaur safaris. I would like to thank Hillary Gillanders, Stuart McHugh, Rick Montague, Sophia Wang, Claudette Bradley, Sue Ann Bilbey, and John Laferriere for reviewing the manuscript. I would also like to thank Yvonne Costa for helping me assemble the maps in this book. A special thanks to Hillary Gillanders, who coached me on my English grammar. Finally, a special thanks to all the museums that made this guide possible by providing information and having a dinosaur exhibit in the first place.

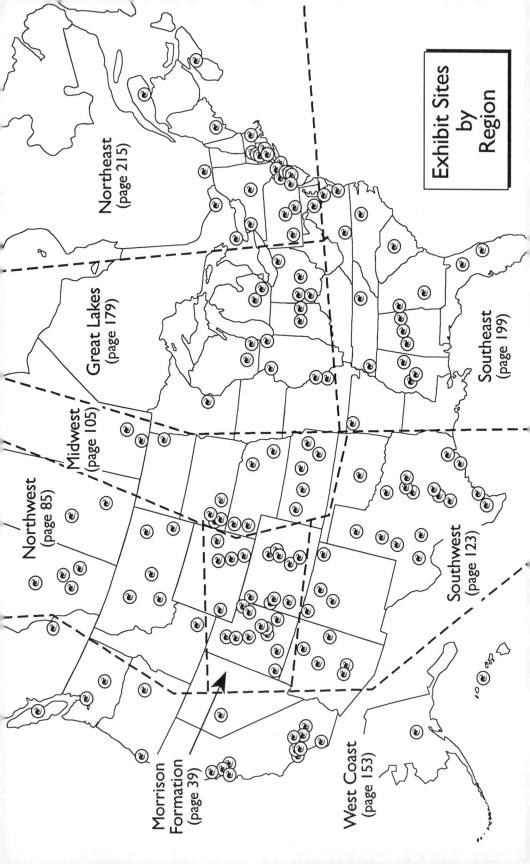

Exhibit Sites
by
Region

Northeast
(page 215)

Great Lakes
(page 179)

Midwest
(page 105)

Northwest
(page 85)

Southeast
(page 199)

Southwest
(page 123)

Morrison
Formation
(page 39)

West Coast
(page 153)

Contents

2. The Northwest   85

3. The Midwest   105

4. The Southwest   123

12

5. The West Coast   153

6. The Great Lakes Region   179

7. The Southeast   199

8. The Northeast   215

How to Plan Your Dinosaur Safari

Welcome to *Dinosaur Safari Guide: Tracking North America's Prehistoric Past*. Here, you'll find everything you need to find exhibits featuring dinosaurs and other prehistoric animals from the Mesozoic Era—the Age of Dinosaurs. This book also contains descriptions of many fascinating paleontological exhibits from the Paleozoic (before dinosaurs) and Cenozoic (after dinosaurs) eras.

Exhibits are continually changing. Typically, they are expanding and improving, although some close down. The information contained in this book is as up-to-date as possible. Exhibits may change their fees, hours, features, and more. Phone numbers and addresses are included with each description, and experienced dinosaur (and other prehistoric creature) hunters know to contact the site or exhibit before finalizing plans. Because this guide's maps give you general directions and are not exactly to scale, bring highway and city maps for complete road details.

The Organization

Dinosaur Safari Guide: Tracking North America's Prehistoric Past features more than 170 exhibits and sites in both the United States and in Canada, making it the most comprehensive dinosaur- and prehistoric-animal-site guide you can find. The book is organized geographically, but you will also find an alphabetical index at the back of the book in case you are looking for a specific site.

Each site description lists what you need to know to plan your visit. (Note opposite page, which shows the layout.)

1.1 College of Eastern Utah Prehistoric Museum
Price, UT

Price, Utah, makes up the southwestern corner of the Dinosaur Triangle, and the College of Eastern Utah (CEU) Prehistoric Museum has an excellent display of dinosaurs.

The museum is the result of a very successful community effort. In 1961, local geologist Don Burge and his friends bought an Allosaurus skull for $50. They thought, "Why stop with a skull when we can have the whole dinosaur!" So $50 and $500 at a time they bought "Al" the Allosaurus—bone by bone—from the nearby Cleveland-Lloyd Dinosaur Quarry. When there was no other way to transport the hugedinosaur bones, "Al" rode into Price on a beer truck. Soon the entire community wanted to help build a museum to display the dinosaurs discovered so close to their town.

Thirty years later the museum operates five quarries. In 1991, scientists from the CEU museum discovered an enormous relative of Velociraptor. This "Utahraptor" was 20 feet long and weighed about 1,000 pounds. Equipped with 12-inch claws it would leap into the air and kick its prey. Discovered near the Jurassic-Cretaceous border, "Utahraptor" is much older than Velociraptor or another of its relatives, Deinonychus.

Articulated Skeletons:
• Allosaurus, Camptosaurus, Camarasaurus, Prosaurolophus, Chasmosaurus, and Stegosaurus.

Exhibit Features:
• Cretaceous dinosaur tracks from nearby coal mines.
• Individual bones from several large apatosaurus.
• Bone dig for children.
• Full size upper-torso model Allosaurus and scale models of dinosaurs.

Hours:
    Tuesday–Saturday   10:00 a.m.–4:00 p.m.
    Summer hours (Memorial Weekend–Labor Day weekend):
        Monday–Saturday   10:00 a.m.–5:00 p.m.
        Sunday   Noon–5:00 p.m.
    Closed: Sundays, Mondays, Thanksgiving, Christmas, New Year's Day.
    Minimum time required to see exhibit: 1 hour

Entrance Fees:
    (Recommended donation)
    Adults $1.00
    Families $2.00

Location Address:
    College of Eastern Utah, Prehistoric Museum
    155 East Main, Price, UT 84501
    Telephone: (801)637-5060

Mailing Address:
    451 East 400 North, Price, UT 84501

Directions:
    Price is located 125 miles southeast of Salt Lake City. From Salt Lake City take I-15 south to Highway 6. Take either the 240 or 243 exit from Highway 6 and follow the signs to the museum. The museum is on the north side of the Price Municipal Building, on the corner of 200 East and Main Street in downtown Price.

Title: *Includes site name and its town and state or province.*

Description: *What to look for when you visit the site.*

Minimum time: *An estimate of how long you would want to spend at a site. Some exhibits have small but fascinating features that take a few minutes to visit. Others are considerably larger. If you're pressed for time, stop at the larger sites anyway; you can concentrate on what interests you most, and save the rest for the return safari.*

The Basics (Entrance Fees, Hours, Address, and Directions, and Nearby): *Includes days the sites are closed, phone numbers, general directions, nearby sites of interest, and more.*

If you are a U.S. traveler visiting Canadian sites, or vice versa, you will need to convert a few measurements. Use this table as your guide.

Conversion	Example
1 inch = 2.540 centimeters	5 in x 2.540 = 12.7 cm
1 centimeter = 0.394 inch	5 cm x 0.394 = 1.97 in
1 foot = 0.3048 meter	5 ft x 0.3048 = 1.524 m
1 meter = 3.281 feet	5 m x 3.281 = 16.405 ft
1 yard = 0.914 meter	5 yds x 0.914 = 4.57 m
1 meter = 1.094 yards	5 m x 1.094 = 5.47 yds
1 mile = 1.609 kilometers	5 miles x 1.609 = 8.045 km
1 kilometer = 0.621 mile	5 km x 0.621 = 3.105 miles
1 pound = 0.454 kilogram	5 lbs x 0.454 = 2.27 kg
1 kilogram = 2.205 pounds	5 kg x 2.205 = 11.025 lbs
1 U.S. ton = 907.18 kilograms	5 tons x 907.18 = 4,535.9 kg
1 U.S. ton = 0.90718 metric tons	5 tons x 0.90718 = 4.5359 metric tons

While you're at—or on your way to—the sites, get to know the dinosaurs and other prehistoric creatures by referring to the following pronunciation guide and introduction.

Now you're on your way!

Speak the Language

It is important to learn the native language before embarking on a journey to faraway places. Your dinosaur safari is no exception. I have provided you with a translation and pronunciation guide for many of the dinosaurs and other prehistoric animals listed in this guide. Place more emphasis on the italicized syllables. In no time at all you should be able to communicate with the natives.

Term	Phonetic Pronunciation	Translation
Abelisaurus	A *bell* eh *sore* us	Abel's Lizard
Alamosaurus	*Al* ah moe *sore* us	Alamo Lizard
Albertosaurus	Al *bur* toe *sore* us	Alberta Lizard
Allosaurus	*Al* o *sore* us	Strange Lizard
Altispinax	*Al* ti *spine* axe	High Spine
Ammosaurus	*Am* oh *sore* us	Sand Lizard
Anatosaurus	Ah *nat* o *sore* us	Duck Lizard
Anchiceratops	*Ain* key *sare* a tops	Near Horn Face

Name	Pronunciation	Meaning
Ankylosaurus	An *kyle* o *sore* us	Fused Lizard
Apatosaurus	A *pat* o *sore* us	Illusory Lizard
Archaeopteryx	Arc e *op* ter icks	Ancient Wing
Archosaurs	Arch o *sores*	Ruling Lizards
Aristosaurus	A *rist* o *sore* us	Best Lizard
Aristosuchus	A *rist* o *sue* cus	Best Crocodile
Arrhinoceratops	Ar *rine* o *sare* a tops	Without Nose Horn Face
Avaceratops	Ah va *sare* a tops	Ava's Horned Face
Avimimus	Ah vee *my* mus	Bird Mimic
Avisaurus	Ah vee *sore* us	Bird Lizard
Barapasaurus	Bah *rap* ah *sore* us	Big Leg Lizard
Barosaurus	*Bear* o *sore* us	Heavy Lizard
Betasuchus	Be ta *sue* cuss	B Crocodile
Brachiosaurus	Brak ee o *sore* us	Arm Lizard
Brontosaurus	*Brawn* toe *sore* us	Thunder Lizard (old name for Apatosaurus)
Caenagnathus	See nag *nay* thus	Recent Jaw
Camarasaurus	Cam are a *sore* us	Chamber Lizard
Camptosaurus	*Camp* toe *sore* us	Bent Lizard
Carnosauria	*Carn* o *sore* e ah	Flesh Eating Lizards
Carnosaurus	*Carn* o *sore* us	Flesh Eating Lizard
Ceratopsians	*Sare* a *tops* e yans	Horn Face Lizards
Ceratosaurus	Sare *at* o *sore* us	Horn Lizard
Cetiosauriscus	See tee o *sore* iss kus	Whale Lizard
Chasmosaurus	*Kaz* mo *sore* us	Space Lizard
Coelophysis	See low *phi* sis	Hollow Bag
Coelosaurus	See low *sore* us	Hollow Lizard
Compsognathus	*Comp* sog *nay* thus	Elegant Jaw
Compsosuchus	*Comp* sew *sue* kus	Elegant Crocodile
Corythosaurus	Co *rith* o *sore* us	Helmet Lizard
Daspletosaurus	Das *pleat* o *sore* us	Frightful Lizard
Deinocheirus	Die no *kie* rus	Terrible Hand
Deinonychus	Die *no* nike us	Terrible Claw
Denversaurus	Den ver *sore* us	Denver Lizard
Desmatosuchus	Des matt o *sue* kus	Bond Crocodile

Diceratops	Die *sare* a tops	Two-Horned Face
Dilophosaurus	Die *low* foe *sore* us	Two Crest Lizard
Dimetrodon	Die *met* ro don	Two Size Tooth
dinosaur	die no *sore*	Terrible Lizard
Diplodocus	Dip *lah* doe kus	Double Beam
Dromaeosaurus	*Droe* me ah *sore* us	Swift Lizard
Dromiceiomimus	Dro *mice* e o *mime* us	Emu Mimic
Edaphosaurus	Ed *af* o *sore* us	Earth Lizard
Edmontosaurus	Ed *mon* toe *sore* us	Edmonton Lizard
Eucentrosaurus	You *sent* ro *sore* us	Spike Lizard
Euoplocephalus	*You* o ploe *sef* a lus	Well Armored Head
Hadrosaurus	*Had* row *sore* us	Haddonfield Lizard
Hypselosaurus	*Hip* sel o *sore* us	High Lizard
Hypsilophodon	*Hip* sel *o* foe don	High Ridge Tooth
Ichthyosaurus	Ik thee o *sore* us	Fish Lizard
Iguanodon	Ig *wan* o don	Iguana Tooth
Kentrosaurus	Ken trow *sore* us	Spike Lizard
Kritosaurus	Cry toe *sore* us	Noble Lizard
Lambeosaurus	*Lamb* e o *sore* us	Lambe's Lizard
Maiasaura	My ah *sore* uh	Mother Lizard
Mamenchisaurus	Maw *men* chee *sore* us	Mamenchi Lizard
Megalosaurus	*Meg* a low *sore* us	Giant Lizard
Monoclonius	Mon o *clone* e us	One Horned
Montanoceratops	Mon *tan* uh *sare* uh tops	Horned Face of Montana
Mosasaurus	*Moz* ah *sore* us	Meuse Lizard
Nanosaurus	*Nan* o *sore* us	Dwarf Lizard
Nanotyrannus	*Nan* o tie *ran* us	Tiny Tyrant
Ornithischia	Orn ith *iss* key ya	Bird Hip
Ornitholestes	Orn ith o *les* tease	Bird Robber
Ornithomimus	Orn ith o *mime* us	Bird Mimic
ornithopod	or *nith* o pod	Bird Foot
Oviraptor	O vee *rap* tor	Egg Thief
Pachyrhinosaurus	*Pack* e *rye* no *sore* us	Thick Nose Lizard
Panoplosaurus	Pan op low *sore* us	Full Armor Lizard
Parasaurolophus	*Pair* ah *sore* o low fus	Beside Lizard Crest
Pentaceratops	Pen tah *sare* a tops	Five Horn Face
Phobosuchus	Foe boe *sue* kus	Fear Crocodile
Phytosaurus	*phi* toe *sore* us	Plant Lizard
Platecarpus	*Play* teh *car* pus	Flat Wrist
Plateosaurus	*Play* te o *sore* us	Flat Lizard

Plesiosaurus	*Plee* see o *sore* us	Near Lizard
Procompsognathus	Pro *comp* sog *nay* thus	Before Elegant Jaw
Prosaurolophus	*Pro* sore *ol* uh fuss	Before Lizard Crest
Prosauropoda	Pro *sore* o pod ah	Before Lizard Foot
Protoceratops	Pro toe *sare* a tops	First Horn Face
Psittacosaurus	Sit a coe *sore* us	Parrot Lizard
Pteranodon	Teh ran o don	Winged and Toothless
Pterosauria	Tare o sore e ah	Wing Lizard
Quetzalcoatlus	Kwet sel co at lus	Aztec God
Rhamphorhynchus	Ram fo rink us	Bill Snout
Rutiodon	Roo tee o don	Wrinkle Tooth
Saurischia	Sore iss key ya	Lizard Hip
Saurolophus	Sore o low fuss	Lizard Crest
sauropod	sore o pod	Lizard Foot
Saurornitholestes	Sore or nith o les tees	Lizard Stealing Bird
Scelidosaurus	Skel e doe sore us	Rib Lizard
Scolosaurus	Skoal o sore us	Thorn Lizard
Scutellosaurus	Skew tell o sore us	Little Shield Lizard
Seismosaurus	Size moe sore us	Earth-shaking Lizard
Stegoceras	Steg ah sare as	Roof Head
Stegosaurus	Steg o sore us	Roof Lizard
Stenonychosaurus	Stee non ike o sore us	Narrow Clawed Lizard (old name for *Troodon*)
Struthiomimus	Strooth e o mime us	Ostrich Mimic
Styracosaurus	Sty rack o sore us	Spiked Lizard
Supersaurus	Soo per sore us	Super Lizard
Syntarsus	Sin tar sus	Together Flat of the Foot
Tarbosaurus	Tar bo sore us	Fear Lizard
Tenontosaurus	Tee non toe sore us	Tendon Lizard
Thecodontia	Thee coe dont e ah	Socket Tooth
therapsid	thare ap sid	Wild Beast Arch
theropod	thare o pod	Wild Beast Foot
Torosaurus	Tor o sore us	Bull Lizard
Triceratops	Try sare a tops	Three Horn Face
Troodon	Troe o don	Wounding Tooth
Typothorax	Tie poe thor axe	Impression Breast
Tyrannosaurus rex	Tie ran o sore us rex	Tyrant Lizard King
Ultrasaurus	Ul truh sore us	Ultra Lizard
Utahraptor	You tah rap tor	Utah Thief
Velociraptor	Ve los e rap tor	Fast Thief

Introduction

You can read about dinosaurs in books, and you can see them in the movies, but nothing compares to staring eye to eye with a forty-foot *Tyrannosaurus rex* skeleton. Shivers run up your spine when you walk in the footsteps of giant flesh-eating prehistoric animals. Dinosaurs leap from imagination to reality when you visit the bone quarries in the "Dinosaur Triangle," southeast of Salt Lake City, Utah.

Although the last dinosaur roamed across North America sixty-five million years ago, footprints, fossils, and bones remain scattered across the continent. *The Dinosaur Safari Guide* provides everything you need to know so that *you* can discover these mysterious and fantastic creatures.

What Were the Dinosaurs?

Dinosaurs! The name conjures up images of a vanished world filled with fantastic creatures. Almost everything we know about dinosaurs is shrouded with mystery. What was this ancient world really like? How did it get that way? Where did it go? Each of the exhibits, sites, and museums in *The Dinosaur Safari Guide* will help you piece together this magnificent puzzle. To get you started on your journey—so that you have an idea of what you'll find as you track North America's dinosaurs—we must travel to the beginning of time, even billions of years before the Mesozoic Era, taking our clues from prehistoric rocks and fossils and modern-day theories.

Setting the Stage for Dinosaurs
The Origin of the Universe, and the Formation of Earth
According to the Big Bang Theory of the origin of the universe, the beginning of time occurred approximately fifteen billion years ago (BYA). Initially the universe was infinitesimally small and infinitely hot. The universe began to expand, and the expansion caused the universe to cool. Each time the universe doubled in size, its temperature was cut in half.

Within a second of the moment the universe began to expand its temperature had dropped to 10,000,000,000 degrees, which was still too hot to allow the formation of anything more complex than simple sub-atomic particles. However, within a few minutes, the ex-panding universe had cooled enough to al-low the formation of simple elements like hydrogen and helium. The universe contin-ued to grow larger and cooler, which allowed increasingly larger at-oms to form. Eventually the universe cooled enough to allow so-lar systems and planets to form. The universe continues to expand today, just as it has for fifteen billion years.

The earth coa-lesced from the cloud of hot matter that orbited our sun 4.8 to 4.4 BYA. The newly formed earth was a ball of hot, molten lava. Gravity caused the denser elements to move to the center of the earth while the lighter ele-ments moved to the surface. The earth was still too hot to hold an atmosphere. Without a protective atmo-sphere, the earth was continually bombarded by comets and mete-orites. As time passed, the surface of the earth cooled enough to allow a relatively thin layer of solid rock to form on the surface. The old-est known rocks that we find today were formed 4.1 to 4.2 BYA, their age deter-mined by radioactive dating.

The earth's thin layer of solid rock, called the crust, is broken up into pieces called plates. The plates float on top of the mantle, which surrounds the core of the earth. The crust supports both the continents and the oceans. The plates have continuously moved since their formation, causing the continents to separate. You might have noticed that the continents we see on a modern world map fit together like the pieces of a jigsaw puzzle: northwest Africa fits into North America's southeastern coast-line, southwest Africa fits into South America, and so forth. When the first dinosaurs appeared on earth 225 million years ago (MYA), all the continents were joined into one great super-continent, which we now call Pangaea. By the end of the Age of Dinosaurs sixty-five MYA, Pangaea had broken up into the separate continents we know today.

It was around four BYA when the earth's surface cooled enough to allow liquid water to form. Soon after, the earth's first oceans appeared. Yet the earth remained barren and devoid of life. The earth's first atmosphere also formed around this time, although this early atmosphere was far different from the one we have today. The air was toxic; you would quickly die if you breathed it. There was no free oxygen; instead, this atmosphere consisted of gases like methane, ammonia, and hydrogen.

Stanley L. Miller performed an interesting experiment in 1953. He subjected a mixture of methane, ammonia, and hydrogen to an electrical discharge, producing a reddish brown mixture of organic molecules. These molecules included the amino acids, which are the building blocks of life. In the real world billions of years ago, the electrical discharge could have been caused by lightning from a primeval storm. Miller's experiment proved that organic compounds could be formed in an inorganic world similar to what we believe the early earth was like.

Although the early earth was devoid of life, the ocean was a soup of complex organic molecules. The first life on earth began somewhere in this organic soup 3.5 to 3.7 BYA. One of the combinations of atoms formed a very special molecule, a "replicator" molecule that made copies of itself from the atoms and molecules that surrounded it. Soon these replicator molecules filled the sea.

Sometimes an error in replication would occur, resulting in a new type of replicator. These errors in replication are called mutations. Most mutations would cause the new replicator to stop replicating and die. But on rare occasions, the "error" improved the replicator's ability to reproduce itself. Replicators that were more effective at replication became more common, and those that were less effective became less common. This process of continual improvement was repeated over and over again. With time, it led to the development of organisms that are increasingly more effective at reproduction. (This process of evolution, discovered by Charles Darwin in 1859, is on display at The Royal Ontario Museum in Toronto, the Royal Tyrrell Museum in Drumheller, the Smithsonian Museum in Washington, D.C., and the San Francisco Academy of Sciences, among other sites.)

Life probably began at some specific location in the primeval ocean, a vast place that offers many different environments, some warm and others cold, some rich in food and others not. Replicators with specific mutations adapted best to specific locations. When environments changed, organisms would adapt to the new environment. The wide variety of continuously changing habitats is responsible for the great diversity in life through the ages, and affected life forms such as the dinosaurs in ways we may never understand.

So How Do We Know All This?

Our knowledge of ancient organisms comes from the study of fossils. The earliest remains of life are bacteria found as fossils in rocks 3.5 billion years old. Fossils may be as magnificent as an entire *Tyrannosaurus rex* skeleton or as subtle as the impression of a leaf in stone. Sometimes entire nests of dinosaurs are discovered, complete with eggs and babies. Traps like the La Brea Tar Pits in California lure animals to their death and then preserve them in the sticky tar. Sometimes insects are trapped in the sap of trees, and in time, the sap turns to amber, perfectly preserving the insect. Dinosaurs sometimes left their footprints in the mud around lakes. Eventually, the mud hardened and turned to stone. (Today, we can see such footprints at Dinosaur State Park in Rocky Hill, Connecticut.)

For the skeleton of an entire dinosaur to be preserved, it must have been covered by sediment shortly after the animal's death. This was most likely to happen in an ancient lakebed, riverbed, or ocean floor. Most animals occasionally cross streams and rivers, particularly during migrations, and occasionally one will die along the riverbank. Other possibilities were that a dinosaur might have been trapped by a spring flood and the body carried to the bottom of a riverbed. Once the dead dinosaur sank to the bottom, its body was covered by sediment. Water percolating through the sediment carried minerals to penetrate and preserve the bone. Minerals may have either filled in all the empty spaces in the bone (permineralization) or completely replaced the bone (petrifaction). With luck, erosion will someday expose the fossil, allowing it to be discovered.

South Dakota's Badlands, with their rapidly eroding cliffs of sedimentary rock, is a good place to look for fossils. Dinosaur Provincial Park in Alberta is another excellent site. Entire herds of dinosaurs are found here, and some of the trails are literally paved with dinosaur bone. (If you know a junior paleontologist who would like to spend the afternoon prospecting for dinosaur bones you might try the Fort Worth Museum of Science and History in Texas. If you want to dig up real dinosaur bones you should contact the Dinamation International Society. They accept volunteers for excavations that take place all over the world.)

Normally, only the hard parts of animals—shells, bones, and teeth—fossilize. However, Charles Sternberg and his sons discovered a duckbilled dino-

Formation of earth & moon
c. 4.5 BYA

Oldest known rocks
c. 3.8 BYA

Oldest known fossils
c. 3.2 BYA

saur (or hadrosaur) complete with fossilized skin near Lusk, Wyoming. This dinosaur "mummy" may be seen at the American Museum of Natural History in New York.

The Age of Dinosaurs

The history of the earth is divided into three eons. The most recent is the Phanerozoic Eon (540 MYA to the present), which is divided into three eras: the Paleozoic (the Age of Ancient Life), the Mesozoic (the Age of Middle Life, also called the Age of Reptiles, of which a large part is called the Age of Dinosaurs), and the Cenozoic (the Age of Modern Life). The Mesozoic is divided into three periods: the Triassic, the Jurassic, and the Cretaceous.

Just as you need maps when you travel across the roads of North America, you will need a geological time scale to guide you as you travel back in time. The geological time scale is your road map through time.

The Triassic Period—Enter the Dinosaurs

The Triassic Period lasted from 245 to 208 million years ago (MYA). The name comes from the word *trias*, due to the threefold nature of Triassic-age rocks in Europe. During the Triassic Period, all the continents were joined in one massive continent, Pangaea. The first dinosaurs—who appeared in the Triassic Period—could walk from New York to London, that is, from one present-day site to the other. Consequently, the Triassic dinosaurs found in England are similar to the ones found in North America.

Fossils tell us about the dinosaurs' world. Forests of giant conifer trees extended throughout much of Pangaea. These trees were similar to today's monkey puzzle and Norfolk Island pine, both species of *Araucaria*. The remains of one of these forests is at the Petrified Forest National Park in Arizona. The west coast of North America was under the ocean during the Triassic Period. What is now a mountain range in Nevada was once a sea home to fifty-six-foot-long ichthyosaurs, which were not dinosaurs but dolphin-shaped marine reptiles. The fossil remains of these enormous sea creatures may be seen at the Berlin-Ichthyosaur State Park in Austin, Nevada.

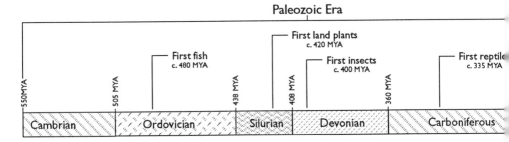

Paleozoic Era

First land plants
c. 420 MYA

First fish
c. 480 MYA

First insects
c. 400 MYA

First reptile
c. 335 MYA

550 MYA

505 MYA

438 MYA

408 MYA

360 MYA

Cambrian   Ordovician   Silurian   Devonian   Carboniferous

The Triassic Period was a very exciting time in the history of life. The therapsid reptiles, which had dominated the Permian Period (just prior to the Triassic), evolved into true mammals during the Triassic. A new group of reptiles, the archosaurs, also appeared during the Triassic.

The archosaurs diverged into two distinct groups that differ in the construction of their ankles and wrist joints. One group became the crocodiles and phytosaurs. They were cold blooded, walked on all fours (were quadrupedal), and lived a low metabolic life. The other group, the Ornithodira, were much more active; they walked on two legs (were bipedal), and some could even fly. They evolved into birds, dinosaurs, and pterodactyls.

At the Ghost Ranch Quarry in New Mexico, a mass graveyard of the Triassic dinosaur *Coelophysis* was discovered. Typical of the first dinosaurs, *Coelophysis* was slender, agile, and fast. *Coelophysis* also had a mouth filled with dangerously sharp teeth.

At the beginning of the Triassic, the ancestors of the mammals dominated the world. By the beginning of the Jurassic, the middle period of the Mesozoic, dinosaurs ruled the earth and pterodactyls ruled the skies. Mammals were relegated to a minor role in the drama of Mesozoic life.

The Jurassic Period

The Jurassic Period, extending from the end of the Triassic (208 MYA) to the beginning of the Cretaceous (144 MYA), is named for the Jura Mountains in Europe, where rocks of this age were first studied. During the Jurassic, the supercontinent Pangaea began to split apart. Tectonic forces separated Europe from North America and formed the Atlantic Ocean. A shallow sea separated Europe from Asia, and the west coast of North America remained at the bottom of the ocean.

The Jurassic is sometimes called the "Age of Cycads." Cycads are plants that look like palms, but are more closely related to conifers. Cycads still exist today and make excellent house plants; they survive outdoors in temperate climates and are a common site in Balboa Park near the San Diego Museum of Natural History. The conifers, particularly *Araucaria*, continued to be abun-

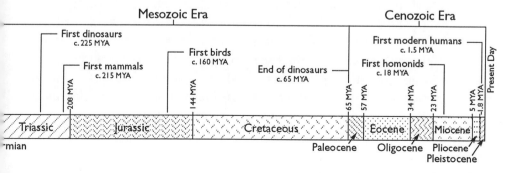

28 28

dant in the Jurassic. There were also dense forests of tree ferns. In Golden Gate Park near the San Francisco Academy of Sciences are groves of giant tree ferns. Exactly which plants the dinosaurs ate is still unknown but ferns, cycads, and conifers are the most likely guesses.

This was an age of giants. The great sauropod dinosaurs flourished during the Jurassic. Sauropods adapted to eating the tops of trees; some sauropods could eat the tops of trees forty-five feet in the air!

The Cretaceous Period

The final geological period in "The Age of Dinosaurs" is the Cretaceous. The word *Cretaceous* is derived from the Latin word *creta* meaning "chalk" because rocks of the Cretaceous Period were first studied along the white chalk cliffs of England. The Cretaceous Period extends from the end of the Jurassic (144 MYA) until the end of the Mesozoic Era (65 MYA).

During the Cretaceous, a vast body of water called the Western Interior Seaway extended from northern Canada to the Gulf of Mexico. Most of the southern states were also under water. (The University of Kansas Museum of Natural History in Lawrence, Kansas, showcases numerous marine fossils from this age.) The seaway separated the east coast of North America from the Rocky Mountain states. North America was separated from South America and Europe during the Cretaceous, but was connected to Asia by way of Alaska.

The first angiosperms (flowering plants) appeared during the early Cretaceous, and new kinds of dinosaurs adapted to the new types of plants.

What is a Dinosaur?

Through the years, excavations and accidental discoveries unearthed mysterious formations that looked like bones, but it wasn't until the spring of 1822 that Mary Ann Mantell discovered the first fossils that were later identified as a dinosaur. The creature was named *Iguanodon* because the teeth resembled those of an iguana. Soon other specimens were discovered, and the term *dinosaur*, meaning "terrible lizard," was coined by Sir Richard Owen in 1841.

The classification of dinosaurs as reptiles is based on the construction of the animals' skulls and teeth. The term *reptile* cannot be rigorously defined, but refers to a catch-all class that includes all amniotes (vertebrates that lay eggs with shells) except for those with feathers or fur (birds and mammals) but includes pterodactyls (although pterodactyls had fur).

Surprisingly, birds are the closest living relatives to dinosaurs. Based on recent discoveries, many prominent paleontologists argue that dinosaurs and birds should be grouped together, separate from reptiles. *Archaeopteryx*, the oldest bird ever discovered, is very similar to a small dinosaur. So, when you think of dinosaurs, think of birds—birds without wings, birds with the heads and tails of crocodiles.

A Quick Mention of Some Dinosaurs

Many textbooks will tell you that dinosaurs belong to the kingdom Animalia, the phylum Chordata, and to the class Reptilia. However, in order to show closer degrees of relationships, the current trend is to base animal groupings on evolutionary trends and to avoid rigid adherence to Linnaean categories, which may be outdated especially as far as dinosaurs are concerned. In many ways, dinosaurs were very different from the kinds of reptiles that live today. Newer taxonomic theories suggest that dinosaurs and pterosaurs evolved from the archosaurs, a major group of reptiles, into a group known as the Ornithodira. Most paleontologists believe that birds were the direct descendants of dinosaurs. Crocodiles were not directly related to the Ornithodira and evolved from a separate group of archosaurs. The newer groupings classify dinosaurs in this way: All belong to the superorder Dinosauria. They are then grouped into two orders, the Saurischia and the Ornithiscia, depending on the shape of the hip. (*The Dinosaur Society Dinosaur Encyclopedia* lists nearly all of the known dinosaurs, over six hundred of them.)

SAURISCHIA

The Saurischia, dinosaurs whose hips superficially resembled those of lizards, evolved along two separate paths, the Theropoda and Sauropoda. The theropods kept the meat-eating ways of their ancestors. Paleontologists believe that birds evolved from theropod dinosaurs. The sauropods ate plants and grew to become the largest creatures to ever walk the earth.

A few of the saurischians are described below, but you'll want to visit the dinosaur exhibits to learn about all of them.

Theropoda

The theropods include the ferocious meat-eating dinosaurs, both large and small, such as *Tyrannosaurus rex*. These dinosaurs had large jaws with teeth serrated like steak knifes. But not all the theropods were ferocious. Many were no bigger than an ostrich, and *Compsognathus* was no bigger than a chicken.

The Theropoda include dinosaurs in such infraorders as the Tetanurae, which in turn includes the Tyrannosauridae, Allosauridae, and Dromeosauridae. The Ceratosauridae dinosaurs belong to the infraorder Ceratosauria.

Tyrannosauridae. *Tyrannosaurus rex*, the most famous member of the family Tyrannosauridae, may have weighed ten thousand pounds and had jaws that could take a six-foot bite with teeth that were half a foot long. *Tyrannosaurus rex* had an earlier relative called *Albertosaurus*, who was similar to *Tyrannosaurus* but weighed less and was more graceful. Both lived during the Late Cretaceous Period.

Allosauridae. The most common dinosaur skeleton found in museums is *Allosaurus*, of the family Allosauridae. Most of these skeletons come from the Cleveland-Lloyd Quarry near Price, Utah.

Seventy-five million years before *Tyrannosaurus* caught his first meal, *Allosaurus* was North America's top carnivore. *Allosaurus* was king of the late Jurassic. This dinosaur had long arms with sickle-shaped claws and jaws filled with sharp teeth. Allosaurus grew to thirty-five feet in length and weighed from three thousand to seven thousand pounds.

Dromeosauridae. The family Dromeosauridae, sometimes called "the raptors," includes some of the most ferocious flesh eaters on earth. These intelligent dinosaurs hunted in packs and were armed with wicked claws on their hands and feet. *Velociraptor* was discovered in the Gobi Desert of Mongolia by an expedition headed by the famous adventurer Roy Chapman Anderson of the American Museum of Natural History. *Velociraptor* weighed only seventy to 150 pounds and was about six to ten feet in length. The expedition also discovered complete nests with eggs of a small ceratopsian dinosaur, *Protoceratops* (from the order Ornithischia). Fossils of *Velociraptor* and *Protoceratops* were discovered locked in a fight to the death.

In 1991, scientists from the College of Eastern Utah were working with Dinamation scientist Jim Kirkland. Together they discovered an enormous raptor near Price, Utah. Named *Utahraptor*, this dinosaur was twenty feet long and weighed around one thousand pounds. Equipped with twelve-inch claws, *Utahraptor* would leap into the air and kick its prey to shreds.

Ceratosauridae. The Ceratosauridae were the most common theropod dinosaurs during the late Triassic and early Jurassic. The ceratosaurs include *Coelophysis*, a very slim dinosaur that was approximately twelve feet in length, and *Dilophosaurus*. *Dilophosaurus* had a bony crest on its snout, which males could have used when they fought over females. Although *Dilophosaurus* was discovered in Arizona, footprints of what is believed to be *Dilophosaurus* are found throughout North America. Some of the best *Dilophosaurus* footprints may be seen at Dinosaur State Park in Rocky Hill, Connecticut.

Sauropoda

The sauropods were giant plant-eating dinosaurs characterized by their long necks and small skulls. They had four massive legs to support their great bulk. They lived from the early Jurassic Period until the end of the Cretaceous. The largest sauropods lived during the Jurassic.

Supersaurus, Ultrasaurus, Seismosaurus, and *Brachiosaurus* are the biggest of the sauropods. These dinosaurs weighed eighty tons and grew to a length of eighty to 140 feet. A few of them could fill a football stadium. In fact, the catacombs beneath the Brigham Young University football stadium in Utah are filled with giant sauropods and other dinosaurs.

The sauropods also include favorites like *Barosaurus* (eighty-foot length, twenty-five tons), *Diplodocus* (eighty-five-foot length, thirteen tons), *Camarasaurus* (sixty-foot length, thirty tons), and *Apatosaurus* (seventy-five-foot length, thirty-four tons). *Apatosaurus* is commonly called *Brontosaurus*.

The sauropods are commonly portrayed as swamp-dwelling animals, but nothing could be further from the truth. Sauropods preferred dry land and fed on the tops of trees like giraffes. However, they were big and bulky like elephants. While some sauropods had whiplike tails and large thumb claws, their main protection was their enormous size.

Many sauropod reconstructions portray them as sluggish animals, dragging their long tails on the ground. However, when you visit the trackways at Moab, Utah, and Glen Rose, Texas, you will see that sauropods did not drag their tails on the ground but proudly held their tails out straight.

Visit the dinosaur exhibits to learn about the rest of the sauropods, especially the Carnegie Museum of Natural History in Pittsburgh, Pennsylvania, which has complete skeletons of *Apatosaurus, Diplodocus,* and *Camarasaurus.*

ORNITHISCHIA

The ornithischians were dinosaurs whose hips superficially resembled those of birds. All ornithiscians were plant eaters. They include many well-known dinosaurs like *Stegosaurus, Triceratops,* and the duckbills (hadrosaurs). The Ornithischia were particularly dominant during the Cretaceous, which was when flowering plants appeared. The ornithischians include the Stegosauria, Ankylosauria, and Ceratopsia, and ornithopods.

Visit the dinosaur exhibits to learn about the many ornithischian dinosaurs not listed here, especially the Royal Tyrrell Museum in Drumheller, Alberta, and the Royal Ontario Museum in Toronto, Ontario.

Stegosauria. *Stegosaurus* (the most famous of the Stegosauria) is known for the unusual upright plates on its back and the spikes on the end of its tail. The placement and purpose of the plates has baffled scientist for over a hundred years. In 1992, a *Stegosaurus* was uncovered at the Garden Park Fossil Area near Canon City, Colorado, with the plates still in place and staggered, answering the question of location. However, the purpose of the plates is still subject to a heated debate.

One suggestion is that the plates were used for cooling. Others feel they were used for sexual display similar to a peacock's feathers. Certainly the thick bony plates provided a measure of protection against predators. The plates could have been covered with a layer of horn. Perhaps they could have been wiggled and moved as an active defense system. *Kentrosaurus* (who was discovered in Africa and is also in the Stegosauria) had large spikes where *Stegosaurus* had plates. The plates and spikes probably evolved from a common ancestor and served the same purpose: defense.

Stegosaurus weighed about four thousand to seven thousand pounds and grew to a length of twenty-five feet. Although *Stegosaurus* was primarily a quadruped, it could rise up on its hind legs to eat the tops of trees. The *Stegosaurus* skeleton at the Dinosaur Valley Museum in Grand Junction, Colorado, is mounted rearing up on its hind legs.

Ankylosauria. The Ankylosauria were the armored tanks of the Mesozoic Era. The largest grew to a length of twenty-five to thirty feet. The Ankylosauria is divided into two groups: the ankylosaurids (animals with wide heads and clubbed tails), which includes the genus *Ankylosaurus* and others, and the nodosaurids (animals with small heads and pointed tails), including *Nodosaurus, Edmontonia,* and others. While all the ankylosaurs lived during the Cretaceous, some nodosaurs are known from the Jurassic.

Eating one of these Mesozoic tanks was not an easy thing to do. They had bony plates covering their backs and frills of spikes protecting their sides. The head was thick bone as well. The ankylosaurids sported a bony club at the end of the tail to ward off predators. Ankylosauria reconstructions may be seen at the Calgary Zoo's Prehistoric Park and at the Royal Tyrrell Museum in Alberta. The ankylosaur model at the Dinosaur Park in Ogden, Utah, is appropriately displayed in the sandbox. Fossils of entire families of ankylosaurs have been found in the Gobi Desert of Mongolia.

Ceratopsia. Ceratopsians are the horned dinosaurs. During the Late Cretaceous 50 to 75 percent of the known dinosaurs were ceratopsians. The ceratopsians include many kinds such as *Triceratops, Chasmosaurus, Centrosaurus* (or *Eucentrosaurus*), and *Monoclonius.* Most ceratopsians were almost the size of an elephant, had horns like a rhinoceros, and the temperament of a bull.

The horns and shields that characterized the ceratopsians may have been used by the males when fighting over females. The wide variety in horns and frills within a species are often attributed to sexual dimorphism (in the simplest terms, the boys look different from the girls).

While some species of ceratopsians may have lived solitary lives, herds of ceratopsians have been discovered at Dinosaur Provincial Park in Alberta. These herds were very similar to the herds of buffalo and wildebeest today.

Imagine a herd of *Triceratops* roaming through the plains of Cretaceous Alberta. The herd is being stalked by a pack of tyrannosaurids, just as the herds of wildebeest are stalked by prides of lions today. Suddenly the pack of tyrannosaurs rushes into the *Triceratops* herd. The herd stampedes. Hundreds of animals, each the size of a pickup truck, race about. One of the old *Triceratops* is not fast enough to dodge the carnivores. The tyrannosaurs' huge jaws slash at the elderly *Triceratops,* who is still too big and dangerous for the carnivore to tackle alone. Suddenly another tyrannosaur takes a slashing bite, again wounding the *Triceratops.* The tyrannosaurs isolate their wounded prey from the rest of the herd, and like a pack of wolves they use their jaws to wear down and weaken the trapped animal.

The tyrannosaurs, like most theropods, had teeth with serrated edges, perfect for slashing. A big cat will suffocate its prey with a bite to the neck, but jumping onto the back of a *Triceratops* would be far too dangerous a maneuver. Instead the tyrannosaur slashes and waits. When the bleeding *Triceratops* weakens, the tyrannosaurs will eat.

Ornithopoda. The Ornithopoda includes a diverse group of primarily bipedal, plant-eating ornithiscians. They usually occupied the equivalent ecological niche belonging to today's deer and antelope. Their main defense against predators was speed.

The most well known ornithopod group is the Hadrosauridae, also called the duckbilled dinosaurs. The duckbilled dinosaurs thrived throughout the Cretaceous and are best known from Montana and Alberta. The Royal Ontario Museum in Toronto and the Royal Tyrrell Museum in Drumheller, Alberta, have enormous collections of duckbilled dinosaurs.

The duckbills are known to have communal nesting sites. Nests of the duckbilled dinosaur *Maiasaura* were discovered near Choteau, Montana. Each nest is spaced about twenty-three feet apart, about the length of an adult *Maiasaura*. Birds that nest in colonies tend to space their nests about the width of their wingspan.

Different age *Maiasaura* babies are found in the nests, and the eggshells appear to have been trampled. That means the babies stayed in the nest and the parents cared for their young. The Museum of the Rockies, Bozeman, Montana, runs guided tours to the nesting ground so you can see them for yourself. The New Mexico Museum of Natural History in Albuquerque has an excellent reconstruction of a *Maiasaura* nest.

Many of the duckbilled dinosaurs were quite musical. The crest of *Parasaurolophus* consists of two hollow tubes that were used like trombones. A *Parasaurolophus* weighed seven thousand pounds and had the lung power to fill the Cretaceous night with music. You can see *Parasaurolophus* at the University of California Museum of Paleontology in Berkeley, California.

Where Did They All Go?

Sixty-five million years ago, dinosaurs suddenly disappeared and the Mesozoic Era ended. The dinosaurs ruled the earth for 150 million years, but all that was left to prove they existed were their fossils. Not only did the dinosaurs disappear, so did many other animals large and small, and many plants. Yet, some animals including our own distant ancestors were lucky enough to survive. What happened?

Without a doubt something of global significance happened at the end of the Mesozoic. Many scientists call whatever occurred the "K/T event," K from the German word for Cretaceous (*Kreide*), the last period of the Mesozoic, and T for Tertiary, the first period of the Cenozoic Era. Studies of the K/T event offer paleontologists many different theories about the disappearance of the dinosaurs. Climatic change is the most commonly suggested cause, but how the climate changed and what caused it to change is a hot topic of debate. Some suggest the climate became too hot; others feel that the climate became too cold. In the movie "Fantasia," a drought is depicted as the cause of dinosaur extinction. Rides at Disneyland in California and Disney World's Epcot Center in Florida recreate this movie's view of dinosaur life and extinction.

The asteroid impact theory provides different answers. In rocks that date from the boundary between the Cretaceous and the Tertiary periods exists a thin band of clay with much more than the usual amount of iridium, a very hard and brittle metallic element. This iridium layer is best clue. Iridium finds are usually associated with pacts on earth. Could an asteroid impact, or sev- explain the disappearance of the dinosaurs, and where asteroid craters be found?

our asteroid im- eral impacts, would such

Initially, scientists suggested a site in Iowa, called Manson crater, or possibly undiscovered sites on the floor. But one site is more interesting. A 186-mile-wide Mexico's Yucatan Peninsula named Chicxulub was sixty-five million years ago, exactly the the dinosaurs disappeared. The im- asteroid large enough to create the Chicxulub crater would cover the rich in iridium. It would also release world's nuclear arsenal. The results waves, acid rain, global forest fires, and out the sun for months. Photosynthesis halt for at least one summer, causing most eco- collapse.

the ocean crater in made same time pact of an

globe with a layer of clay enough energy to dwarf the of the impact were tidal enough soot to block would have ground to a logical systems to

That some dinosaurs had already adapted to living throughout the winter in arctic conditions makes this theory seem less plausible. Winter has always been harsh in the Arctic. However, the meteorite impact would have caused the winter at the poles to be far more brutal than normal. The arctic dinosaurs might have been able to survive the comet's winter at the equator, but those dinosaurs were near the poles, where it would have been unbearably cold. If the arctic dinosaurs had migrated to the equator after the asteroid hit they might have survived. Even though dinosaurs may have been much smarter than we give them credit for, they probably did not have the presence of mind to go beyond their normal migratory patterns.

Some scientists still are convinced that the dinosaurs died out slowly over millions of years, as opposed to the sudden extinction that an asteroid would cause. However, a recent survey of dinosaur diversity at the K/T boundary was conducted in the Hell Creek Formation in Montana. The survey included all dinosaur material, and not just complete skeletons. The researchers concluded that dinosaurs flourished right up to the end of the Cretaceous and then suddenly disappeared.

We will get a taste of our own vulnerability when a comet slams into Jupiter during July of 1994. The comet, known as Shoemaker-Levy 9, was first sighted in 1993. The comet will blast Jupiter with more energy than that of the Chicxulub comet, which devastated the earth sixty-five million years ago.

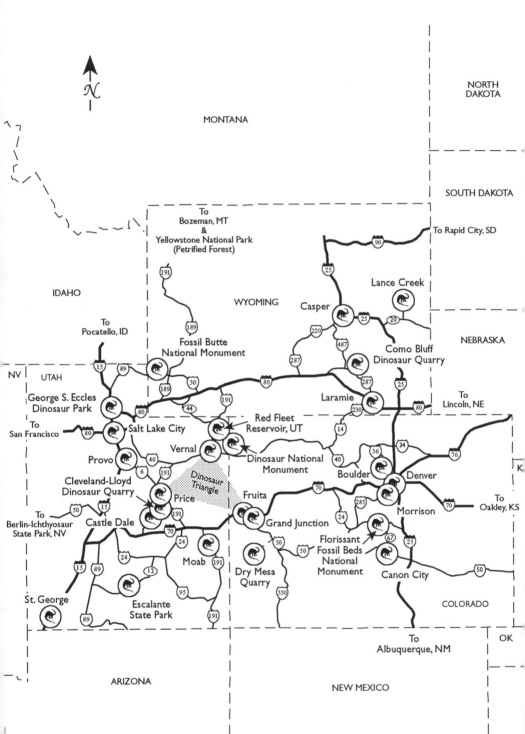

1.
The Morrison Formation
A Window to the Jurassic

To find Jurassic dinosaurs, you need to look in Jurassic-period rocks. In 1877, Arthur Lakes discovered dinosaur bones near the little town of Morrison, Colorado. The rock formation that the bones were discovered in is the Morrison Formation.

The Morrison Formation is rich with Jurassic dinosaur fossils. The Cleveland-Lloyd Quarry, Como Bluff, Dinosaur National Monument, Garden Park Quarry, and many other spots in the region have become windows to the Jurassic. The largest outcrops of the Morrison Formation are found in Utah, Colorado, and Wyoming; traces of the formation also are found in the nearby states of New Mexico and Oklahoma. At these places, brief instants in time are frozen and preserved for us to see, 145 million years later.

The cities of Vernal, Utah; Price, Utah; and Grand Junction, Colorado, form the Dinosaur Triangle. The approximately two-thousand-square-mile region of the Dinosaur Triangle is one of the world's richest deposits of Jurassic dinosaurs. What better place to start your Jurassic Safari?

1.1 College of Eastern Utah Prehistoric Museum Price, UT

Price, Utah, makes up the southwestern corner of the Dinosaur Triangle. The College of Eastern Utah (CEU) Prehistoric Museum in Price has an excellent display of dinosaurs.

The museum is the result of a very successful community effort. In 1961, local geologist Don Burge and his friends bought an *Allosaurus* skull for $50. They thought, "Why stop with a skull when we can have the whole dinosaur?" So $50 and $500 at a time they bought "Al" the *Allosaurus*—bone by bone—from the nearby Cleveland-Lloyd Dinosaur Quarry. When there was no other way to transport the huge dinosaur bones, "Al" rode into Price on a beer truck. Soon the entire community wanted to help build a museum to display the dinosaurs discovered so close to their town.

Today the museum operates five quarries. In 1991, scientists from the CEU museum discovered an enormous relative of *Velociraptor* in a rock formation near the Jurassic-Cretaceous border. Named *Utahraptor*, this terrifying monster was 20 feet long and weighed about 1,000 pounds. Equipped with 12-inch claws, it would leap into the air and kick its prey to shreds

Articulated Skeletons:
- *Allosaurus, Camptosaurus, Camarasaurus, Prosaurolophus, Chasmosaurus,* and *Stegosaurus.*

Exhibit Features:
- Cretaceous dinosaur tracks from nearby coal mines.
- Individual bones from several large *Apatosaurus.*
- Bone dig for children.
- Full-size upper-torso model *Allosaurus* and scale models of dinosaurs.

Hours:
Tuesday–Saturday 10:00 a.m.–4:00 p.m.
Summer hours (Memorial Weekend to Labor Day weekend):
Monday–Saturday 10:00 a.m.–5:00 p.m.
Sunday Noon–5:00 p.m.
Closed: Sundays, Mondays; Thanksgiving, Christmas, New Year's Day.
Minimum time required to see exhibit: 1 hour

Entrance Fees:
(Recommended donation)
Adults $1.00
Families $2.00

Location Address:
College of Eastern Utah, Prehistoric Museum
155 East Main, Price, UT 84501
Telephone: (801)637-5060

Mailing Address:
451 East 400 North, Price, UT 84501

Directions:
Price is located 125 miles southeast of Salt Lake City. From Salt Lake City take I-15 south to Highway 6. Take either the 240 or 243 exit from Highway 6 and follow the signs to the museum. The museum is on the north side of the Price Municipal Building, on the corner of 200 East and Main Street in downtown Price.

Map to College of Eastern Utah Prehistoric Museum

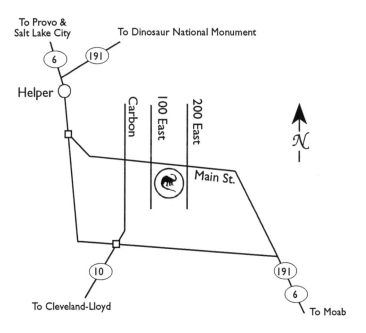

1.2 Cleveland-Lloyd Dinosaur Quarry near Price, UT

Nicknamed the "Dinosaur Department Store," the Cleveland-Lloyd Dinosaur Quarry has provided dinosaurs for museums the world over. To fund excavations at Cleveland-Lloyd, scientists from the University of Utah sold specimens to other museums and universities. This enterprise provided scientists and students around the world with the opportunity to study Jurassic dinosaurs. Seventy of the slate black dinosaurs found at this site have been shipped to 43 exhibits, from Paris, France, to Osaka, Japan.

Articulated Skeletons:
- *Allosaurus.*

Exhibit Features:
- A metal shed covers the quarry, and visitors can walk inside to observe the excavation site.
- Displays of individual dinosaur elements found at the quarry.

Hours:
Easter to Memorial Day:
Saturday–Sunday 10:00 a.m.–5:00 p.m.
Memorial Day to Labor Day:
Daily 10:00 a.m.–5:00 p.m.
Closed: Labor Day through Easter.
Minimum time required to see exhibit: 1 hour

Entrance Fees: free

Mailing Address:
U.S. Department of the Interior
Bureau of Land Management
P.O. Drawer A.B.
900 North 700 East, Price, UT 84501
Telephone: (801)637-4584

Directions:
Price is in central Utah. From Price take Route 10 south about 14 miles. Turn left on Route 155 and continue to Elmo. Follow the signs for the quarry. The road from Elmo to the quarry is a graded dirt road. The quarry also may be reached from I-70 near Moab by a dirt road that passes through the San Rafael Campground.

Map to Cleveland-Lloyd Dinosaur Quarry

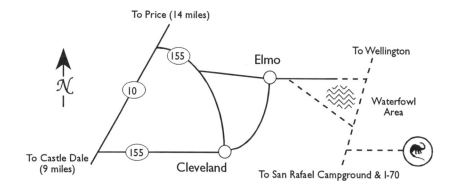

1.3 Emery County Museum
Castle Dale, UT

The Emery County Museum has a small collection of fossils found locally.

Articulated Skeletons:

- *Allosaurus.*

Exhibit Features: Local paleontology

Hours:

Monday–Friday 9:00 a.m.–5:00 p.m.
Saturday 10:00 a.m.–5:00 p.m.
Closed: Sundays; July 4, Thanksgiving, Christmas.
Minimum time required to see exhibit: 20 minutes

Entrance Fees: $1 donation suggested

Address:

Emery County Museum
City Hall, 61 East 100 South, Castle Dale, UT 84513
Telephone: (801)381-2115

Directions:

Castle Dale is 30 miles south of Price, Utah, on Highway 10.

1.4 Sauropod Tracksite near Moab, UT

About 150 million years ago, dinosaurs walked across an ancient river channel near Moab. In 1989 this site was discovered by Linda-Dale Jennings Lockley. These unique tracks show a large sauropod making a sharp turn to the right. You can also see the tracks of four different theropod dinosaurs here; one of the theropods appears to be limping. It is easiest to see the tracks when the sun is low on the horizon.

You probably have seen many reconstructions of dinosaurs with their tails dragging on the ground and their legs spayed out like a crocodiles. Note that there is absolutely no evidence of any tail dragging at this tracksite. The narrow width and long stride of the footprints indicate that dinosaurs were not sprawling reptiles, but walked with their legs underneath them as mammals do today.

Hours: always open, but road is impassable when wet

Minimum time required to see exhibit: 1 hour

Entrance Fees: free

Mailing Address:
Bureau of Land Management, c/o Grand Resource Area
885 S. Sand Flats Road, Moab, UT 84532
Telephone: (801)259-8193

Directions:
The tracks are in an exposure of the Salt Wash Member of the Morrison Formation, between the town of Moab and I-70 in southeastern Utah. From Highway 191 about 23 miles north of Moab, a dirt road between mile markers 148 and 149 will lead you to the tracks. The dirt road is just north of the microwave tower on Highway 191. You will cross railroad tracks and then see signs directing you to the tracks.

Map to Moab Area fossil sites near Moab, UT

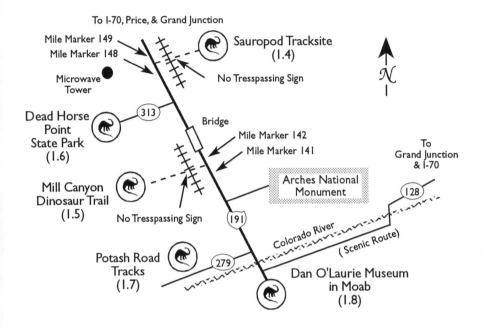

1.5 Mill Canyon Dinosaur Trail near Moab, UT

Mill Canyon Dinosaur Trail offers an opportunity to see dinosaur fossils in the "wild." You will see the bones of several Jurassic dinosaurs embedded in the rock. Please do not abuse this rare privilege by stealing or vandalizing the fossils. Leave the trail for others to enjoy as they have left it for you.

The nearby area is excellent hiking and mountain biking terrain, punctuated by scenic rock formations.

Exhibit Features:

- A self-guided interpretive trail that takes you past dinosaur bones in the "wild."
- Bones of *Camarasaurus* and *Allosaurus*.
- Petrified wood.

Hours: always open

Minimum time required to see exhibit: 1 hour

Entrance Fees: free

Mailing Address:

Bureau of Land Management c/o Grand Resource Area
855 S. Sand Flats Road, Moab, UT 84532
Telephone: (801)259-8193

Directions:

From Highway 191, look for a dirt road about 15 miles north of Moab, near mile marker 141. Cross the railroad tracks and continue two miles on the dirt road (the No Trespassing sign refers to the railway easement). The road may be difficult to pass and may require either a high-clearance vehicle or a short hike. (The area around Moab is particularly well suited to mountain bikes.) A sign marks the Mill Canyon Dinosaur Trail.

1.6 Dead Horse Point State Park near Moab, UT

Exhibit Features:
- The Visitor Center has a small display of dinosaur bones.
- The park offers spectacular views of the Mesozoic section of the surrounding canyonlands.
- The land surrounding the park contains numerous fossils.

Hours:
Daily 9:00 a.m.–5:00 p.m.
Summer hours (May 16 to September 15):
Daily 8:00 a.m.–6:00 p.m.
Visitor Center closed Thanksgiving, Christmas, and New Year's Day
Minimum time required to see exhibit: 30 minutes

Entrance Fees:
Per vehicle $3.00
Per person $1.00
Camping (per vehicle) $7.00

Mailing Address:
Dead Horse Point State Park
P.O. Box 609, Moab, UT 84532
Telephone: (801)259-2614

Directions:
Take Highway 191 north of Moab to Highway 313. The park is on State Route 313, about 18 miles from the intersection of Highway 191 and State Route 313.

1.7 Potash Road Dinosaur Tracks near Moab, UT

These dinosaur tracks, made by two theropods, are in the red sandstone of the Kayenta Formation, which was deposited during the early Jurassic Period about 200 million years ago and represents a semiarid environment. You can see the tracks from the side of the road or you can climb to them.

Hours: always open
Minimum time required to see exhibit: 15 minutes

Entrance Fees: free

Mailing Address:
Bureau of Land Management, c/o Grand Resource Area
855 S. Sand Flats Road, Moab, UT 84532
Telephone: (801)259-8193

Directions:
Take Highway 191 north from Moab to Highway 279. The tracks are found on red sandstone blocks upturned on the side of a cliff above Highway 279 and the Colorado River. The tracks are about 4.5 miles from the junction with Highway 191. The tracks are on the right (towards the mountain, opposite the river), about 60 feet above the road. Look for the sign marking the tracksite (the overgrowth of shrubs sometimes hides the sign). A spotting scope is available to help you locate the tracks.

Driving along Highway 128 along the Colorado River is the closest thing to driving through the Grand Canyon. If you are headed to Grand Junction, this is the way to go.

1.8 Dan O'Laurie Museum Moab, UT

Exhibit Features:
- Dinosaur tracks and a dinosaur femur.

Hours:
Monday–Thursday 3:00 p.m.–5:00 p.m. and 7:00 p.m.–9:00 p.m.
Friday–Saturday 1:00 p.m.–5:00 p.m. and 7:00 p.m.–9:00 p.m.

Summer hours (April 1 to October 31):
Monday–Saturday 1:00 p.m.–5:00 p.m. and 7:00 p.m.–9:00 p.m.
Closed: Sundays; Thanksgiving, Christmas, New Year's Day.
Minimum time required to see exhibit: 10 minutes

Entrance Fees: free

Address:

The Dan O'Laurie Museum
118 East Center Street, Moab, UT 84532
Telephone: (801)259-7985

Directions:

From Main Street in Moab, turn east on Center Street (by First Security Bank). The museum is in the second block on the right, across the street from the courthouse.

1.9 Escalante State Park
near Escalante, UT

Escalante State Park offers a 1.5-mile hike through a petrified forest from the Jurassic Period. Collecting fossil wood is NOT allowed in the park. Nearby there are several places where collecting petrified wood is legal (see map). Campsites with showers are available in the park.

Exhibit Features:

- A pair of self-guided interpretive trails through a petrified forest.
- Dinosaur paintings in the Visitor Center.

Hours:

The park is always open. The Visitor Center usually open during the day, but only when the ranger is available.
Minimum time required to see exhibit: 2 hours

Entrance Fees:

Per vehicle $3.00
Individuals $1.00
Camping $9.00

Address:

Escalante State Park
P.O. Box 350, Escalante, UT 84726-0350
Telephone: (801)826-4466 or (801)538-7221

Directions:

Escalante is 250 miles south of Salt Lake City and about 75 miles east of Cedar City. Escalante State Park is off Highway 12, between Bryce Canyon National Park and Capitol Reef National Park. The park is about 1.5 miles southeast of the town of Escalante.

Do not collect wood at the park. The fossil wood collecting area is 0.4 miles southeast from Escalante State Park. There is a minor road on the south side of Highway 12. Drive as far as you can on the road and park at the end. Hike about a mile south on the trail. If you explore the area you will find many pieces of petrified wood. Petrified wood may be collected on public land in quantities up to 25 pounds per day. Be sure to leave some for the next visitor!

Map to Escalante State Park

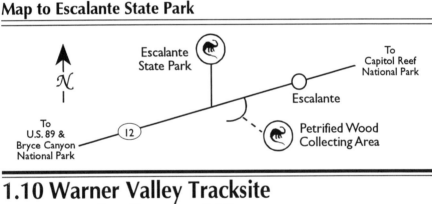

1.10 Warner Valley Tracksite near St. George, UT

Discovering dinosaur tracks in the "wild" is exciting. There are some excellent dinosaur footprints in Warner Valley near St. George. The tracks are preserved in a fine-grained, reddish sandstone. The fine grain of the sandstone implies that the tracks were made in a lower flood plain. As they walked across the moist sand, dinosaurs left their footprints to be preserved. The tracks are easiest to see when the sun is low on the horizon.

The sandstone is part of the Dinosaur Canyon member of the Moenave Formation, which means the tracks were made in the late Triassic or early Jurassic, about 213 million years ago. Fragments of petrified wood found nearby suggest that this was a wooded area at that time.

Hours: always open, but road is impassable when wet

Minimum time required to see exhibit: 2 hours

Entrance Fees: free

Mailing Address:

Bureau of Land Management, c/o Dixie Resource Area
225 North Bluff Street, St. George, UT 84770
Telephone: (801)673-4654

Directions:

St. George is in the far southwestern corner of Utah, about 300 miles southwest of Salt Lake City on I-15. The tracks are in Warner Valley, which is southeast of St. George. The heat of the desert in this region can be very harsh, so bring plenty of water.

From I-15 in St. George, take exit 6 east onto St. George Road and drive east. Turn right on Red Cliffs Drive, which becomes River Road. Immediately after crossing the bridge over the Virgin River, turn left onto 1450 South and head east. Follow the signs to Fort Pierce. Signs will indicate the way to the tracks and the parking area. A short hike takes you to the tracksite.

Map to the Warner Valley Tracksite

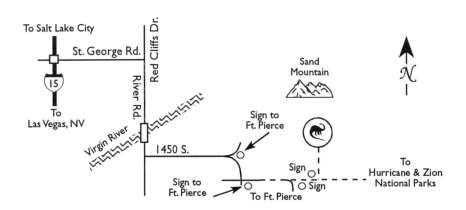

1.11 BYU Earth Science Museum Provo, UT

The BYU (Brigham Young University) Earth Science Museum has one of the world's largest collections of Jurassic dinosaurs. Unfortunately, the funds to prepare and display most of the fossils are unavailable. The majority of the collection languishes in the catacombs under the football stadium awaiting scientific examination. Even so, the display features some of the finest dinosaur fossils in the world.

Articulated Skeletons:
- A dynamic camptosaur mount created by "Dinosaur Jim" Jenson.
- *Allosaurus, Nanosaurus, Dimetrodon, Edaphosaurus.*
- A large *Pterodactyl* and an ichthyosaur.

Exhibit Features:
- Skulls of *Tyrannosaurus rex* and *Dinosuchus* (a ferocious 50-foot Mesozoic crocodile).
- An excellent *Triceratops* skull. Look for the ball joint on the underside of the skull. The cervical vertebrae would have a corresponding socket to connect to the ball on the skull. The massive *Triceratops* skull is perfectly balanced on this ball and socket joint.
- Elements of *Ultrasaurus, Supersaurus,* and *Apatosaurus.*
- An *Apatosaurus* bone showing the teeth marks of *Allosaurus.*
- A Jurassic dinosaur egg containing the oldest known dinosaur fetus (150 million years old).
- Dinosaur skin impressions found in Utah.
- Glass walls allowing you to see into one of the world's most productive paleontology labs in action.
- A beautiful palm frond and fossil fish from the Green River shale.
- A 20-by-11-foot wall mural showing life in the late Jurassic.

Hours:
Monday 9:00 a.m.–9:00 p.m.
Tuesday–Friday 9:00 a.m.–5:00 p.m.
Saturday Noon–4:00 p.m.
Closed: Sundays; July 4, Thanksgiving, Christmas Eve, Christmas, New Year's Day; all school holidays.
Minimum time required to see exhibit: 2 hours

Entrance Fees: Donation requested

Address:

Brigham Young University, Earth Science Museum
1683 North Canyon Road, Provo, UT 84602
Telephone: (801)378-3680

Directions:

Provo is 45 miles south of Salt Lake city on I-15. Take exit 272 from I-15 and head east on 1200 S. The road bends south and becomes University Parkway as you continue east. Look to the northeast (your left) for the BYU football stadium. At the stadium, turn left on North Canyon Road. The museum is across the street from the stadium. The museum is on North Canyon Road west of the BYU football stadium.

Map to BYU Earth Science Museum

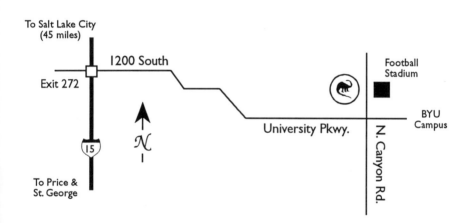

1.12 Utah Museum of Natural History Salt Lake City, UT

The Utah Museum of Natural History has an excellent collection of Jurassic dinosaurs and Ice Age mammals. Children can practice their excavation skills on an entire mammoth buried in peat. The peat is rather dirty, so don't dress the kids in their best clothes on this day.

Articulated Skeletons:
- Two *Allosaurus, Camptosaurus, Stegosaurus*, and a *Dimetrodon*.
- Casts of *Archaeopteryx* and other Solenhoffen fossils.
- First cast of Columbian Mammoth (adult bull found near Huntington, Utah).
- Ice Age mammals.

Exhibit Features:
- A full-size *Apatosaurus* drawing with some leg bones in place.
- Displays highlighting fossil collecting in Utah.
- Dinosaur footprints.

Hours:
Monday–Saturday 9:30 a.m.–5:30 p.m.
Sundays and holidays Noon–5:00 p.m.
Closed: July 4, July 24, Thanksgiving, Christmas, New Year's Day.
Minimum time required to see exhibit: 2 hours

Entrance Fees:
Adults $3.00
Children (3–14) $1.50
Seniors $1.50

Address:
Utah Museum of Natural History, University of Utah
President's Circle, Salt Lake City, UT 84112
Telephone: (801)581-4303 or (801)581-6928

Directions:
The museum is on the University of Utah campus. From I-15 take the 600 South exit (exit 310) and head due east. Turn left (north) at 1300 East; turn right at 200 South, which ends at President's Circle. Turn right onto the Circle. The museum is in the George Thomas Building, the first building on the right. Park in front of the museum.

Map to Utah Museum of Natural History

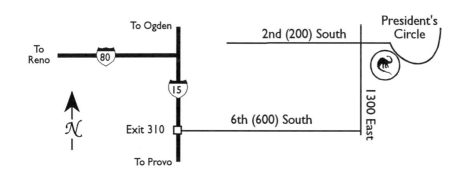

1.13 Weber State Museum of Natural Science Ogden, UT

You can stand right next to the *Allosaurus* skeleton at the Weber State Museum, so be careful not to knock it over!

Articulated Skeletons:
- *Allosaurus*, partial *Dimetrodon*, and a sabertoothed cat.

Exhibit Features:
- Skulls of *Allosaurus*, *Camarasaurus*, and *Camptosaurus*.
- Examples of local plant and invertebrate fossils.

Hours:
Monday–Friday 8:00 a.m.–5:00 p.m.
Closed: Thanksgiving; beginning of December to beginning of January, and beginning of August to end of September.
Minimum time required to see exhibit: 30 minutes

Entrance Fees: free

Address:
Weber State University Museum of Natural Science
3750 Harrison Boulevard, Ogden, UT 84408-2504
Telephone: (801)626-6653

Directions:
The museum is on the Weber State University campus in Ogden, about 35 miles north of Salt Lake City. From I-15 take exit 344 and head east on 31st Street. Turn right on Wall Avenue. Turn left on 36th Street and continue to the top of the hill. Turn right on Harrison Boulevard. The

museum is on the northeastern corner of the campus, in the Lind Lecture Hall of Science.

Map to Weber State University and the Dinosaur Park

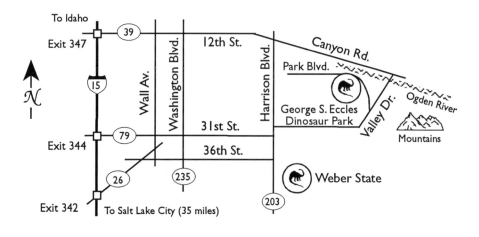

1.14 George S. Eccles Dinosaur Park Ogden, UT

The George S. Eccles Dinosaur Park opened in April of 1993 with 26 life-size prehistoric animal statues. Many of the concrete and plaster replicas represent the latest scientific findings.

Some of the dinosaurs at this park were only recently discovered. *Utahraptor,* for example, was first identified in 1991.

Exhibit Features:

- Models of *Utahraptor, Pteranodon, Archaeopteryx, Stegosaurus, Ankylosaurus, Deinonychus,* a plesiosaur, an ichthyosaur, *Camarasaurus, Allosaurus,* an erythrosuchid, *Dimetrodon, Euparkeria, Alamosaurus, Dryosaurus, Camp-tosaurus, Triceratops, Marshosaurus, Tyrannosaurus,* and *Parasaurolophus.*
- A dinosaur playground where children can climb on an ankylosaur and dig for fossils.
- An outdoor fossil exhibit.

Hours:

Daily 10:00 a.m.–7:00 p.m.

Closed: November to April and when snow covers the ground.

Minimum time required to see exhibit: 1 hour

Entrance Fees:
Adults $2.50
Children (6–17) $1.00
Young children (2–5) $.50
Seniors (62+) $2.00

Mailing Address:
Weber State University, c/o Continuing Education Dept. PT #316
Ogden, UT 84408-4010

Location Address:
George S. Eccles Dinosaur Park
1544 E. Park Boulevard, Ogden, UT 84401
Telephone: (801)393-DINO

Directions:
Ogden is about 35 miles north of Salt Lake City. From I-15 take exit 347 east onto 12th Street (Route 39). Follow 12th Street onto Canyon Road. Just before you enter the mouth of the canyon, turn right and cross over the Ogden River. Turn right again to Park Boulevard.

1.15 Utah Field House of Natural History State Park, Vernal, UT

The Utah Field House of Natural History State Park houses a good selection of local fossils including a 70-foot *Diplodocus*. The Field House is also the home of Dinosaur Gardens, which contain 16 life-size models of dinosaurs and prehistoric animals sculpted by Elbert Porter.

The Field House also serves as the Dinosaurland Travel Information Center. Vernal, Utah, forms the northeastern corner of the Dinosaur Triangle, and the place is "Dino-Crazy" (you'll see lots of names like the Dine-A-Ville Hotel and the Dinosaur Inn). Vernal is an excellent base for exploring the Dinosaur National Monument area.

Articulated Skeletons:
- The giant sauropod dinosaur *Diplodocus*.
- A new *Stegosaurus* skeleton will be displayed in 1995.

Exhibit Features:
- Life-size models of *Tyrannosaurus rex*, *Diplodocus*, *Protoceratops*, *Pteranodon*, *Ornithomimus*, *Triceratops*, *Rhamphorhynchus*, *Stegosaurus*, *Edaphosaurus*, a woolly mammoth, and *Moschops* in the Dinosaur Gardens.

- Local fossil material.
- Life-size concrete statues of *Stegosaurus*, *Ceratosaurus*, and *Camarasaurus* by Millard F. Malin.

Hours:

Daily 9:00 a.m.–5:00 p.m.
Closed: Thanksgiving, Christmas Eve, Christmas, New Year's Day.
Summer hours (Memorial Day to Labor Day):
Daily 8:00 a.m.–9:00 p.m.
Minimum time required to see exhibit: 90 minutes

Entrance Fees:

Adults $1.50
Families $6.00
Children (6–15) $1.00

Address:

Utah Field House of Natural History
235 East Main, Vernal, UT 84078
Telephone: (801)789-3799 OR (800)477-5558

Directions:

Vernal is 175 miles east of Salt Lake City in northeastern Utah, near the Colorado border. The Utah Field House of Natural History is on the north side of Main Street (235 East) as you drive through the town of Vernal. Look for the concrete statues of *Stegosaurus*, *Ceratosaurus*, and *Camarasaurus* on the lawn in front of a large brick building.

Map to the Dinosaur National Monument area

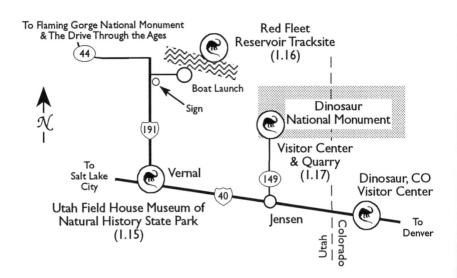

1.16 Red Fleet Reservoir Tracksite near Vernal, UT

During the early Jurassic, this area was an oasis in a land of desert sand dunes. Preserved in the sandstone of the Navajo/Nugget Formation are more than 200 dinosaur tracks. The tracks are exposed along the shoreline of the reservoir and were made by at least two different types of bipedal dinosaurs. The Jurassic tracks near the reservoir were found in 1987; tracks dating from the Triassic and Cretaceous also have been found near the reservoir.

Hours:

Open 24 hours a day. The tracks may be covered by water during the spring runoff or by snow in the winter.

Minimum time required to see exhibit: 2 hours

Entrance Fees:

Per vehicle $3.00

Address:

Red Fleet State Park
Steinaker Lake North 4335, Vernal, UT 84078-9500
Telephone: (801) 789-6614

Directions:

Vernal is 175 miles east of Salt Lake City in northeast Utah, near the Colorado border. To reach the tracksite, go 10 miles north of Vernal on Highway 191. Turn right at the big sign for the state park. The reservoir is about two miles into the park; the tracks are on the opposite bank of the reservoir from the boat launch. Trail maps to the tracksite are available in the park office. You can also reach the tracks by boat or by swimming. The swim across the reservoir is approximately 400 yards in deep water. Often in winter the reservoir will freeze, and you can walk across to the tracks—but check in the park office first.

Nearby:

Just north of Red Fleet Reservoir, signs along Highway 191 and Highway 44 identify the rock formations visible from the road. The route is known as the "Drive Through the Ages." To take the Drive Through the Ages, follow Highway 191 from Vernal to Flaming Gorge. At Flaming Gorge follow Highway 44 west towards Fossil Butte. For more information, inquire at the Dinosaurland Information Center at the Utah Field House of Natural History.

1.17 Dinosaur National Monument near Dinosaur, CO

In 1909, paleontologist Earl Douglass found eight perfectly articulated tail bones of an *Apatosaurus* (formerly called *Brontosaurus*) near Vernal, Utah. At the time Douglass was working for the Carnegie Museum of Natural History in Pittsburgh. Douglass was so excited by his discovery that he brought his family to Jensen, Utah, and made exploring the quarry his life's work. To protect this valuable scientific resource, the quarry was proclaimed a national monument in 1915.

The exposed wall of bones is a cross-section of the late Jurassic Period, approximately 145 million years old. Although it was long believed that Dinosaur National Monument was a sand bar in a river, a recent study indicates that it might originally have been the bottom of a river when the dinosaurs were deposited. Eventually, tectonic forces caused the land to rise up and fold over. Excavations have exposed one of the most spectacular sights in the world, a 200-foot rock wall of dinosaur bones.

Articulated Skeletons:
- *Allosaurus* and *Camarasaurus*.

Exhibit Features:
- A 200-foot rock wall covered with over 1,600 dinosaur bones. The exposed bones include *Apatosaurus* (once known as *Brontosaurus*), *Stegosaurus*, *Camarasaurus*, and *Camptosaurus*.
- Excellent murals painted by John Dawson depicting life in the late Jurassic. The murals portray the latest in scientific theory and depict colorful, active, and exciting dinosaurs.
- A full-size *Stegosaurus* model and finely crafted scale models of *Apatosaurus* (formerly *Brontosaurus*), *Diplodocus*, *Camarasaurus*, and *Stegosaurus*.
- Full-size *Camarasaurus* "billboards."
- Individual skulls of several dinosaurs, including *Allosaurus*.

Hours:
Daily 8:00 a.m.–4:30 p.m.
Closed: Thanksgiving, Christmas, New Year's Day.
Summer hours (Memorial Day to Labor Day):
Daily 8:00 a.m.–7:00 p.m.
Minimum time required to see exhibit: 3 hours

Entrance Fees:
Per vehicle $5.00
Camping $8.00

Mailing Address:
Dinosaur National Monument
P.O. Box 210, Dinosaur, CO 81610
Telephone: (303)374-2216
For quarry: (801)789-2115

Directions:
Dinosaur, Colorado, is 38 miles east of Vernal, Utah, on Highway 40. To get to the quarry of Dinosaur National Monument from Dinosaur, take Highway 40 west 21 miles to Jensen, Utah. Turn north on Highway 149. The quarry is seven miles north of Jensen.

Nearby:
The Visitor Center for Dinosaur National Monument is in Dinosaur, Colorado. As you drive down the main street in town, known as the Stegosaurus Highway, you will see dinosaur statues. There also is a Visitor Center at the quarry, inside the National Monument.

The Dinosaur Nature Association (DNA) is a nonprofit organization that supports educational and scientific operations at both Dinosaur and Fossil Butte National Monuments. The DNA is headquartered in the Dinosaur National Monument bookstore. For more information write:
Dinosaur Nature Association
1291 East Highway 40, Vernal, UT 84078
Telephone: (801)789-8807 or (800)845-DINO

1.18 Dinosaur Valley Museum of Western Colorado, Grand Junction, CO

Grand Junction, Colorado, is the southeastern corner of the Dinosaur Triangle. The Dinosaur Valley Museum of Western Colorado operates several quarries in the area and has become a showcase for the fossil finds from the Grand Junction area. New discoveries made by the museum staff and the people of Grand Junction keep the exhibit on the cutting edge of dinosaur technology.

Articulated Skeletons:
- *Stegosaurus*, posed rearing up on her hind legs as modern dinosaur theory suggests.
- *Allosaurus* and *Camptosaurus*.

Exhibit Features:
- Half-size animated models of *Triceratops*, *Stegosaurus*, *Apatosaurus*, *Iguanodon*, and *Pachycephalosaurus*.
- A viewing area where you can watch paleontologists prepare fossils.
- A model of *Pteranodon*.
- Dinosaur footprints and individual bones.

Volunteer Opportunities:
The museum accepts volunteers to help with preparation of exhibits and fossils, and field work. A long-term commitment is desired.

Hours:
Tuesday–Saturday 10:00 a.m.–4:30 p.m.
Closed: Sundays, Mondays; Thanksgiving, Christmas, New Year's Day; first or second week of January for refurbishing.
Summer hours (Memorial Day to Labor Day):
Daily 9:00 a.m.–5:30 p.m.
Minimum time required to see exhibit: 90 minutes

Entrance Fees:
Adults $4.00
Children (2–12) $2.50

Location Address:
Dinosaur Valley Museum of Western Colorado
362 Main Street, Grand Junction, CO 81502-5020
Telephone: (303)243-DINO, (303)242-0971, (303)241-9210

Mailing Address:

Dinosaur Valley Museum of Western Colorado
P.O. Box 20,000-5020, Grand Junction, CO 81502-5020

Directions:

The Dinosaur Valley Museum of Western Colorado is located in downtown Grand Junction at the corner of Main Street and 4th Street. When coming from the east on I-70 take exit 31; when coming from the west on I-70 take exit 26.

Map to the Grand Junction, CO, area

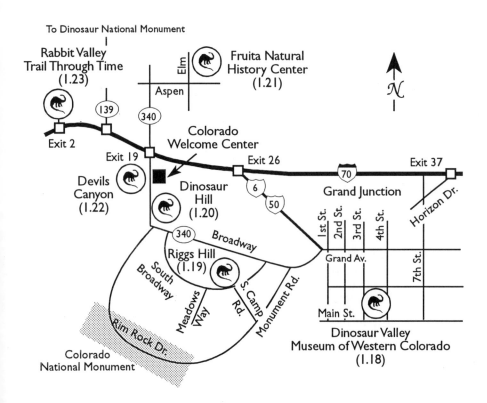

1.19 Riggs Hill
Grand Junction, CO

In 1899, Elmer S. Riggs made one of the first direct-mail searches for dinosaurs. Riggs, who was the Assistant Curator of Paleontology at the Field Museum in Chicago, sent letters to western towns inquiring about fossils for his museum. Dr. S. M. Bradbury, president of the Western Colorado Academy of Science, responded to Riggs's inquiry, describing the many fossils that ranchers had collected. Riggs went to Grand Junction and found the bones of a *Camarasaurus* in what was to become Colorado National Monument.

Riggs continued his search until he came to the area now known as Riggs Hill. On this hill in 1900, Riggs discovered the fossils of the largest dinosaur in existence, *Brachiosaurus altithorax*.

In 1937, Edward Holt, a school teacher, discovered partial skeletons of four dinosaurs at Riggs Hill. Holt tried to make the new discovery into an outdoor display of dinosaur bones. Unfortunately, souvenir hunters stole the fossils, piece by piece. Please, help prevent this from happening at other interpretive fossil sites.

Exhibit Features:
- A three-quarter-mile hiking trail takes you past historical markers showing former locations of bones.

Hours: always open
Minimum time required to see exhibit: 30 minutes

Entrance Fees: free

Mailing Address:
Dinosaur Valley Museum of Western Colorado
362 Main Street P.O. Box 20,000-5020, Grand Junction, CO 81502-5020
Telephone: (303)243-DINO, (303)242-0971, (303)241-9210

Directions:
Riggs Hill is about five miles northwest of Grand Junction, Colorado. From I-70, exit at Route 340 going south. (You might want to stop at the Colorado Welcome Center, at the intersection of I-70 and Route 340.) Route 340 becomes Broadway. Continue on Broadway to South Broadway. Turn right. Riggs Hill is near the intersection of Meadows Way and South Broadway.

To reach Riggs Hill from Dinosaur Hill (section 1.20), continue east on Broadway to South Broadway. Turn right (southwest) on South Broadway and follow the road around to your right. Riggs Hill is on your right near the intersection of Meadows Way and South Broadway.

1.20 Dinosaur Hill
near Grand Junction, CO

In 1901, Elmer S. Riggs prospected for dinosaurs at an area south of Fruita, Colorado. Here he discovered fossilized remains, which he named *Brontosaurus excelsus*. We now call *Brontosaurus* by its scientifically correct name, *Apatosaurus*, but the words *Brontosaurus excelsus* still have a wonderful ring to them.

To remove the fossils from the rock, Riggs tunneled his way into the hillside using mining equipment. In fear of the mountainside collapsing on top of them, workers abandoned the excavation. The remainder of the *Apatosaurus* tail is probably still buried in the mountainside that has entombed it for the last 147 million years.

The skeleton Riggs found showed evidence that, during the animal's lifetime, its ribs had been broken and had healed. The mounted *Apatosaurus* now stands in the Field Museum of Chicago (section 6.12).

In 1992, a family from Kansas was walking along Dinosaur Hill when they discovered vertebrae, freshly exposed in the ground. They reported the find to the Dinosaur Valley Museum. Scientists were then able to expose the delicate bones and prepare them for study. If you discover bones, please report them to the museum as each bone is a valuable piece in the dinosaur puzzle.

Exhibit Features:
- A one-mile hiking trail that takes you past historical markers showing the former locations of dinosaur bones.
- The impression of a *Diplodocus* femur, visible in a boulder along the trail.

Hours: always open

Minimum time required to see exhibit: 45 minutes.

Entrance Fees: free

Mailing Address:

Dinosaur Valley Museum of Western Colorado
362 Main Street P.O. Box 20,000-5020,
Grand Junction, CO 81502-5020
Telephone: (303)243-DINO, (303)242-0971, (303)241-9210

Directions:

Dinosaur Hill is just south of the town of Fruita and about five miles
northwest of Grand Junction. Take exit 19 from I-70 at Fruita and head
south on Highway 340. You might want to stop at the Colorado Welcome
Center to pick up maps and information on the surrounding area. Continue south across the Colorado River and Dinosaur Hill is to your left
(east).

1.21 Fruita Natural History Center
Fruita, CO

The museum features finds from the Grand Junction area.

Exhibit Features:

- Museum visitors can watch scientists prepare and study fossil specimens.
- Exhibits on *Utahraptor*, *Apatosaurus*, and a nodosaur.

Volunteer Opportunities:

The museum accepts volunteers to help with preparation and repair of
exhibits, field work, and fossil preparation.

Hours:

Monday–Friday 9:00 a.m.–5:00 p.m.
Closed: Thanksgiving, Christmas, New Year's Day.
Minimum time required to see exhibit: 20 minutes

Entrance Fees: free

Address:

Dinamation International Society
Fruita Natural History Center
325 W. Aspen, P.O. Box 307, Fruita, CO 81521
Telephone: (800)DIG-DINO or (303)858-7282

Directions:

Take exit 19 from I-70 and head north on Highway 340. Take a right on Aspen and head east through town. There is a large *Allosaurus* statue in the park on Aspen. The museum is on near the corner of Elm and Aspen.

Nearby:

When the big names in paleontology are in town, they can't resist eating at Dinosaur Pizza, a restaurant that includes paleontology memorabilia as part of its decor. Dinosaur Pizza is located across the street from the museum.

1.22 Devils Canyon
Fruita, CO

Dinamation International Society is opening a new museum of paleontology in Fruita. The exhibit is expected to be open by July 4, 1994.

Dinamation is one of the few private corporations that is funneling the profits made from marketing dinosaur products back into dinosaur research. Chris Mays, the founder of Dinamation, is genuinely committed to dinosaur research.

The Dinamation International Society has been involved in the discovery of *Utahraptor*, the world's largest *Apatosaurus*, and one of the few known Jurassic dinosaur nesting sites. The society is organizing some of the first dinosaur hunting expeditions to Mexico.

Volunteer Opportunities:

Dinamation International Society sponsors field expeditions throughout North America; participants dig dinosaurs with professional paleontologists.

Address:

Dinamation International Society
P.O. Box 307, Fruita, CO 81521
Telephone: (800)DIG-DINO or (303)858-7282

Directions:

The Devils Canyon exhibit will be located directly across from the Colorado Welcome Center on the way to Dinosaur Hill (see directions to Dinosaur Hill, section 1.20).

1.23 Rabbit Valley Trail Through Time near Grand Junction, CO

The Rabbit Valley Trail Through Time is a 1.5-mile hike along a trail where you will see dinosaur fossils in the rocks just as nature has revealed them to us. The discovery sites of *Camarasaurus* and *Diplodocus* fossil remains are marked on the trail. Plant fossils are also visible on this trail.

Unthinking visitors who steal souvenirs threaten the existence of interpretive sites like Rabbit Valley. Please do not try to collect or alter the fossils in any way. By leaving the fossils alone so that everyone might enjoy them, you will encourage the opening of other fossil areas. The commercial collection of fossils on state or federal land is prohibited by law. Unfortunately, this law is difficult to enforce. You can help by reporting those who appear to be collecting souvenirs to park rangers or officials at nearby museums. Those who steal fossils on public land steal from you and give legitimate commercial collectors a bad name.

Hours: always open
> (From June 1 to September 30, a quarry host is on hand Mondays and Tuesdays from 9:00 a.m. to 4:00 p.m. to explain the on-going excavations at the Mygatt-Moore quarry.)
> **Minimum time required to see exhibit:** 1 hour

Entrance Fees: free

Mailing Address:
> Dinosaur Valley Museum of Western Colorado
> 362 Main Street, P.O. Box 20,000-5020, Grand Junction, CO 81502-5020
> Telephone: (303)243-DINO, (303)242-0971, (303)241-9210

Directions:
> The Rabbit Valley Trail Through Time is 30 miles west of Grand Junction and two miles east of the Utah border. Take the Rabbit Valley exit off I-70 and head north across the frontage road. The parking lot is about 500 feet from the highway.

1.24 Dry Mesa Quarry
near Delta, CO

Dry Mesa Quarry is the site where "Dinosaur Jim" Jensen found the remains of *Ultrasaurus* and *Supersaurus*. These were the biggest animals to ever walk the earth. The shoulder blade of an *Ultrasaurus* is nearly 9 and one-half feet long. Although neither dinosaur was ever fully recovered, estimates based on other giant sauropods put the creatures at 80 to 140 feet in length.

There are plans underway to make this important paleontological site an interpretive display for the public. Your cooperation in preserving this site is extremely important. All the fascinating things we learn about the behavior of dinosaurs comes from meticulous fossil collection. These methods require interpretation based on the exact relative location of every bit of fossil material. Do not move or disturb anything in the quarry area; you could ruin the next great dinosaur discovery. If you wish to visit the quarry, contact one of these museums.

Mailing Address:

USDA Forest Service
2505 S. Townsend, Montrose CO 81401
Telephone: (303)249-3711

Directions:

Delta, Colorado, is 40 miles southeast of Grand Junction on Highway 50. The Dry Mesa Quarry is located in the Uncompahgre National Forest, near the east fork of Escalante Creek. From Delta follow 5th W. west to 501; take 501 southwest. At the Cottonwood Basin head north about three miles on 502; then turn left. Follow this road about two and a half miles to the quarry at the end of the road.

Map to the Dry Mesa Quarry

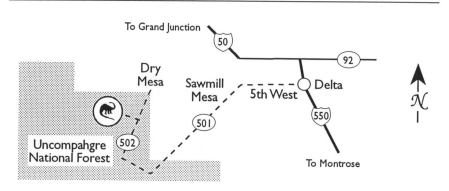

1.25 Garden Park Fossil Area
Canon City, CO

Local school teacher O.W. Lucas discovered dinosaur fossils in the spring of 1876 while hiking in Garden Park. Lucas realized the importance of his findings and sent word to E. D. Cope, a wealthy man who was known to pay handsome rewards for information on the location of dinosaur bones. Cope encouraged Lucas to dig for more bones.

It wasn't long before Cope's rival, O. C. Marsh, heard of the discovery. Marsh was a professor of paleontology at Yale University and nephew of the wealthy industrialist George Peabody. Both Cope and Marsh were obsessed with dinosaurs. Marsh sent his chief field collector, Benjamin Mudge, to investigate the area. Mudge, in turn, hired Kansan Sam Williston to set up a rival excavation site near the Lucas site. Thus, Garden Park became a battlefield in the Cope-Marsh "Bone Wars." The battle resulted in the discovery of 17 new dinosaur species.

One of the greatest finds at Garden Park during the 1890s was *Stegosaurus*. For over a century, controversy raged over whether the plates running down this dinosaur's back were arranged in pairs or staggered. Today researchers at the Garden Park Fossil Area continue to make discoveries; in 1992 a *Stegosaurus* was uncovered with the plates still in place, ending the controversy: The plates on this *Stegosaurus* were staggered. Other recent finds at Garden Park include egg shell fragments, a juvenile *Dryosaurus*, and a massive *Haplocanthosaurus* which is now on display at the Cleveland Museum of Natural History.

The Garden Park Paleontology Society is establishing an educational center at the Garden Park Fossil Area. A temporary educational center is being set up at the old firehouse in Canon City, where visitors can see the latest Garden Park *Stegosaurus* being prepared for display.

Exhibit Will Feature:
- 18 drawings and two scale models.

Volunteer Opportunities:
The Garden Park Paleontology Society provides an excellent opportunity to assist paleontologists with field research.

Hours: open daily
(From Memorial Day to Labor Day, a slide show and tour of the Garden Park fossil area is conducted Saturday evenings at 6 p.m.)

Minimum time required to see exhibit: 2 hours

Entrance Fees: free

Mailing Address:
Garden Park Paleontology Society
P.O. Box 313, Canon City, CO 81215-0313
or
Canon City Chamber of Commerce
1032 Royal Gorge Boulevard, Canon City, CO 81212
Telephone: (719)275-2331

Directions:
The slide show is at the Bureau of Land Management office in Canon City, 35 miles west of Pueblo on Highway 50, in south-central Colorado. The fossil quarry is about seven miles north of Canon City on County Road 1 (Shelf Road) near where the road crosses the creek in the Four Mile Creek Canyon.

Map to Garden Park Fossil area and Florissant Fossil Beds

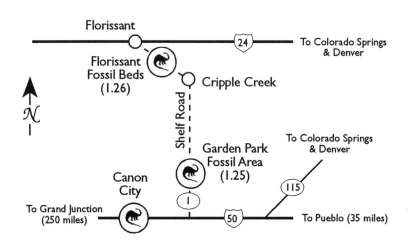

1.26 Florissant Fossil Beds National Monument Florissant, CO

Florissant Fossil Beds National Monument contains some of the finest deposits of fossils from the Oligocene Epoch (35 million years ago). Fossils of over 1,100 insects and 114 plant species have been identified here. Insect fossils are quite rare, so this represents a unique collection of fossils.

Exhibit Features:

- A one-mile hiking trail through a scenic petrified forest. Some of the petrified tree stumps are 38 feet in circumference.
- Insect fossils on exhibit in the Visitor Center.

Hours:

Daily 8:00 a.m.–4:00 p.m.
Closed: Thanksgiving, Christmas, New Year's Day.
Summer hours (June to August):
Daily 8:00 a.m.–7:00 p.m.
Minimum time required to see exhibit: 1 hour

Entrance Fees:

Walk-in $2.00
Per family $4.00

Address:

Florissant Fossil Beds National Monument
P.O. Box 185, Florissant, CO 80816
Telephone: (719)748-3253

Directions:

Take U.S. 24 west 40 miles from Colorado Springs to the town of Florissant. At the town center, turn south toward Cripple Creek on County Road 1 (a dirt road). The park is a half-mile from the town of Florissant.

1.27 Dinosaur Ridge
near Morrison, CO

In 1877, teacher Arthur Lakes was hiking near Morrison, Colorado, when he discovered huge bones along a sandstone ridge. He sent word of the bones to O.C. Marsh, a wealthy man who would pay for dinosaur bones. While Lakes waited for Marsh's reply, he excavated numerous fossil bones. Lakes grew impatient and sent samples of the bones to both Marsh and E.D. Cope, Marsh's rival. When Marsh heard this, he immediately sent Lakes $100 and told him to keep the discovery a secret. Lakes made all future shipments of bones to Marsh and instructed Cope to send the bones he had received to Marsh.

In the 1930s dinosaur tracks were discovered on the east side of Dinosaur Ridge. Recent research revealed that this area is the shoreline of an ancient sea. The track-bearing formation extends along the length of the Colorado Front Range. The area is frequently referred to as the "Dinosaur Freeway."

Exhibit Features:
- Historic Morrison Formation dinosaur quarries.
- Dinosaur footprints from the 100-million-year-old Dakota Group (Cretaceous period).
- Numbered roadside markers indicate the location of quarries, tracksites, and fossils.

Minimum time required to see exhibit: 1 hour

Entrance Fees: free

Address:
Friends of Dinosaur Ridge, Morrison Natural History Museum
P.O. Box 564, Morrison, CO 80465
Telephone: (303)697-1873

Directions:
Dinosaur Ridge is two miles north of Morrison, a few miles west of Denver, and two and one-half miles south of Golden. From I-70, exit at Hog Back–Vernon Canyon State Route 26 and head south towards Morrison. Dinosaur Ridge is about a mile south of the exit.

Nearby:
There is a small natural history museum near Dinosaur Ridge in the town of Morrison, open Wednesday through Saturday, 1 p.m.–4. p.m.

Map to Dinosaur Ridge and Morrison Museum

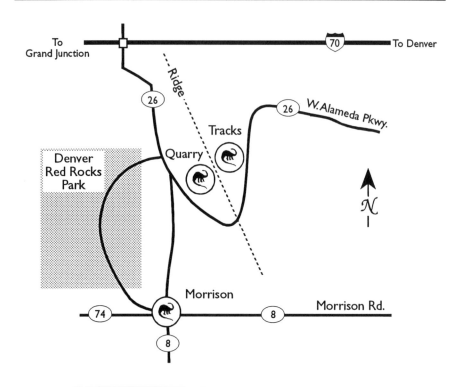

1.28 Denver Museum of Natural History Denver, CO

An incredible skeleton of *Tyrannosaurus rex* dominates the Denver Museum of Natural History. *Tyrannosaurus* is rearing up on one foot with the other foot outstretched, baring vicious claws. Preparators are currently working on a recently discovered *Stegosaurus* in Dinosaur Hall, where visitors can watch and ask questions.

In October 1995, the museum will open "Prehistoric Journey," an exhibition presenting the history of life on earth through 3.5 billion years, using fossil evidence from Colorado, the Rocky Mountain region, and other areas of the world. The exhibit will include walk-through environments of ancient plants, mammals, and dinosaurs and hands-on computer games.

Articulated Skeletons:

- *Tyrannosaurus rex* and a *Diplodocus*.

After October 1995:

- *Stegosaurus, Coelophysis,* and *Edmontosaurus.*
- Two plesiosaurs and a mosasaur.

Exhibit Features:

- Museum visitors can watch through a window as scientists prepare fossils. A special close-up video camera has been installed to provide visitors with a detailed view of the fossil preparation. Denver's proximity to the Morrison Formation provides the museum with a fresh supply of dinosaur fossils.
- Walk-through environments.

After October 1995:

- Scale models of dinosaurs and several dinosaur murals.
- Paleozoic fossils, fossil fish, and many individual dinosaur fossils.

Volunteer Opportunities:

- Volunteers prepare fossils for display and help in field excavations.
- The museum offers a certification program in paleontology, a rigorous one-year crash course.
- Volunteers act as docents and help out with children's programs.

Hours:

Daily 9:00 a.m.–5:00 p.m.

Closed: Christmas.

Minimum time required to see exhibit: 3 hours

Entrance Fees:

Adults $4.50

Seniors $2.50

Children (4–12) $2.50

Address:

Denver Museum of Natural History

2001 Colorado Boulevard, Denver, CO 80205

Telephone: (303)370-6387 or (800)925-2250

Directions:

From I-70 take the Colorado Boulevard exit south. Turn right on Montview after 22nd Street. Or, from I-25 take the Colorado Boulevard exit and head north. Turn left on Montview, after 19th Street. The museum is on the west side of Colorado Boulevard near 21st Street.

Map to Denver Museum of Natural History

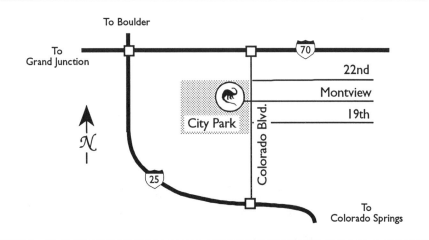

1.29 University of Colorado Museum Boulder, CO

The University of Colorado Museum at Boulder features a new exhibit entitled "Dinosaurs & Sea Monsters of the Ancient Rockies."

Exhibit Features:
- Skulls of *Triceratops*, *Diplodocus*, and *Corythosaurus*.
- A *Tylosaurus* skull and a *Dolichorhynchops* flipper.
- *Pterodactyl*, a *Camptosaurus* forepaw, and a sabertoothed cat.

Hours:
Monday–Friday 9:00 a.m.–5:00 p.m.
Saturday 9:00 a.m.–4:00 p.m.
Sunday 10:00 a.m.–4:00 p.m.
Closed: all university holidays.
Minimum time required to see exhibit: 30 minutes

Entrance Fees:
(Recommended donation)
Adults $2.50
Students and Seniors $1.50
Children over 6 $1.00

Address:

University of Colorado Museum
Henderson Building, 15th and Broadway
Campus Box 218, Boulder, CO 80309
Telephone: (303)492-6165

Directions:

From Denver take Highway 36 to Baseline and 28th Street. Follow Baseline west to 15th Street. The museum is at the Intersection of 15th and Broadway, on the University of Colorado campus.

Or, to reach the museum from the north, take 119 to 28th Street. Follow 28th Street to Baseline and then follow Baseline west to 15th Street.

Map to University of Colorado Museum

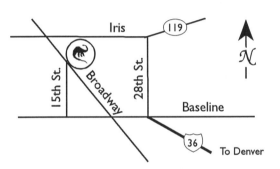

1.30 University of Wyoming Geological Museum, Laramie, WY

The University of Wyoming opened in 1887 in the frontier town of Laramie. In 1893, Dr. W. C. Knight was hired to teach at the university. When Knight became curator of the museum in 1896, he set to work collecting over 70 tons of Jurassic plant and reptile fossils. In 1901, Charles Gilmore, a student at the university, collected the *Brontosaurus* that is now the museum's centerpiece. Charles Gilmore eventually became the curator of the Smithsonian Museum in Washington, D.C.

Articulated Skeletons:

- Complete *Apatosaurus* (formerly called *Brontosaurus*).
- Juvenile *Maiasaura* and a full-grown mammoth.
- Ichthyosaurs, *Mosasaurus*, and plesiosaurs.

Exhibit Features:

- Remains of *Anchiceratops*, *Anatosaurus*, and plesiosaurs.
- A dinosaur nest with eggs, dinosaur skin, and related dinosaur fossils.
- A 47-foot copper statue of *Tyrannosaurus rex* sculpted by W. C. Knight.
- A *Triceratops* skull and murals of the prehistoric past.
- Some of America's oldest fossils, 1.7-billion-year-old stromatolites.

Hours:

Monday–Friday 9:00 a.m.–5:00 p.m.

Closed: weekends; July 4, Thanksgiving, Christmas, New Year's Day.

Minimum time required to see exhibit: 1.5 hours

Entrance Fees: free (donations accepted)

Address:

The University of Wyoming Geological Museum
Laramie, WY 82071-3006
Telephone: (307)766-4218

Directions:

Laramie is 50 miles west of Cheyenne on I-80. From I-80 exit at 3rd Street and go north. Take a right at Lewis Street. The museum is located at Lewis and 11th streets on the University of Wyoming campus.

Map to University of Wyoming Geological Museum

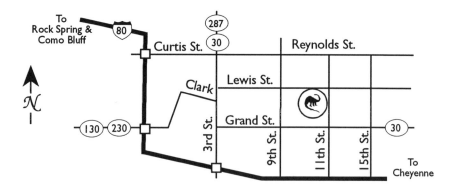

1.31 Como Bluff Dinosaur Quarry near Medicine Bow, WY

In 1877, O. C. Marsh received a box of bones with a mysterious letter post-marked Laramie, WY. The letter described a fossil find of magnificent proportions and included an offer to reveal the location for the right price. The letter was signed "Harlow and Edwards." Marsh sent a check for $75 (in 1877, $75 was more than most people made in a month) with instructions for further excavation and shipment of bones.

"Harlow and Edwards" urged Marsh to come to Como Bluff. The letter warned that other men were near the site. Marsh feared that his despised rival, E.D. Cope, was closing in on the bones, so he immediately sent his assistant, Sam Williston, to Como Bluff.

Upon his arrival, Williston discovered that "Harlow and Edwards" were actually William H. Reed and William E. Carlin. The two men were railroad employees and would spend company time hunting for fossils. Afraid of losing their jobs, Reed and Carlin used aliases. Unfortunately, they were unable to cash a check made out to "Harlow and Edwards."

Williston wired back to Marsh, telling him that fossil bones extended seven miles along Como Bluff. Frantic to collect the bones before Cope's men heard of the discovery, Marsh's crew worked through the winter.

When Cope's men finally arrived at Como Bluff, a fierce "Bone War" erupted. The rivalry was so bitter that some of Marsh's men were known to smash uncollected bones rather than risk them falling into Cope's hands.

In 1898, Henry Osborn of the American Museum of Natural History began a methodical scientific study of the area. One of the amazing things that Osborn discovered here was a cabin built of dinosaur bones. The giant dinosaur bones were so plentiful that a shepherd had used them to construct his home. You can see a replica of the bone cabin here.

Hours: always open

Minimum time required to see exhibit: 15 minutes

Entrance Fees: free

Address: none

Directions:

Como Bluff is 50 miles northwest of Laramie and 7 miles southeast of Medicine Bow on Highway 30 at the Carbon-Albany county line.

Nearby:

There is a small natural history museum in Rock River.

Map to Como Bluff Dinosaur Quarry

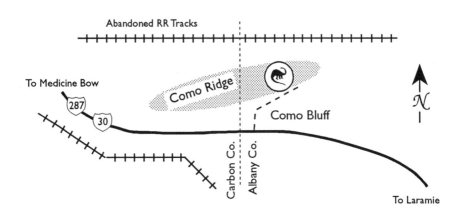

1.32 Lance Creek
Lance Creek, WY

In 1888, on a tip from a cowboy, John Bell Hatcher discovered *Triceratops* near Lance Creek (geographically part of the Lance Formation). *Triceratops* was the most famous of the ceratopsians, or horned dinosaurs. Most ceratopsians had horns like a bull or rhinoceros and were the size of an elephant; the ceratopsian's temperament was probably similar to that of a bull.

The remains of more than 30 *Triceratops* and *Torosaurus* were discovered in the 200-square-mile area just north of the town of Lance Creek during the period from 1888 to 1897.

Many different species of *Triceratops* are found here. It is unusual to find so many closely related but distinct species in the same location. Some scientists believe that the variation in specimens represents variation within a species rather than several different species. This difficulty in distinguishing fossils at the species level or even genera level cloud arguments for a gradual decline in dinosaur diversity towards the end of the Cretaceous.

Hours: always open

Entrance Fees: free (Although this area is open range, there is not always access to locations on private land. Before venturing into the badlands, be sure to check with authorities in the town of Lance Creek.)

Address: none

Directions:

Lance Creek is in eastern Wyoming, about 100 miles east of Casper. The remains were discovered at several sites in the region between Crazy Woman Creek and Lance Creek, 2 to 15 miles north of Lance Creek.

Map to Lance Creek Historical area

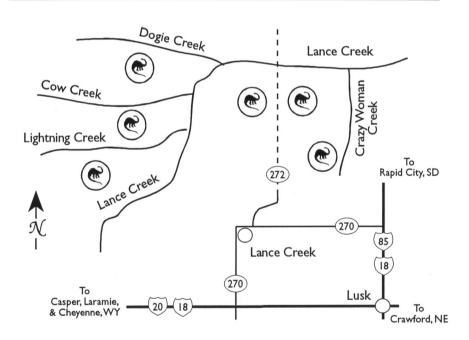

1.33 Fossil Butte National Monument near Kemmerer, WY

Fifty million years ago, during the Eocene Epoch of the Cenozoic Era, Fossil Butte (part of the Eocene Green River Formation) was a large lake. Animals died and fell to the bottom of the lake. Calcium carbonate precipitated out of the water and covered their remains. When the waters of the lake receded, they left behind fossils in the shale.

Articulated Skeletons:
- Crocodile, turtle, stingray, and countless fish fossils.

Exhibit Features:
- A mural depicting the lake life during the Eocene Epoch.
- Hiking to historic fossil collection sites.

Hours:
Daily 8:00 a.m.–4:30 p.m.
Closed: Thanksgiving, Christmas, New Year's Day.
Summer hours (Memorial Day to Labor Day):
Daily 8:00 a.m.–7:00 p.m.
Minimum time required to see exhibit: 30 minutes

Entrance Fees: free

Address:
Fossil Butte National Monument
Box 592, Kemmerer, WY 83101
Telephone: (307)877-4455

Directions:
Fossil Butte National Monument is a few hours' drive northwest of Vernal, Utah, in far southwestern Wyoming. From I-80, exit at U.S. 30 North. Fossil Butte National Monument is 80 miles northwest on U.S. 30, just beyond Kemmerer.

Map to Fossil Butte National Monument

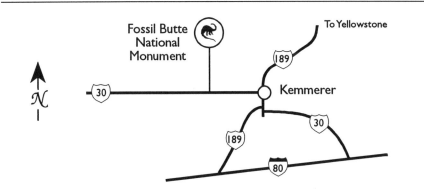

1.34 Tate Mineralogical Museum
Casper, WY

Exhibit Features:
- Some local fossils, dinosaur footprints, and a mosasaur skull.

Hours:
Monday–Friday 2:00 p.m.–5:00 p.m.
Summer hours:
Monday–Friday 9:00 a.m.–5:00 p.m.
Closed: weekends; all holidays.
Minimum time required to see exhibit: 15 minutes

Entrance Fees: free

Address:
Tate Mineralogical Museum
Casper Community College, Casper, WY 82062

Directions:
From I-25 take exit 188B south. Follow Poplar Street to College Drive and turn left. Head east towards the college. The museum is located on the Casper Community College campus.

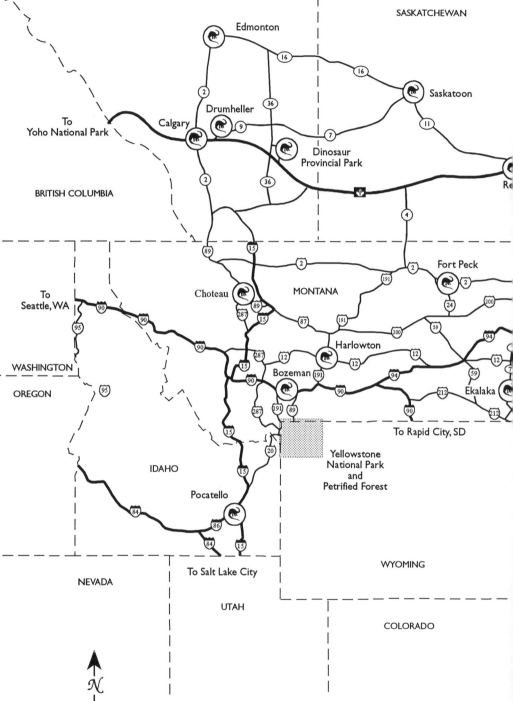

2.
The Northwest
The Hunting Grounds
of *Tyrannosaurus rex*

The final geological period in "The Age of Dinosaurs" is the Cretaceous (144 million years ago to 65 million years ago). The word *Cretaceous* is derived from the Latin word *creta*, which means "chalk." Rocks of the Cretaceous Period were first studied along the white chalk cliffs of England.

During the Cretaceous Period, the northwestern United States and much of western Canada was next to an inland sea now known as the Mid-Continental Cretaceous Seaway. The region's close proximity to this sea, along with a paleo-latitude much closer to the equator, made for a more temperate climate than this region has today. Angiosperms (flowering plants) appeared early in the Cretaceous. The new plants did not grow as tall as previous ones, they had different types of leaves, and many had berries. Dinosaurs adapted to eat these new plants.

The sauropods and stegosaurs that dominated the Jurassic become relatively rare during the Cretaceous. Duckbills with their elaborate crests and ceratopsians with horns and spiky frills became the common dinosaurs. Sauropods had been designed to eat the tops of trees; ceratopsians were designed to eat low-growing vegetation.

Carnivorous dinosaurs adapted to the challenge of eating new types of herbivorous dinosaurs. Bringing down a full-grown *Triceratops* must have been quite a challenge, but *Tyrannosaurus rex* was more than capable. *Tyrannosaurus rex* weighed nearly 10,000 pounds, had six-inch serrated teeth in jaws that could take a six-foot bite, and may have been able to run at a speed of 40 miles per hour.

2.1 Dinosaur Provincial Park near Patricia, AB

Seventy-five million years ago, Dinosaur Provincial Park was a series of deltas and river flood plains extending into a warm shallow sea to the east. Then, 10,000 to 15,000 years ago, flash floods from melting glaciers carved the area into the badlands that now expose a fantastic wealth of dinosaur bones. In 1979 the United Nations recognized Dinosaur Provincial Park as a World Heritage Site. Other World Heritage Sites include the Pyramids in Egypt and Mount Everest National Park in Nepal.

Camping is available in the park and you should probably spend the night and plan an early morning hike (before the heat) through dinosaur country.

The Field Station of the Royal Tyrrell Museum of Paleontology is located within Dinosaur Provincial Park.

Articulated Skeletons:
- *Chasmeosaurus, Albertosaurus,* and several duckbilled dinosaurs.
- *Corythosaurus* and other duckbilled and ceratopsian dinosaurs, displayed *in situ* at various locations in the park.
- A pack of small carnivorous dinosaurs attacking a duckbilled dinosaur.

Exhibit Features:
- A paleontology laboratory where visitors can see the fossils being prepared.
- A model of *Styracosaurus.*
- A theater showing dinosaur videos.
- Outdoor exhibits of dinosaurs *in situ.*
- Guided hikes and bus tours on trails paved with dinosaur bones.

Hours:
(Museum hours; park is always open)
Mid-October to May 14
Monday–Friday 8:15 a.m.–4:30 p.m.
May 15 to Labor Day
Daily 8:15 a.m.–9:00 p.m.
Labor Day to Mid-October
Monday–Friday 8:15 a.m.–4:30 p.m.
Friday, Saturday, Sunday 8:15 a.m.–6:00 p.m.

Closed: New Year's Day, Alberta Family Day (3rd Monday in February), Good Friday, Easter Monday, Remembrance Day (November 11), Christmas Day, Boxing Day (December 26).

Minimum time required to see exhibit: 2 hours to 2 days

Entrance Fees:

$1.00/person recommended donation at the Field Station
Camping $10.75

Address:

Dinosaur Provincial Park
Field Station of the Royal Tyrrell Museum of Paleontology
P.O. Box 60, Patricia, Alberta, Canada T0J 2K0
Telephone: (403)378-4342

Directions:

The park is 49.6 kilometers (31 miles) northeast of Brooks and 160 kilometers (100 miles) east of Calgary. From Highway 1 take either Highway 550 or Highway 884 to Highway 544. Head towards Patricia on Highway 544. At Patricia head northeast to the park. (Signs mark the way to the park along both Highway 544 and Highway 884.)

Map to Dinosaur Provincial Park

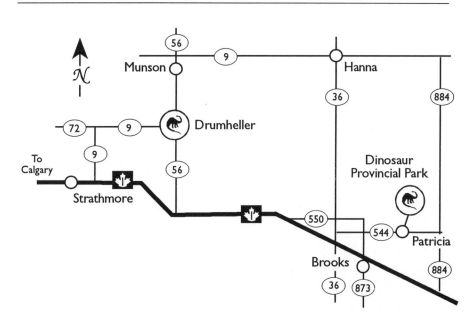

2.2 The Royal Tyrrell Museum of Paleontology near Drumheller, AB

The Royal Tyrrell Museum of Paleontology is one of the world's most magnificent dinosaur museums. The collection is large, the displays are well designed, and the surrounding area is rich in fossils. The museum, which opened in 1985, is located in the badlands along the Red Deer River. A century earlier, Joseph Tyrrell discovered dinosaurs just west of the museum. News of this discovery triggered the Great Canadian Bone Rush. Paleontologists would float down the Red Deer River and fill their barges with dinosaur bones.

Today, the badlands around the museum are as important as ever. Every year, scientists and museum volunteers make new dinosaur discoveries.

Articulated Skeletons:

- 35 complete dinosaur skeletons including *Tyrannosaurus rex*, *Triceratops*, *Albertosaurus*, *Eucentrosaurus*, *Coelophysis*, *Corythosaurus*, *Dromaeosaurus*, *Hadrosaurus*, *Hypacrosaurus*, *Lambeosaurus*, *Ornitholestes*, *Saurornitholestes*, *Dilophosaurus*, *Camarasaurus*, *Stegosaurus*, *Camptosaurus*.
- *Dimetrodon*, *Ichthyosaurus*, *Plesiosaurus*, *Mosasaurus*.

Exhibit Features:

- 200 dinosaur specimens and over 800 fossils.
- The Palaeoconservatory, a wonderful indoor garden of 110 species of plants that lived during the Age of Dinosaurs.
- Life-size models of *Albertosaurus* and an ankylosaur.
- Spectacular murals and lighting accentuate the fossil collection.
- Mini-theaters, slide shows, and interactive computers.
- Displays explaining fossilization, evolution, and biomechanics.
- The display of Mesozoic sea life includes sound effects and special lighting.

Hours:

Tuesday–Sunday 10:00 a.m.–5:00 p.m.

Closed: Mondays; Christmas.

Summer hours (Victoria Day weekend to Labor Day):
Daily 9:00 a.m.–9:00 p.m.

Minimum time required to see exhibit: 1 day

Entrance Fees:
Adults $5.00
Children (7–18) $2.00

Address:
Royal Tyrrell Museum of Paleontology
Box 7500 Drumheller, Alberta, Canada T0J 0Y0
Telephone: (403)823-7707

Directions:
Drumheller is about 144 kilometers (90 miles) northeast of Calgary. Take Highway 1 east from Calgary to Highway 9 North. Highway 9 leads to Drumheller. The museum is located on the Dinosaur Trail (Highway 838) about 6.4 kilometers (4 miles) northwest of Drumheller near Munson and on the north side of the Red Deer river.

Map to Drumheller, Alberta

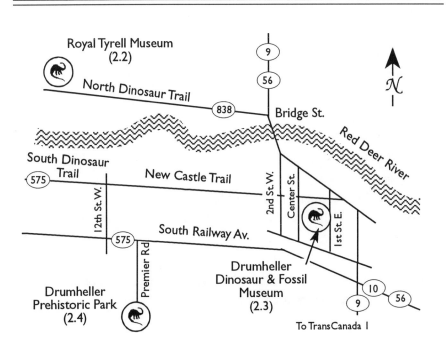

2.3 Drumheller Dinosaur and Fossil Museum Drumheller, AB

Although overshadowed by the magnificent Royal Tyrrell Museum, the Drumheller Museum has several dinosaur exhibits. All of the dinosaurs exhibited here are genuine fossils.

Articulated Skeletons:

- *Edmontosaurus*, unearthed locally in 1923.

Exhibit Features:

- *Pachyrhinosaurus* skull, unearthed locally in 1960.
- Invertebrate fossils, leaf imprints, and fossil fragments.

Hours:

Daily 10:00 a.m.–5:00 p.m.

Summer hours (July 1 to August 31):

Daily 10:00 a.m.–6:00 p.m.

Closed: Thanksgiving; October 15 to May 1.

Minimum time required to see exhibit: 20 minutes

Entrance Fees:

Adults $2.00

Children (6–18) $0.75

Seniors $1.00

Address:

Drumheller Dinosaur and Fossil Museum

Box 2135, 335 1st Street East, Drumheller, AB, Canada T0J 0Y0

Telephone: (403)823-2593

Directions:

Located in downtown Drumheller, the museum is south of the intersection of 3rd Avenue and 1st Street East.

2.4 Drumheller Prehistoric Park Drumheller, AB

This is a small park with picnic tables and dinosaur models.

Hours:
April 1 to April 30:
Daily 10:00 a.m.–6:00 p.m.
May 1 to Labor Day:
Daily 9:00 a.m.–9:00 p.m.
Labor Day to Thanksgiving:
Daily 10:00 a.m.–6:00 p.m.
Minimum time required to see exhibit: 30 minutes

Entrance Fees: vary

Address:
Drumheller Prehistoric Park
Prehistoric Park, Box 2686, Drumheller, AB T0J 0Y0
Telephone: (403)823-6144

Directions:
Follow New Castle Trail west from downtown Drumheller. Head south on Premier Road. The park is at the end of Premier Road.

2.5 Calgary Zoo's Prehistoric Park Calgary, AB

The 1930s saw the opening of what was to become the world's largest Prehistoric Park at the Calgary Zoo. The life-size dinosaur models are accurate and painted in realistic colors. It's easy to forget that you are stuck in the Pleistocene when you take a walk through the Calgary Zoo's Prehistoric Park.

Exhibit Features:
- Life-size models of *Tyrannosaurus rex*, *Triceratops*, *Styracosaurus*, *Eucentrosaurus*, *Ankylosaurus*, *Iguanodon*, *Edmontosaurus*, *Corythosaurus*, *Struthiomimus*, *Ornitholestes*, *Elasmosaurus*, *Nothosaurus*, *Placodus*, *Tanystropheus*, *Tylosaurus*, *Pteranodon*, *Stegosaurus*, *Apatosaurus*, and *Archaeopteryx*.

Hours:

Daily 9:00 a.m.–4:00 p.m.
Summer hours (Memorial Day to Labor Day):
Daily 9:00 a.m.–6:00 p.m.
Minimum time required to see exhibit: 2 hours

Entrance Fees:

Adults $7.50
Children (2–15) $3.75
Seniors $4.75 ($2.00 on Tuesdays)

Address:

Calgary Zoo's Prehistoric Park
P.O. Box 3036, Station B, Calgary, AB, Canada T2M 4R8
Telephone: (403)232-9300

Directions:

The Calgary Zoo is located on an island in the Bow River at the south end of Calgary. From Highway 2 (Deerfoot Trail) take the Memorial Drive West exit. The zoo will be to your left (south) and the parking area to your right. A tunnel takes you from the parking area north of Memorial Drive under the road and the river to the zoo.

Map to Calgary Zoo's Prehistoric Park

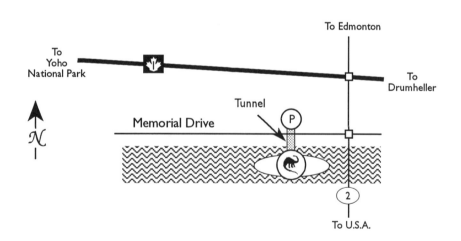

2.6 Provincial Museum of Alberta
Edmonton, AB

The Provincial Museum of Alberta is a showcase for a few of the many dinosaurs that once roamed Alberta.

Articulated Skeletons:

- *Albertosaurus*, *Lambeosaurus*, sabertoothed cat, and a Columbian Mammoth.

Exhibit Features:

- Full-size models of *Hadrosaurus* and *Ankylosaurus*.
- Fossils and fossil casts representing *Ankylosaurus*, *Hadrosaurus*, a lankeosaur, and a eucentrosaur.

Hours:

Tuesday–Sunday 9:00 a.m.–5:00 p.m.
Summer hours (Victoria Day to Labor Day):
Daily 9:00 a.m.–8:00 p.m.
Minimum time required to see exhibit: 45 minutes

Entrance Fees:

Adults $3.25
Children (6–17) $1.25
Families $8.00

Address:

Provincial Museum of Alberta
12845 102nd Avenue, Edmonton, AB, Canada T5N 0M6
Telephone: (403)453-9100 or (403)427-1786

Directions:

Heading north into Edmonton from Calgary on Highway 2, exit at Whitemud Drive going west. Follow Whitemud across the river and turn right on 149th Street. Turn right at 102nd Avenue (Stony Plain Road) and follow signs to the museum.

Map to Provincial Museum of Alberta

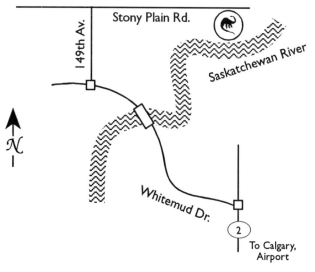

2.7 Museum of Natural Sciences Saskatoon, SK

The centerpiece of this museum is a magnificent *Tyrannosaurus rex* skeleton. In keeping with current scientific thinking, the *Tyrannosaurus* is mounted with its tail upright as an agile, aggressive hunter on the attack

The museum's theme is "Evolution Through Geologic Time." Therefore, it is fitting that the museum forms a physical link between the geology and biology buildings. To illustrate the role of evolution in shaping our planet's history, the museum contrasts living animals with fossils.

Articulated Skeletons:
- *Tyrannosaurus rex, Stegosaurus, Pteranodon,* and *Triceratops.*
- *Eryops* and several prehistoric horses.

Exhibit Features:
- The dinosaur reconstructions are displayed among living plants that are similar to prehistoric plants.
- Several of the museum's walls are clad with slabs of fossiliferous rock from Canada and Germany.
- Casts of two baby *Protoceratops* and an *Archaeopteryx.*
- Invertebrate fossils and parts of an ichthyosaur.

Hours:

Monday–Friday 9:00 a.m.–4:30 p.m.

Saturday–Sunday Noon–5:00 p.m.

Closed: Good Friday, Easter, Victoria Day, Labor Day, July 1, August Civic Holiday; from Christmas Eve through early January.

Minimum time required to see exhibit: 45 minutes

Entrance Fees: free

Address:

Museum of Natural Sciences

University of Saskatchewan, Saskatoon, SK, Canada S7N 0W0

Telephone: (306)966-8385 or (306)966-5683

Directions:

Saskatoon, Saskatchewan, is 251 kilometers (157 miles) northwest of Regina on Highway 11 and 400 kilometers (250 miles) northeast of the Royal Tyrrell Museum in Drumheller. From the south, follow Highway 16 into Saskatoon. Turn left on College Drive. Take the first right into the University of Saskatchewan campus, at Wiggins Road. Follow the signs to the museum.

Map to Museum of Natural Sciences

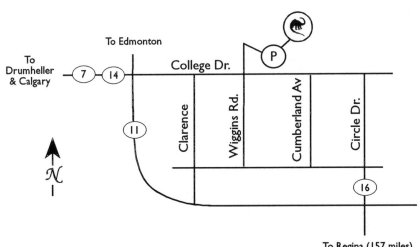

2.8 Saskatchewan Museum of Natural History Regina, SK

Exhibit Features:
- "Megamunch," an animated half-size replica of *Tyrannosaurus rex*.

Hours:
Daily 10:00 a.m.–5:00 p.m.
Summer hours (May 1 to Labor Day):
Daily 9:00 a.m.–8:30 p.m.
Closed: Christmas.
Minimum time required to see exhibit: 15 minutes

Entrance Fees: free

Address:
Saskatchewan Museum of Natural History
College Avenue and Albert Street
2445 Albert Street, Regina, SK, Canada S4P 3V7
Telephone: (306)787-2815

Directions:
Regina is in south-central Saskatchewan. The museum is located on the corner of Albert (Highway 6) and College Avenue. All main highways entering Regina intersect Highway 6.

2.9 Fort Peck Project Fort Peck, MT

Exhibit Features:
- *Triceratops, Trachodon,* and a mosasaur.

Hours:
Daily 9:00 a.m.–5:00 p.m.
Minimum time required to see exhibit: 30 minutes

Entrance Fees: free

Address:
Fort Peck Project, U.S. Army Corps of Engineers
Box 208, Fort Peck, MT 59223-0208
Telephone: (406)526-3431

Directions:
Fort Peck is in northeastern Montana, 22 miles south of Glasgow. The museum is at the Fort Peck power plants. Follow Highway 24 to the power plant.

2.10 Carter County Museum
Ekalaka, MT

The museum features mostly local fossils from Cretaceous dinosaurs. Ekalaka is an out-of-the-way town, but on the way there you'll pass through unique geological formations.

Articulated Skeletons:
- *Anatosaurus* (discovered 35 miles west of the museum).

Exhibit Features:
- Skulls of *Triceratops*, *Nanotyrannus*, *Pachycephalosaurus*, and an Ice Age bison.
- Dinosaur tracks, fossil turtles, marine fossils.

Hours:
Tuesday–Friday 9:00 a.m.–12:00, 1:00 p.m.–5:00 p.m.
Saturday–Sunday 1:00 p.m.–5:00 p.m.
Closed: Mondays; July 4, Thanksgiving, Christmas Eve, Christmas, New Year's Day.
Minimum time required to see exhibit: 1 hour

Entrance Fees: free

Address:
Carter County Museum
100 Main Street, Ekalaka, MT 59324
Telephone: (406)775-6886 or (406)775-6327

Directions:
Ekalaka is 35 miles south of Baker on Highway 7, in the southeast corner of Montana.

Nearby:

There are fossil beds about 10 miles east of Baker on the north side of Highway 12 near the North Dakota border.

Map to Ekalaka and fossil beds

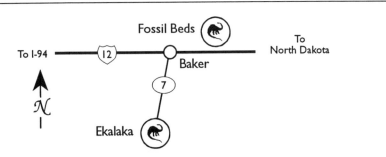

2.11 Upper Musselshell Museum Harlowton, MT

Although this museum is primarily dedicated to pioneer history, it does include a mounted skeleton of *Avaceratops*. The skeleton is a cast of the original, which is on display at the Academy of Sciences in Philadelphia. *Avaceratops* was a small horned dinosaur found north of Shawmut, Montana, in 1981. About 72 million years ago this area was a coastal lowland that supported a great diversity of dinosaurs.

Articulated Skeletons:

- Cast of *Avaceratops*.

Hours:

Tuesday–Saturday 10:00 a.m.–5:00 p.m.
Monday 1:00 p.m.–5:00 p.m.
Closed: Sundays; November 1 through April 30.
Minimum time required to see exhibit: 15 minutes

Entrance Fees: Recommended donation $1.00

Address:

Upper Musselshell Museum
11 South Central, Harlowton, MT 59036
Telephone: (406)632-5519

Directions:

Harlowton is 150 miles northeast of Bozeman, Montana. Take Highway 191 north from Bozeman to Harlowton. The museum is at the corner of Central and Division streets.

2.12 Egg Mountain Tour near Choteau, MT

In 1978, Jack Horner was spending his vacation the way he always had, hunting for dinosaurs. He was browsing through a rock shop when he stumbled across the fossils of tiny, baby duckbilled dinosaurs. The shopkeeper, Marion Brandvold, agreed to show Horner where she had found the baby duckbill fossils. Brandvold had discovered the communal nesting site of a herd of duckbilled dinosaurs. They named the site "Egg Mountain."

Egg Mountain was a dinosaur nursery. Evidence found here indicates that at least some dinosaurs cared for their young in the same way that most birds care for theirs: The babies stayed in the nest while the parents brought them food and guarded them. The teeth of the baby dinosaurs show plenty of wear, but the structure of their kneecaps suggest that they did little traveling. Some of the nests contain babies that were only 14 inches long, while other nests had fossil babies that were over three feet long.

The nests found on Egg Mountain were evenly spaced about 23 feet apart, the approximate length of a full-grown maiasaur. Similarly, ground-nesting birds usually space their nests the length of their outstretched wings.

Near the egg fossil site, Horner and his team discovered evidence of dinosaur herds. The remains of 10,000 dinosaurs of the same species were found together, apparently killed by the sudden eruption of a volcano.

The site has also yielded complete growth sequences of duckbilled dinosaurs. The analysis of these growth sequences indicates that dinosaurs grew rapidly when young and then more slowly as they aged. This is similar to the growth pattern of birds and mammals and unlike that of reptiles. Turtle and crocodile fossils found nearby exhibit the characteristic growth rings of cold-blooded animals.

The discoveries at this site have changed the way we think about dinosaurs. The Old Trail Museum (Section 2.13) and the Museum of the Rockies (Section 2.14) offer guided tours of the famous Egg Mountain dinosaur nesting site.

Hours: Tours start at 2:00 p.m. July through August

Minimum time required to see exhibit: 2 hours

Entrance Fees:

Adults $7.50

Children (under 12) $4.00

Telephone: (406)494-2251

Directions:

Choteau, Montana, is about 100 miles north of Helena and 50 miles northwest of Great Falls. Egg Mountain tours meet on the road in Choteau. Egg Mountain is 21 miles west of Choteau.

Map to Egg Mountain and Old Trail Museum

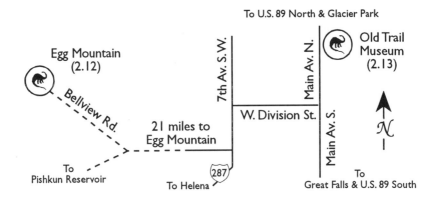

2.13 Old Trail Museum
Choteau, MT

This museum displays local fossils and runs a tour of the area around Egg Mountain. Tours are subject to a minimum booking so call ahead for latest information.

Hours:
Tuesday–Sunday 10:00 a.m.–3:00 p.m.
Closed: Monday–Wednesday
Summer hours (Memorial Day to Labor Day):
Daily 9:00 a.m.–6:00 p.m.
Minimum time required to see exhibit: 15 minutes

Entrance Fees: free

Address:
Old Trail Museum
Choteau, MT 59422
Telephone: (406)466-5332

Directions:
Choteau, Montana, is about 100 miles north of Helena and 50 miles northwest of Great Falls.

2.14 Museum of the Rockies
Bozeman, MT

The Museum of the Rockies displays the latest dinosaur discoveries of Montana. Montana is famous for its Cretaceous dinosaurs. Jack Horner discovered the nesting grounds of vast herds of *Hadrosaurus* just 180 miles northwest of the museum. In 1990, two more *Tyrannosaurus rex* remains were discovered near Hell Creek, Montana.

Exhibit Features:
- Models of *Maiasaura*, a hypsilophodontid, and a *Pterodactyl*.
- A diorama of *Pterodactyl*, *Orodromeus*, and *Maiasaura* nesting grounds.
- Public fossil preparation lab.
- Dinosaur eggs.

- Robotic models of a mother *Triceratops* with two juveniles.
- Mosasaur skull.
- Inquire at the museum about guided tours to *Maiasaura* nesting site.
- Other research specimens on rotating exhibition.

Hours:

Monday–Saturday 9:00 a.m.–5:00 p.m.
Sunday 12:30 p.m.–5:00 p.m.
Summer hours (Memorial Day to Labor Day):
Daily 9:00 a.m.–9:00 p.m.
Closed: Thanksgiving, Christmas, New Year's Day.
Minimum time required to see exhibit: 1 hour

Entrance Fees:

Adults $5.00
Young adults (13–18) $3.00
Children (5–12) $2.00

Address:

Museum of the Rockies
600 West Kagy Boulevard, Bozeman, MT 59717
Telephone: (406)994-2251 or (406)994-DINO

Directions:

Bozeman, Montana, is about halfway between Butte and Billings. The museum is in Bozeman at the southern end of the Montana State University campus. From I-90, take the Main Street exit west. Near the center of town, take Wilson Avenue south (left). Follow Wilson south to Kagy. The museum is near the intersection of Wilson and Kagy.

Map to Museum of the Rockies

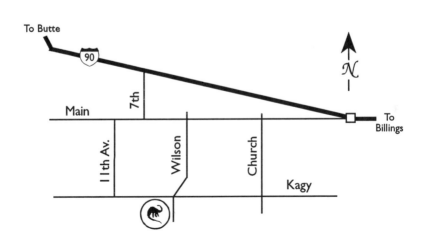

2.15 Idaho Museum of Natural History Pocatello, ID

Exhibit Features:
- A few fragmentary dinosaur remains including some eggshells.

Hours:
Monday–Saturday 10:00 a.m.–5:00 p.m.
Closed: Sundays; July 4, Thanksgiving, Christmas, New Year's Day.
Minimum time required to see exhibit: 10 minutes

Entrance Fees: free

Address:
Idaho Museum of Natural History
Box 8096, I.S.U., Pocatello, ID 83209
Telephone: (208)236-3168

Directions:
Pocatello is in southeastern Idaho, 250 miles east of Boise. From I-15, take the Clark Street exit and head west. Turn left on S. 4th Street and then left again on Dillion. The museum is on Dillion.

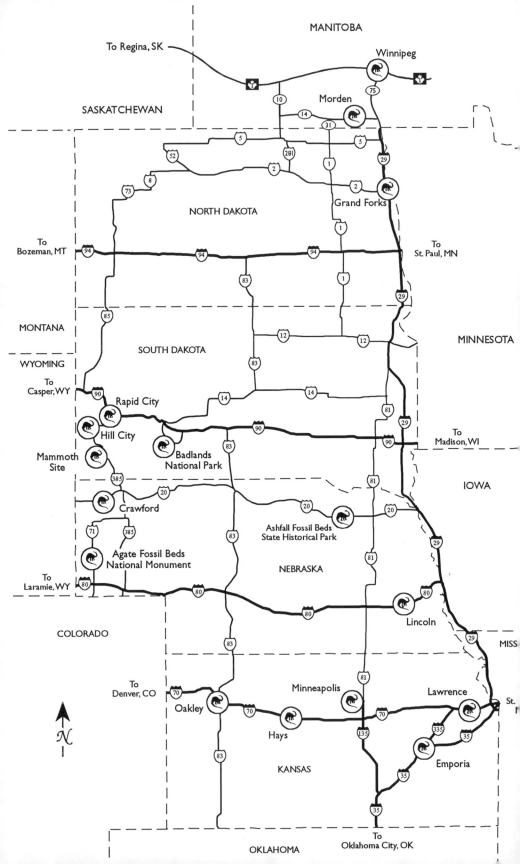

3.
The Midwest
The Mid-Continental Cretaceous Seaway

During the Cretaceous Period, a vast body of water known as the Western Interior Seaway extended from the northern reaches of Canada to the Gulf of Mexico. At that time, the Gulf of Mexico covered much of the southern United States. Sea monsters filled the warm, shallow waters. *Pterodactyl* ruled the skies.

Throughout the Cretaceous the level of the shallow sea would rise and fall. At the close of the Cretaceous the sea disappeared. We know there was an ocean here because of the plentiful fossils of sea reptiles, marine invertebrates, and fish that are found here.

3.1 University of Kansas Museum of Natural History, Lawrence, KS

The museum has an excellent display of Cretaceous pterosaurs and sea reptiles. These creatures were contemporaries of the dinosaurs. Dinosaurs ruled the land, pterosaurs ruled the skies, and incredible sea reptiles ruled the oceans. Kansas is very rich in Cretaceous marine fossils. The University of Kansas Museum of Natural History has over 100,000 specimens in its collection.

Articulated Skeletons:
- *Parasaurolophus* and *Archaeopteryx*.
- Numerous examples of ichthyosaurs, plesiosaurs, and mosasaurs.
- Several pterosaur examples including *Pteranodon*, whose 25-foot wingspan holds the record for the largest complete pterosaur fossil.

Exhibit Features:
- *Triceratops* skull, pieces of *Silvisaurus*, and assorted bones.

Hours:
Monday–Saturday 8:00 a.m.–5:00 p.m.
Sunday 1:00 p.m.–5:00 p.m.
Closed: July 4, Thanksgiving, Christmas Eve, Christmas, New Year's Day.
Minimum time required to see exhibit: 1 hour

Entrance Fees:
(Recommended donation)
Adults $2.00
Children $1.00

Address:
University of Kansas Museum of Natural History
Dyche Hall, 14th and Jayhawk Boulevard, Lawrence, KS 66045
Telephone: (913)864-4540

Directions:
Lawrence is 30 miles west of Kansas City, Kansas. The museum is located on the University of Kansas campus next to the Kansas Union, at 14th Street and Jayhawk Boulevard. Enter the campus at 13th Street and Jayhawk Boulevard.

3.2 Emporia State University Geology Museum, Emporia, KS

This museum features exceptionally well-preserved specimens from the Hamilton Quarry. Hamilton Quarry fossils are from the Pennsylvanian Period (320 to 2860 million years ago). The fossils of early reptiles, fish, plants, and insects are on display.

Articulated Skeletons:

- A mosasaur.

Exhibit Features:

- *Pteranodon* wing and Cretaceous fish and plant fossils.
- Hamilton Quarry fossils as well as invertebrates from Kansas.

Hours:

Monday–Friday 8:00 a.m.–10:00 p.m.
Saturday 8:00 p.m.–12:00 p.m.
Closed: Sundays; July 4, Thanksgiving; last week of December through the first week of January, and whenever the university is not in session.
Minimum time required to see exhibit: 30 minutes

Entrance Fees: free

Address:

Emporia State University Geology Museum
1200 Commercial Street, Emporia State University, Emporia, KS 66801
Telephone: (316)341-5978

Directions:

Emporia is about 100 miles southwest of Kansas City. From U.S. 50, take exit 133. From I-35, take the Merchant Street exit. The museum is on Merchant Street, four blocks south of I-35 in the Science Hall.

3.3 Ottawa County Historical Museum Minneapolis, KS

Although dinosaurs are rare in Kansas, the armored dinosaur *Silvisaurus* was found nearby the museum in 1955. The museum has a display featuring *Silvisaurus*. The museum also displays local fossils.

Hours:
Monday–Friday 10:00 a.m.–Noon and 1:00 p.m.–5:30 p.m.
Saturday 10:00 a.m.–Noon and 1:00 p.m.–5:00 p.m.
Closed: Sundays; July 4, Thanksgiving, Christmas, New Year's Day.
Minimum time required to see exhibit: 15 minutes

Entrance Fees: free

Address:
Ottawa County Historical Museum
110 South Concord, Minneapolis, KS 67467
Telephone: (913)392-3621

Directions:
The museum is about 20 miles north of Salina, Kansas. Just after northbound U.S. 81 narrows to a two-lane highway, turn left on Highway 93. Continue into Minneapolis to Concord. Head south to the museum.

3.4 Sternberg Museum Hays, KS

The Sternberg Museum displays some of the many Cretaceous marine fossils found in Kansas.

Articulated Skeletons:
- *Pterodactyl*, mosasaurs, and a plesiosaur.
- The perfectly preserved remains of a large fish (*Xiphactinus*) with a smaller fish (*Gillicus*) inside it.

Exhibit Features:
- Dinosaur skin impressions, footprints, and assorted teeth and bones.
- Skull casts of a several dinosaurs.
- An excellent collection of Cretaceous marine fossils.

Hours:

Monday–Friday 9:00 a.m.–5:00 p.m.

Saturday–Sunday 1:00 p.m.–5:00 p.m.

Closed: all state holidays.

Minimum time required to see exhibit: 30 minutes.

Entrance Fees: free

Address:

Sternberg Museum, Fort Hays State University

Campus Drive, Hays, KS 67601

Telephone: (913)628-4286

Directions:

Hays is in central Kansas, 270 miles west of Kansas City. The museum is on the Fort Hays State University campus. From I-70, take exit 159 and head south on Highway 183. Turn right at 8th Street and head northwest. Take a left on to Park Street and then a right onto Campus Drive.

Map to Sternberg Museum

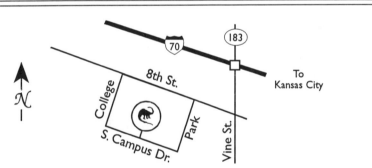

3.5 Fick Fossil and History Museum Oakley, KS

This museum displays local Cretaceous marine fossils.

Exhibit Features:

- Fossils of a 15-foot fish, a plesiosaur paddle, and a mosasaur skull.
- 11,000 Cretaceous shark teeth.

Hours:

Monday–Saturday 9:30 a.m.–5:00 p.m.

Sundays & holidays 2:00 p.m.–4:00 p.m.

Summer hours (Memorial Day to Labor Day):

Monday–Saturday 8:30 a.m.–6:00 p.m.

Sundays & holidays 2:00 p.m.–4:00 p.m.

Closed: Thanksgiving, Christmas, New Year's Day.

Minimum time required to see exhibit: 20 minutes.

Entrance Fees: free

Address:

Fick Fossil and History Museum

700 West Third Street, Oakley, KS 67748

Telephone: (913)672-4839

Directions:

Oakley is in northwest Kansas, about 85 miles west of Hays, Kansas, on I-70. From I-70, exit south on U.S. 83. At 8th Street turn left and head east. Turn right on Maple and then left on 3rd Street.

3.6 University of Nebraska State Museum Lincoln, NE

"Elephant Hall" is the museum's big attraction. The display includes the world's largest mounted mammoth and the plesiosaur with the longest neck.

In 1995 the museum will open a new dinosaur gallery called "Mesozoic Monsters, Mammals, and Magnolias." The new hands-on exhibit will feature interactive video displays.

Articulated Skeletons:

- *Allosaurus* and *Stegosaurus*.
- More than 10 ancient elephants as well as fossils of a prehistoric ground sloth, camel, and giant beaver.
- A plesiosaur, a mosasaur, and fossil fish.

Exhibit Features:

- Life-size model of *Allosaurus*.
- A *Triceratops* skull and bones, and casts of *Tyrannosaurus* parts and a *Coelophysis*.

- A new Ice Age mammoth mural.
- Fossil shark material.

Hours:

Monday–Saturday 9:30 a.m.–4:30 p.m.
Sundays and holidays 1:30 p.m.–4:30 p.m.
Closed: Thanksgiving, Christmas, New Year's Day.
Minimum time required to see exhibit: 45 minutes

Entrance Fees:

(Recommended donation)
Over 2 years of age $1.00

Address:

University of Nebraska State Museum
Morrill Hall, Lincoln, NE 68588-0338
Telephone: (402)472-6302

Directions:

Lincoln is in the southeast corner of Nebraska, 60 miles southwest of
Omaha. From I-80, take the 27th Street exit and head south. Follow 27th
to Vine Street. Turn right on Vine into the University of Nebraska campus. The museum is to your left.

Map to University of Nebraska State Museum

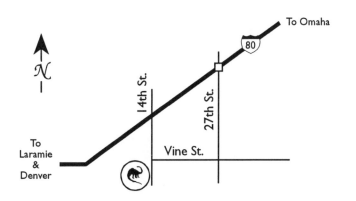

3.7 Ashfall Fossil Beds State Historical Park Royal, NE

Ten million years ago, a volcanic eruption killed hundreds of animals around a small watering hole. The remains of those animals were discovered at Ashfall Fossil Beds. The park opened in 1991 to display the fossil remains as they are being excavated. Hundreds of skeletons of Cenozoic mammals are in this quarry. The animals include rhinoceros, elephants, and a "giraffe-camel."

Exhibit Features:

- Numerous Cenozoic mammal fossils displayed *in situ*.

Hours:

Memorial Weekend to Labor Day:
Monday–Saturday 9:00 a.m.–5:00 p.m.
Sunday 11:00 a.m.–5:00 p.m.
May & September:
Wednesday–Saturday 10:00 a.m.–4:00 p.m.
Sunday 1:00 p.m.–4:00 p.m.
Minimum time required to see exhibit: 45 minutes.

Entrance Fees: Over 2 years $1.00

Address:

Ashfall Fossil Beds State Historical Park
P.O. Box 66, Royal, NE 68773
Telephone: (402)893-2000

Directions:

The park is about 90 miles due west of Sioux City, Iowa, in northern Antelope County.

Map to Ashfall Fossil Beds State Historical Park

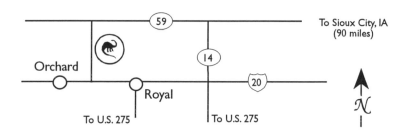

3.8 Museum at Trailside
Crawford, NE

This museum displays a pair of mammoths that fought to the death. Discovered 10,000 years later, the mammoths are displayed just as they were found.

Articulated Skeletons:
- Mammoths.

Exhibit Features:
- Paintings of Nebraska's prehistoric past.

Hours:
May and September:
Wednesday–Sunday 10:00 a.m.–4:00 p.m.
June to August:
Daily 9:00 a.m.–5:00 p.m.
Minimum time required to see exhibit: 20 minutes

Entrance Fees:
Individuals $1.50

Address:
University of Nebraska State Museum at Trailside
Fort Robinson State Park
Box 462, Crawford, NE 69339
Telephone: (308)665-2900

Directions:
U.S. 20 runs through Fort Robinson State Park in far northwestern Nebraska, about three miles west of Crawford. The Museum at Trailside is located off U.S. 20, inside the State Park.

Map to Trailside Museum and Agate Fossil Beds

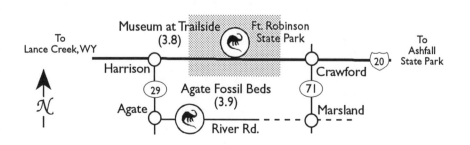

3.9 Agate Fossil Beds National Monument near Gering, NE

The fossils found in this park prove that rhinoceroses, camels, and horses once roamed the Nebraska plains. The fossils are from the Miocene Epoch (20 million years ago) of the Cenozoic Age. You can hike along several self-guided trails to view fossils *in situ*.

Hours:
Daily 8:30 a.m.–5:30 p.m.
Closed: Thanksgiving, Christmas, New Year's Day.
Minimum time required to see exhibit: 45 minutes

Entrance Fees: free

Address:
Agate Fossil Beds National Monument
P.O. Box 27, Gering, NE 69341
Telephone: (308)668-2211

Directions:
Agate Fossil Beds National Monument is off Highway 29, in far northwestern Nebraska. The monument is about 35 miles north of Scottsbluff. From Highway 29, follow the signs to River Road and the monument.

3.10 Museum of Geology Rapid City, SD

Most of the *Tyrannosaurus rex* skulls you see in museums are casts. This museum has one cast and one genuine skull. The museum contains many other local treasures including a long-necked plesiosaur. The museum is closely associated with the South Dakota School of Mines Geology Department, and the museum's research collection is continuously growing.

Articulated Skeletons:
- *Edmontosaurus, Mosasaurus, Plesiosaurus,* and a prehistoric pig.

Exhibit Features:
- Two *Triceratops* skulls, two *Tyrannosaurus rex* skulls, one partial *Iguanodon* skull, and a *Titanothere* skull.
- A great collection of Cycads and Cretaceous marine invertebrates.

Hours:

Monday–Friday 8:00 a.m.–5:00 p.m.
Saturday 9:00 a.m.–4:00 p.m.
Sunday 1:00 p.m.–4:00 p.m.
Closed: Easter, Thanksgiving, Christmas, New Year's Day.
Summer hours (Memorial day to Labor Day):
Monday–Saturday 8:00 a.m.–6:00 p.m.
Sunday Noon–6:00 p.m.
Minimum time required to see exhibit: 45 minutes

Entrance Fees: free

Address:

Museum of Geology
501 E. St. Joseph Street, Rapid City, SD 57701-3995
Telephone: (605)394-2467

Directions:

Rapid City is in southwestern South Dakota, near the Wyoming border.
From I-90, take the I-190 exit into Rapid City. I-190 becomes West Bou-
levard. Follow West Boulevard to St. Joseph Street. The museum is on St.
Joseph on the South Dakota School of Mines campus.

Nearby:

Rapid City's Dinosaur Park is the oldest outdoor display of dinosaurs in
the United States. Six full-size dinosaurs inhabit this public park. It's a
great place for a picnic and is open year-round with no admission fee.
Dinosaur Park is on a hill off Skyline Drive overlooking the city. Heading
south on West Boulevard, turn right on Quincy Street. Quincy becomes
Skyline Drive, and the park is about a mile up Skyline on the right.

Map to the Museum of Geology and Dinosaur Park

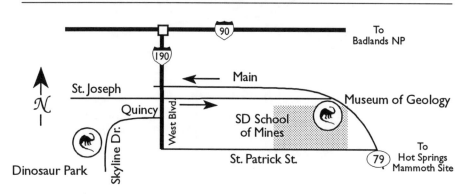

3.11 Black Hills Museum of Natural History Hill City, SD

The museum is preparing a *Tyrannosaurus* for display.

Articulated Skeletons:
- Juvenile duckbilled dinosaur and a whale.

Exhibit Features:
- Museum visitors can watch scientists prepare and study fossil specimens.

Hours:
Monday–Friday 9:00 a.m.–5:00 p.m.
Closed: weekends; July 4, Thanksgiving, Christmas, New Year's Day.
Minimum time required to see exhibit: 20 minutes

Entrance Fees: free

Address:
Black Hills Museum of Natural History
217 Main Street, Hill City, SD 57745
Telephone: (605)574-4289

Directions:
Hill City is 12 miles southwest of Rapid City, on U.S. 385/Highway 16.

Map to the Black Hills area

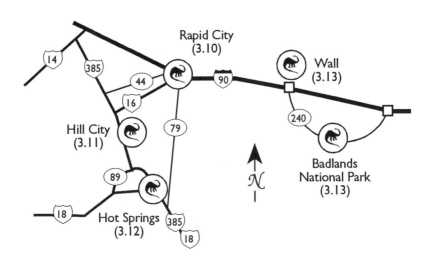

3.12 Mammoth Site
Hot Springs, SD

The Mammoth Site in Hot Springs provides an excellent opportunity to see paleontologists excavating mammoths, elephantlike animals from the Pleistocene. This site houses the largest concentration of woolly and Columbian Mammoth bones discovered in the world. Paleontologists working with local volunteers have uncovered 60 mammoths in the ongoing excavation.

Articulated Skeletons:
- An impressive display of mammoths in *situ* includes articulated skeletons.
- A fiberglass cast of "Sinbad," the Columbian mammoth.

Exhibit Features:
- Bone dig for children.

Hours:
September to October and April to May 14:
Monday–Saturday 9:00 a.m.–5:00 p.m.
Sunday 11:00 a.m.–5:pm
May 15 to August:
Daily 8:00 a.m.–8:00 p.m.
November to March:
Monday–Saturday 9:00 a.m.–3:30 p.m.
Sunday 11:00 a.m.–3:30 p.m.
Minimum time required to see exhibit: 1 hour

Entrance Fees:
Ages 60 and above $3.95 + tax
Ages 13–59 $4.25 + tax
Ages 6–12 $2.25 + tax

Address:
The Mammoth Site of Hot Springs
P.O. Box 606, Hot Springs, SD 57747-0606
Telephone: (605)745-6017

Directions:
Hot Springs is 60 miles south of Rapid City, South Dakota. The Mammoth Site is just to the south of the town of Hot Springs. Take the Highway 18 truck bypass from either U.S. 18 or U.S. 385.

3.13 Badlands National Park near Interior, SD

Erosion of the surrounding prairie here has revealed fossils from the Eocene and Oligocene Epochs (37 to 23 million years ago). The fossils are primarily mammals that roamed a marshy plain. Fossils may be viewed in the Visitor Center and *in situ* along interpretive trails.

The name "badlands" is derived from the Sioux Indians who called this area *Mako Sika* meaning "land bad." French trappers called the White River area *les mauvaises terres*, which means "bad lands to travel across."

The Sioux Indians were always aware of the fossils on their lands. The Sioux believed that the bones were the remains of giant serpents. The "Great Spirit" had slain the serpents with lightning bolts. The bones retained great mystical power and were to be avoided by ordinary mortals. It was believed that only those with extreme spiritual power should dare to venture near the bones.

Hours:

Daily 8:00 a.m.–4:30 p.m.
Summer hours (June 1 to September 4):
Daily 7:00 a.m.–8:00 p.m.
Closed: Thanksgiving, Christmas, New Year's Day.
Minimum time required to see exhibit: 2 hours

Entrance Fees: $5.00 per car

Address:

Badlands National Park
P.O. Box 6, Interior, SD 57750
Telephone: (605)433-5361

Directions:

The park is 35 miles east of Rapid City, South Dakota. From I-90, exit to Highway 240.

Nearby:

There is a statue of an *Apatosaurus* (formerly called *Brontosaurus*) near the drug store in Wall, South Dakota.

3.14 University of North Dakota Grand Forks, ND

This museum is in the lobby of the Geology Department of the University of North Dakota, in Leonard Hall. Some of the exterior walls of the building have silhouettes of *Apatosaurus* and *Triceratops* set into their brickwork. Some of the walls contain fossiliferous limestone.

Exhibit Features:
- Fossils and a *Triceratops* skull.

Hours:
Monday–Friday 8:00 a.m.–5:00 p.m.

Closed: weekends; Martin Luther King Day, Presidents' Day, Good Friday, Memorial Day, July 4, Labor Day, Veterans' Day, Thanksgiving, Christmas Eve, Christmas, New Year's Day.

Minimum time required to see exhibit: 20 minutes.

Entrance Fees: free

Address:
Deptartment of Geology and Geological Engineering
University of North Dakota
Box 8358, Grand Forks, ND 58202
Telephone: (701)777-2811

Directions:
Grand Forks is on the North Dakota–Minnesota border. From I-29, exit at Demers Avenue and head east. Continue on to Columbia Road, and go north. Turn left on 2nd Avenue onto the University of North Dakota campus. Go one block and follow Cornell Street to the left. The exhibit is in Leonard Hall at the end of Cornell, below the watertower. Look for the dinosaurs.

3.15 Morden and District Museum
Morden, MB

Eighty million years ago, the Mid-Continental Seaway covered the town of Morden. In 1972, the Morden Museum began collecting the fossils found in the nearby bentonite quarries. Today the museum claims the largest collection of marine reptiles in Canada. In fact, it is one of the largest in the world.

Articulated Skeletons:
- *Mosasaurus, Ichthyosaurus, Plesiosaurus,* and *Xiphactinus.*

Exhibit Features:
- Excellent paintings and dioramas depicting ancient sea life.
- Remains of toothed sea birds from the late Cretaceous.

Hours:
Saturday and Sunday 1:00 p.m.–5:00 p.m.
Summer hours (June 1 to August 31):
Daily 1:00 p.m.–5:00 p.m., or by appointment
Minimum time required to see exhibit: 2 hours

Entrance Fees:
Adults $2.00
Students $1.00

Mailing Address:
Morden and District Museum
P.O. Box 728, Morden, MB, Canada R0G 1J0
Telephone: (204)822-3406

Location Address:
Morden Rec Center
Gilmore and 2nd streets, Morden, MB

Directions:
Morden is about 128 kilometers (80 miles) southwest of Winnipeg, near the Manitoba–North Dakota border. The museum is located near the corner of Mountain Street and Thornhill in Morden.

Map to Morden and District Museum

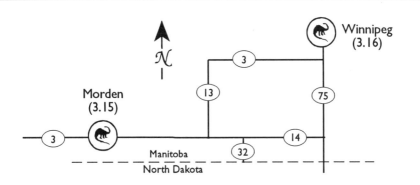

3.16 Manitoba Museum of Man and Nature Winnipeg, MB

The Earth History Gallery takes the visitor from the present to the origin of the universe. Along the way, you will see plesiosaurs and mosasaurs. You can also watch paleontologists prepare a duckbilled dinosaur for display. The dinosaur was excavated near Drumheller, Alberta, in 1991.

Hours:
Tuesday–Friday 10:00 a.m.–5:00 p.m.
Saturday & Sunday 10:00 a.m.–5:00 p.m.
Summer hours (Victoria Day to Labor Day):
Daily 10:00 a.m.–6:00 p.m.
Minimum time required to see exhibit: 1 hour

Entrance Fees:
Adults $3.50
Children (4–12) and seniors $2.25
Students $2.50

Address:
Manitoba Museum of Man and Nature
190 Rupert Ave, Winnipeg, MB, Canada R3B 0N2
Telephone: (204)956-2830

Directions:
The museum is part of the Manitoba Centennial Center. The Center is on Main Street in downtown Winnipeg, across from City Hall and the Historic District.

4.
The Southwest
Dinosaur Tracks

The southwestern portion of the United States holds a special surprise for the Jurassic tourist—dinosaur tracks. This part of the country is covered with dinosaur footprints. You can experience the excitement of walking down the same path that a *Brachiosaurus* stomped down millions of years ago.

4.1 Fort Worth Museum of Science and History, Fort Worth, TX

The Fort Worth Museum of Science and History surveyed the public to find out what kind of exhibits they enjoyed the most. The top three answers were dinosaurs, hands-on activities, and activities that families can do together.

The Fort Worth Museum of Science and History has given people exactly what they wanted. The new outdoor exhibit is an authentic dinosaur dig. Dinosaur bones are hidden in the sand along the banks of a shallow stream. It is up to you to uncover these dinosaur remains. Be careful—research indicates that very few children will voluntarily stop digging and that everyone from toddlers to grandparents quickly becomes addicted to discovering "new" fossils in the sand.

The museum maintains an active scientific research program and is in the process of excavating several dinosaurs. The dinosaurs were found within 50 miles of Fort Worth. During the Early Cretaceous Period (113 million years ago) this area was on the coast of a shallow sea. After being excavated, prepared, and studied, these dinosaurs will go on display at the museum.

Articulated Skeletons:
- A dramatic moment from the Jurassic: a ferocious meat-eating *Allosaurus* has brought down a plant-eating *Camptosaurus*.
- *Tenontosaurus*, found near Fort Worth.

Exhibit Features:
- Full-size models of *Acrocanthosaurus* and *Tenontosaurus*.
- Dino Dig, a re-creation of a dinosaur dig site, for kids.

Volunteer Opportunities:
Call the museum and ask for the Volunteer Services Office.

Hours:
Monday 9:00 a.m.–5:00 p.m.
Tuesday–Thursday 9:00 a.m.–8:00 p.m.
Friday–Saturday 9:00 a.m.–9:00 p.m.
Sunday Noon–9:00 p.m.
Closed: Thanksgiving, Christmas Eve, Christmas.
Minimum time required to see exhibit: 30 minutes

Entrance Fees:
Adults $3.00
Seniors $1.00
Children (5–12) $1.00

Address:
Fort Worth Museum of Science and History
1501 Montgomery Street, Fort Worth, TX 76107
Telephone: (817)732-1631

Directions:
From I-30, exit on to Montgomery Street about three miles west of downtown Fort Worth. The museum is one mile north on Montgomery Street.

Map to Fort Worth Museum of Science and History

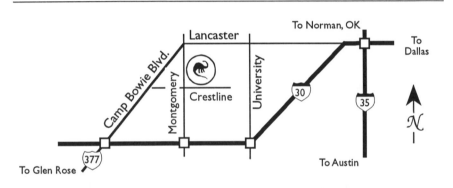

4.2 Dallas Museum of Natural History Dallas, TX

The Dallas Museum of Natural History displays dinosaurs found in Texas. The museum also provides educational activities for children.

Articulated Skeletons:
- *Tenontosaurus*, the first Texas dinosaur to be fully assembled.
- A 31-foot mosasaur, an *Edaphosaurus* (a fin-backed reptile predating dinosaurs), and a Pleistocene mammoth.

Exhibit Features:
- Cretaceous fossils including the second-largest sea turtle fossil in the world; fish and other sea fossils.
- Dinosaur tracks and a *Quetzalcoatlus* wing.

Volunteer Opportunities:

The museum accepts volunteers to help with preparation and repair of exhibits, field work, and to prepare fossils.

Hours:

Daily 9:00 a.m.–5:00 p.m.

Closed: July 4, Thanksgiving, Christmas Eve, Christmas, New Year's Day.

Minimum time required to see exhibit: 45 minutes

Entrance Fees:

Adults $3.00

Seniors and students $2.00

Children (3–12) $1

Children under 3 free

Mailing Address:

Dallas Museum of Natural History

P.O. Box 150349, Dallas, TX 75315

Location Address:

Dallas Museum of Natural History

3535 Grand Avenue in Fair Park, Dallas, TX 75226

Telephone: (214)670-8457

Directions:

The museum is located in State Fair Park. From eastbound I-30, exit on Second Avenue and follow signs. From westbound I-30, exit on First Avenue and follow signs.

Map to Dallas Museum of Natural History

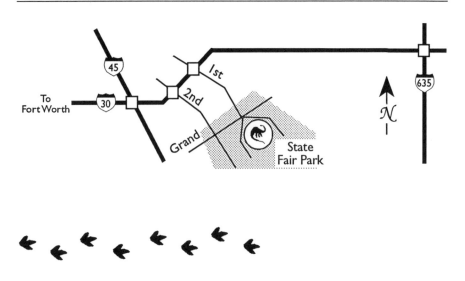

4.3 Houston Museum of Natural Science Houston, TX

Founded in 1909, this exciting museum features a 70-foot *Diplodocus*. Giant sauropods like these are responsible for the many tracks found throughout Texas. In 1994, the 162,000-square-foot museum will grow to 252,000 square feet and will feature an even larger paleontology display.

Articulated Skeletons:

- *Diplodocus* (a late-Jurassic sauropod) and a plesiosaur.
- A sabertoothed cat leaping onto the back of a *Mesohippus*, a prehistoric horse.
- A huge mosasaur skeleton chasing a prehistoric sea turtle.

Exhibit Features:

- A giant armadillo found a few miles from the museum.
- Wing bones from the pterosaur *Quetzalcoatlus*. Discovered in the late Cretaceous rocks of Big Bend National Park, *Quetzalcoatlus*, with a wingspan near 40 feet, was the largest creature ever to fly.
- Dinosaur egg shells.
- A dramatic wall mural depicting life in the Mesozoic Era.
- A reconstruction of an *Ankylosaurus*, and fossil plants.

Hours:

Monday–Saturday 9:00 a.m.–6:00 p.m.
Sunday Noon–6:00 p.m.
Closed: Christmas, New Year's Day.
Minimum time required to see exhibit: 2 hours

Entrance Fees:

(Admission is free on Thursday afternoons from 2:00 p.m. to 6:00 p.m.)
Adults $2.50
Seniors and children under 12 $2.00

Address:

Houston Museum of Natural Science
One Hermann Circle Drive, Houston, TX 77030
Telephone: (713)639-4600

Directions:

Take the I-610 loop to U.S. 59. Follow U.S. 59 east towards the center of the city and exit on Fannin. Follow Fannin south to Hermann Park. The museum is the first building on your left as you enter the park.

Map to Houston Museum of Natural Science

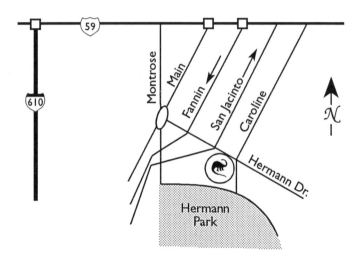

4.4 Vines Environmental Science Center Houston, TX

The Vines Environmental Science Center is primarily an arboretum and bird sanctuary. A distant cousin of the birds, a 33-foot *Allosaurus* skeleton, is also on display.

Articulated Skeletons:

- *Allosaurus*.

Exhibit Features:

- Sauropod footprints, a *Tyrannosaurus rex* skull, and fossil exhibits.

Hours:

Monday–Friday 8:30 a.m.–5:00 p.m.

Closed: Spring Break; July 4, Labor Day, Thanksgiving, Christmas Eve, Christmas, New Year's Day.

Minimum time required to see exhibit: 45 minutes

Entrance Fees: free

Address:

R. A. Vines Environmental Science Center
8856 Westview Drive, Houston, TX 77055
Telephone: (713)465-9628

Directions:

Exit from I-10 at Campbell Street North. Take Campbell to Westview.

4.5 Brazosport Museum of Natural Science Lake Jackson, TX

This small museum has a 25-foot *Allosaurus* on display.

Articulated Skeletons:

- *Allosaurus*.

Exhibit Features:

- A reconstruction of *Dimetrodon*.
- A large collection of shells, fossil fish, and ferns.

Hours:

Tuesday–Saturday 10:00 a.m.–5:00 p.m.
Sunday 2:00 p.m.–5:00 p.m.
Closed: Mondays; Easter, July 4, Thanksgiving, Christmas, New Year's Day.
Minimum time required to see exhibit: 20 minutes

Entrance Fees: free

Address:

Brazosport Museum of Natural Science
400 College Drive, Lake Jackson, TX 77566
Telephone: (409)265-7831

Directions:

The museum is 45 miles south of Houston on Highway 288, in the town of Lake Jackson.

4.6 Corpus Christi Museum of Science & History, Corpus Christi, TX

The museum has a hall devoted to earth science and paleontology.

Articulated Skeletons:

- A mosasaur.

Exhibit Features:

- The Dinoscape: a climb-on exhibit for small children.
- A *Pteranodon* model, a *Tyrannosaurus rex* skull, and a dinosaur egg.
- A dinosaur tailbone showing where an old injury had healed.
- A Pleistocene mammal collection.

Hours:

Tuesday–Saturday 10:00 a.m.–5:00 p.m.

Sunday 1:00 p.m.–5:00 p.m.

Closed: Mondays (future plans include being open on Monday); July 4, Thanksgiving, Christmas, New Year's Day.

Minimum time required to see exhibit: 1 hour

Entrance Fees:

(Admission is free on Saturdays from 10:00 a.m. to noon)

Adults $3.00

Children (6–12) $1.00

Address:

Corpus Christi Museum of Science and History

1900 North Chaparral, Corpus Christi, TX 78401

Telephone: (512)883-2862

Directions:

Corpus Christi is 215 miles southwest of Houston and 150 miles southeast of San Antonio. Follow the signs on I-37 as you come into town.

4.7 John E. Conner Museum
Kingsville, TX

Exhibit Features:
- Fossil mammals.

Hours:
Tuesday–Saturday 9:00 a.m.–5:00 p.m.
Closed: Sundays, Mondays; July 4, Thanksgiving, Christmas Eve, Christmas, New Year's Day.
Minimum time required to see exhibit: 10 minutes

Entrance Fees: Adults $2.00

Address:
John E. Conner Museum, Texas A&I University
821 W. Santa Gertrudis, Kingsville, TX 78363
Telephone: (512)595-2819

Directions:
Kingsville is south of Corpus Christi. The museum is on the Texas A&I campus.

4.8 Fiedler Memorial Museum
Seguin, TX

The museum has a small collection of fossils in the outdoor garden.

Hours:
Outdoor rock garden always open, indoor exhibit open by appointment.
Minimum time required to see exhibit: 10 minutes

Entrance Fees: free

Address:
Fiedler Memorial Museum
Texas Lutheran College, Seguin, TX 78155
Telephone: (210)372-8000

Directions:
Seguin is about 30 miles east of San Antonio. The museum is on the Texas Lutheran College campus, in Langner Hall on Prexy Drive.

4.9 Texas Memorial Museum Austin, TX

Marine invertebrates are visible in the fossiliferous limestone walls of the museum. If you are interested in dinosaur tracksites, this is a good place to do research. The files at the Vertebrate Paleontology Laboratory at the museum list over 50 sites where dinosaur tracks exist in Texas.

Articulated Skeletons:

*   A mosasaur, *Eryops*, *Dimetrodon*, *Glyptodon*.

Exhibit Features:

*   A *Diplodocus* femur and skulls of *Tyrannosaurus* and *Eucentrosaurus*.
*   *Quetzalcoatlus* remains.
*   The original limestone blocks of Dinosaur tracks excavated from the Paluxy River.

Hours:

Monday–Friday 9:00 a.m.–5:00 p.m.
Saturday 10:00 a.m.–5:00 p.m.
Sunday 1:00 p.m.–5:00 p.m.
Closed: Easter, Thanksgiving, Christmas, New Year's Day.
Minimum time required to see exhibit: 1 hour

Entrance Fees: free

Address:

Texas Memorial Museum
University of Texas at Austin
2400 Trinity, Austin, TX 78705
Telephone: (512)471-1604

Directions:

The museum is on the University of Texas campus, approximately two blocks north of Memorial Stadium and three blocks west of the Lyndon Baines Johnson Library. From I-35, take the 26th Street exit west. Then head south on East Campus drive to 23rd Street. Head west on 23rd Street. At Trinity, go north; the museum will be on your left.

Map to Texas Memorial Museum

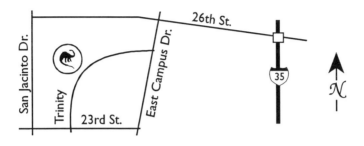

4.10 Inner Space
Georgetown, TX

Inner Space is a privately operated cavern with Cenozoic mammal fossils displayed inside.

Hours:
Daily 10:00 a.m.–5:00 p.m.
Closed: Thanksgiving and the two weeks before Christmas.
Summer hours (Memorial Day to Labor Day):
Daily 9:00 a.m.–6:00 p.m.
Minimum time required to see exhibit: 90 minutes for tour

Entrance Fees:
Adults $6.50 + tax
Seniors $5.50 + tax
Children (5–11) $4.00 + tax

Address:
Inner Space
P.O. Box 451, Georgetown, TX 78627
Telephone: (512)863-5545

Directions:
Georgetown is north of Austin, Texas. From I-35, take exit 259 about a mile south of Georgetown. Inner Space is right at the exit, on the east side of the interstate.

4.11 Dinosaur Valley State Park near Glen Rose, TX

Roland T. Bird was a "dinosaur hunter" for the American Museum of Natural History. In the spring of 1938, while Bird was riding his motorcycle through Texas, he stopped at an Indian trading post and noticed some dinosaur footprints for sale. He soon determined that the footprints were fake. Inquiring around town, Bird was told about some real tracks near the Paluxy River. There, Bird found solid evidence that *Apatosaurus* (formerly called *Brontosaurus*) was not a sprawling reptile but walked with his legs underneath him and his tail held high. The tracks also show that *Apatosaurus* was not swamp bound and could support its own weight on land. Although the tracks appear to show an *Allosaurus* cautiously stalking a giant sauropod, it is also possible that the *Allosaurus* just happened to walk the same path hours later.

Come prepared with good wading boots. When the river is high the tracks are obscured. Try to plan your visit for late summer, when the river is low.

Exhibit Features:
- Lower Cretaceous (105 million year old) dinosaur tracks *in situ*.
- The Visitor Center has an excellent painting of a carnivorous dinosaur attacking a sauropod.
- A 70-foot model of *Apatosaurus* and a 45-foot model of *Tyrannosaurus rex*. Both were originally displayed at the 1964–65 World's Fair in New York City.

Hours:
Park is always open
Visitor Center open daily 8:00 a.m.–5:00 p.m.
Minimum time required to see exhibit: 1 hour

Entrance Fees:
Per vehicle $3.00–$5.00
Camping $6.00–$12.00

Address:
Dinosaur Valley State Park
Box 396, Glen Rose, TX 76043
Telephone: (817)897-4588

Directions:

Glen Rose, Texas, is on Highway 67, a little southwest of Fort Worth. From Glen Rose, take FM205/Park Road 59 about four miles to Dinosaur Valley State Park.

Map to Dinosaur Valley State Park

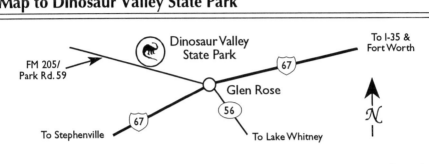

4.12 Annie Riggs Museum
Fort Stockton, TX

The Annie Riggs Museum presents a few local fossils. There are dinosaur footprints on display at a nearby picnic area.

Exhibit Features:

- A mosasaur jaw and Lower Cretaceous marine invertebrate fossils.
- Dinosaur footprint casts.

Hours:

Monday–Saturday 10:00 a.m.–8:00 p.m.
Sunday 1:30 p.m.–8:00 p.m.
Closed: Thanksgiving, Christmas Eve, Christmas, New Year's Day.
Minimum time required to see exhibit: 20 minutes

Entrance Fees:

(for museum; tracks are free)
Adults $1.00
Children (6–12) $0.50

Address:

Fort Stockton Historical Society
301 South Main, Fort Stockton, TX 79735
Telephone: (915)336-2167

Directions:

Fort Stockton is in southwestern Texas. The museum is on Main Street.

Nearby:

Just outside Fort Stockton is a picnic area next to a dry creek bed. In the creek bed are the footprints of a theropod from the Lower Cretaceous. The most likely track-maker is *Acrocanthosaurus*, a 40-foot-long meat-eater that stood 14 feet tall and weighed two to three tons. The tracks are 21 inches long and the stride is almost 6 feet.

The tracks are protected by a steel cage to prevent theft and vandalism. Please remember this steel cage when you visit other tracksites; do not force other fossil sites to erect cages.

Directions:

To get to the picnic area, take I-10 east from Fort Stockton about 14 miles and exit at U.S. 385 North. The picnic area is along the highway, about seven miles from the exit off the interstate. The dinosaur footprints are in a dry creek bed about 150 yards from the picnic area.

Map to the dinosaur tracksite near Fort Stockton

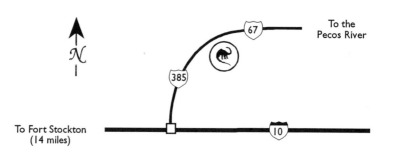

4.13 Archer Museum
Archer City, TX

Exhibit Features:

- Permian fossils, which are plentiful in Archer County.

Hours: by appointment

Minimum time required to see exhibit: 30 minutes

Entrance Fees: free

Address:
201 N. Sycamore
Archer City, TX 76351

Mailing Address:
Archer Museum
Rt. 1, Box 89, Windthorst, TX 76389
Telephone: (817)423-6426

Directions:
Archer City is about 120 miles northeast of Fort Worth and 20 miles south of Wichita Falls on U.S. 281. The museum is one block northeast of the Archer County Courthouse.

4.14 Petroleum Museum
Midland, TX

Exhibit Features:
- The museum has only one dinosaur fossil exhibit. *Camptosaurus* footprints found in the Permian Basin, about 50 miles from museum, can be seen here.

Hours:
Monday–Saturday 9:00 a.m.–5:00 p.m.
Sunday 2:00 p.m.–5:00 p.m.
Closed: Thanksgiving, Christmas Eve, Christmas.
Minimum time required to see exhibit: 10 minutes

Entrance Fees:
Adults $3.00
Seniors $2.50
Children (6–17) $1.50

Address:
Petroleum Museum
1500 I-20 West, Midland, TX 79701
Telephone: (915)683-4509

Directions:
Midland is 150 miles west of Abilene, in southwestern Texas. From I-20, take exit 136 north.

4.15 Panhandle-Plains Historical Museum Canyon, TX

This museum focuses on regional fossils from the Triassic and Tertiary periods. Several dinosaur fossils from other locations are also on display.

Articulated Skeletons:
- *Allosaurus*.

Exhibit Features:
- A *Triceratops* skull.
- Triassic and Tertiary fossils.

Hours:
Monday–Saturday 900 a.m.–5:00 p.m.
Sunday 1:00 p.m.–6:00 p.m.
Summer hours (June 1 to August 31):
Monday–Saturday 9:00 a.m.–6:00 p.m.
Sunday 1:00 p.m.–6:00 p.m.
Closed: Thanksgiving, Christmas Eve, Christmas, New Year's Day.
Minimum time required to see exhibit: 1 hour

Entrance Fees:
(Recommended donation)
Adults $2.00
Children $1.00

Address:
Panhandle-Plains Historical Museum
WTSU Box 967, 2401 Fourth Avenue, Canyon, TX 79016
Telephone: (806)656-2244

Directions:
The museum is 17 miles south of Amarillo and just northeast of Canyon on I-27.

4.16 Museum of Texas Tech University Lubbock, TX

The museum is planning to open a new paleontology gallery.

Articulated Skeletons:
- *Allosaurus*.

Exhibit Features:
- A mural depicting the history of life.
- The thecodont *Desmatosuchus* and a phytosaur skull.

Hours:
Tuesday–Wednesday 10:00 a.m.–5:00 p.m.

Thursday 10:00 a.m.–8:30 p.m.

Friday–Sunday 10:00 a.m.–5:00 p.m.

Closed: Mondays; Spring Break, Martin Luther King Day, Memorial Day, July 4, Thanksgiving, Christmas Eve, Christmas, New Year's Day.

Minimum time required to see exhibit: 15 minutes

Entrance Fees: free

Address:
Museum of Texas Tech University

4th and Indiana Avenue, Lubbock, TX 79409

Telephone: (806)742-2490

Directions:
Lubbock is in western Texas. From L-289, which circles the city, take the Clovis Road southeast exit to Indiana Avenue. Turn right on Indiana and head south. The museum will be on your left at the intersection of Indiana and 4th.

Map to Museum of Texas Tech University

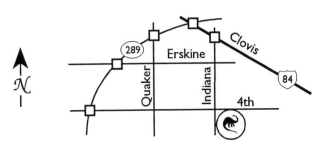

4.17 Crockett County Museum
Ozona, TX

Exhibit Features:
- Mammoth bones found in Ozona.

Hours:
Monday–Friday 9:00 a.m.–5:00 p.m.
Saturday 10:00 a.m.–4:00 p.m.
Closed: Sundays; Thanksgiving, Christmas Eve, Christmas, New Year's Day.
Minimum time required to see exhibit: 20 minutes

Entrance Fees: $1.00 recommended donation

Address:
Crockett County Museum
P.O. Box 1444, 404 Eleventh Street, Ozona, TX 76943
Telephone: (915)392-2837

Directions:
Ozona is in southern Texas, halfway between San Antonio and El Paso. The museum is one block east of Highway 163 on Eleventh Street.

4.18 Oklahoma Museum of Natural History
Norman, OK

The Oklahoma Museum of Natural History was once known as the Stovall Museum, named for J. W. Stovall. During the Great Depression, Stovall obtained 30 workers through the Works Progress Administration to help him excavate dinosaur bones. Their most exciting find is *Saurophagus*, a Jurassic predator the size of *Tyrannosaurus rex*. Some believe that *Saurophagus* is an oversized *Allosaurus*.

One of Stovall's most productive quarries was on the Oklahoma panhandle near Kenton. The Cimarron River cuts through the surface layers of rock here to reveal the Morrison Formation. This is the same formation that has produced so many dinosaur fossils in Utah, Colorado, and Wyoming.

Exhibit Features:
- *Tenontosaurus* (lower jaw), *Triceratops* (jaw), *Saurolophus* (skull), and a baby and adult *Apatosaurus* (leg bones of each).

Hours:
Tuesday–Friday 10:00 a.m.–5:00 p.m.
Saturday and Sunday 2:00 p.m.–5:00 p.m.
Saturdays of home football games 9:00 a.m.–1:00 p.m.
Closed: Mondays; Thanksgiving, Christmas, New Year's Day.
Minimum time required to see exhibit: 45 minutes

Entrance Fees: free

Address:
Oklahoma Museum of Natural History
1335 Asp Avenue, Norman, OK 73019-0606
Telephone: (405)325-4712

Directions:
Norman is south of Oklahoma City. From Interstate 35 south, exit at Lindsey. Turn left on Lindsey and drive about three miles to the University of Oklahoma campus. At Asp, turn right. The museum is about one-half block up on the left.

4.19 Clayton Lake State Park near Seneca, NM

Over 500 footprints representing at least five different species of dinosaurs are exposed at the spillway of the Clayton Lake Dam. Most of the tracks were made by adult ornithopod dinosaurs. However, some of the tracks are very unusual: Some appear to have been made by a *Pterodactyl;* others are believed to have been made by baby dinosaurs. The tracks are in the Mesa Rica Sandstone of the Dakota Group. The tracks date back to the early Cretaceous Period, 120 to 98 million years ago.

Exhibit Features:
- Dinosaur tracks and possible pterosaur tracks.

Hours:
Always open. The tracks are easiest to see in early morning or late afternoon, when the sun is low on the horizon.
Minimum time required to see exhibit: 45 minutes.

Entrance Fees:

Per vehicle $3.00

Camping $6.00–$7.00 per night

Address:

Clayton Lake State Park

R.R. Box 20, Seneca, NM 88437

Telephone: (505)374-8808

Directions:

Clayton Lake State Park off Highway 370 in far northeastern New Mexico, near the Oklahoma border. The tracks are along the spillway of the Clayton Lake Dam, a half-mile hike from the dinosaur tracks parking lot.

Nearby:

Kenton, Oklahoma, Dinosaur Quarry. University of Oklahoma paleontologist J. W. Stovall excavated the remains of several Jurassic dinosaurs near Kenton during the 1930s. A concrete replica of a six-foot-long sauropod femur commemorates the site of the quarries.

Map to Clayton Lake State Park and Kenton, OK

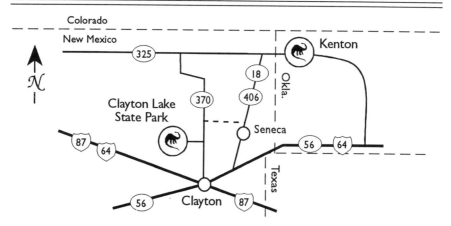

4.20 Ruth Hall Museum of Paleontology Abiquiu, NM

Edwin H. Colbert and a research team from the American Museum of Natural History discovered the famous Ghost Ranch Quarry in 1947. The team uncovered a mass graveyard of *Coelophysis* at the quarry.

Coelophysis was a lightly built, highly active carnivore from the Triassic

Period. Evidence of cannibalism was discovered at this mass graveyard. One of the *Coelophysis* skeletons contained a skeleton of a smaller *Coelophysis* in its rib cage, the remnants of its last meal. What happened at this carnivore graveyard is still a mystery.

The museum is dedicated to preserving and displaying the discoveries made at this important fossil site. You may take the short hike to the quarry, although no excavations are currently in progress.

Articulated Skeletons:

- Several *Coelophysis*.
- A phytosaur in a Triassic diorama.

Exhibit Features:

- Paleontologists preparing specimens in the center of the museum.

Hours:

Tuesday–Saturday 9:00 a.m.–5:00 p.m.
Sunday 10:00 a.m.–5:00 p.m.
Closed: Mondays; Easter, Thanksgiving; the month of December.
Minimum time required to see exhibit: 30 minutes

Entrance Fees: free

Address:

Ruth Hall Museum of Paleontology
Ghost Ranch Conference Center, Abiquiu, NM 87510
Telephone: (505)685-4333

Directions:

Abiquiu is 50 miles north of Santa Fe, New Mexico. The museum is on Ghost Ranch Road, which intersects Highway 84 about two miles south of Ghost Ranch Living Museum. Look for signs marking a Presbyterian conference center. A half-mile dirt road then takes you to the museum.

Map to Ruth Hall Museum of Paleontology

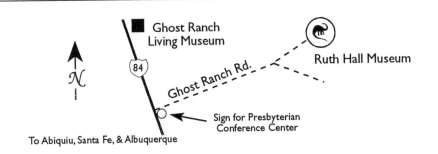

4.21 New Mexico Museum of Natural History Albuquerque, NM

The New Mexico Museum of Natural History is spacious and modern. There are many activities for children including a fossil dig that uses bird seed instead of sand so kids stay clean.

Articulated Skeletons:
- *Stegosaurus, Camarasaurus, Allosaurus,* and *Camptosaurus* are mounted with a mural as a backdrop.
- *Coelophysis* and *Dilophosaurus.*

Exhibit Features:
- Several life-size pterosaur models fill the museum.
- Life-size bronze models of *Albertosaurus* and *Styracosaurus* stand guard at the entrance to the museum.
- The 25-foot leg bones of a *Brachiosaurus.*
- *Seismosaurus* vertebrae found about 60 miles northwest of Albuquerque. At 150 feet in length, *Seismosaurus* may be the world's largest dinosaur.
- An excellent diorama of *Maiasaura* in a steamy jungle with live plants.
- A Cretaceous sea life display including a life-size *Mosasaurus* model.
- Be sure to ride the Evolator, a special effects journey through time.

Volunteer Opportunities:
The museum accepts volunteers to help with preparation and repair of exhibits and fossils, and field work.

Hours:
Daily 9:00 a.m.–5:00 p.m.
Minimum time required to see exhibit: 4 hours

Entrance Fees:
Adults $4.00
Seniors and students $3.00
Children (3–11) $1.00

Address:
New Mexico Museum of Natural History
1801 Mountain Road NW, Albuquerque, NM 87104
Telephone: (505)841-8837 or (505)841-8836

Directions:

From I-40, exit at Rio Grande Boulevard and head south. Take a left at Mountain Road and head east. The museum is just past Old Town.

Map to New Mexico Museum of Natural History

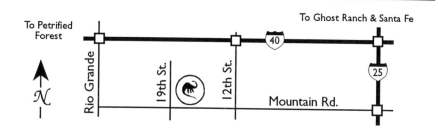

4.22 Farmington Museum
Farmington, NM

The museum has several exhibits on the dinosaurs of New Mexico.

Exhibit Features:

- *Pentaceratops* and *Albertosaurus* fossils.
- A laser disc show takes you to the Cretaceous of the San Juan Basin.
- Displays on the local geology.

Hours:

Tuesday–Friday Noon–5:00 p.m.
Saturday 10:00 a.m.–5:00 p.m.
Closed: Mondays; Easter, Memorial Day, July 4, Labor Day, Thanksgiving, day after Thanksgiving, Christmas, New Year's Day.
Minimum time required to see exhibit: 45 minutes

Entrance Fees: free

Address:

Farmington Museum
302 North Orchard, Farmington, NM 87401
Telephone: (505)599-1179 or (505)599-1173 or (800)448-1240

Directions:

Farmington is in the northwestern corner of New Mexico. The museum is in downtown Farmington, two blocks north of Main Street on the corner of Orchard and LaPlata streets.

Nearby:

The Bisti and De-Na-Zin Wilderness areas are known for their dinosaur fossils. They are located 30 miles south of the museum on Highway 371. Hiking is the only access to the wilderness areas. Bring plenty of water.

Map to Farmington Museum

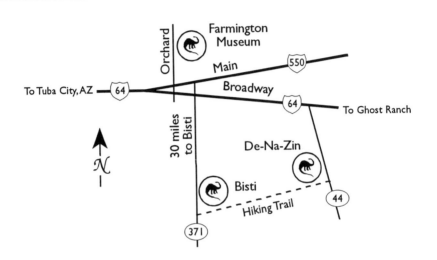

4.23 Petrified Forest National Park Arizona

Let your imagination take you back 225 million years to the Triassic; the beginning of the "Age of Dinosaurs." You see the first dinosaurs in a forest of giant trees. Some of the trees reach 250 feet into the air. The trees are vaguely familiar, closely resembling Monkey Puzzles and Norfolk Island Star Pines.

At Petrified Forest National Park, the secrets of days long past are revealed in massive logs of petrified wood. The park is the largest known concentration of petrified wood in the world. In some places, the fossil-bearing sediment is 300 feet thick.

Every year, thoughtless visitors steal nearly 12 tons of petrified wood from the park. Please do not take souvenirs from the park.

Articulated Skeletons:
- Triassic dinosaurs and reptiles.

Exhibit Features:

- Hiking trails to view petrified logs from the late Triassic.
- Some excellent paintings and dioramas depicting the area as it was 225 million years ago.

Hours:

(open during daylight hours only)
Closed: Christmas, New Year's Day.
Minimum time required to see exhibit: 3 hours

Entrance Fees:

Per vehicle $5.00
Per person (buses) $3.00

Address:

Petrified Forest National Park
P.O. Box 2217, Petrified Forest National Park, AZ 86028
Telephone: (602)524-6228

Directions:

Petrified Forest National Park is near the Arizona–New Mexico border, about 100 miles east of Flagstaff. From I-40, exit at the north entrance to the park. The road goes all the way through the park to U.S. 180.

Map to Petrified Forest National Park

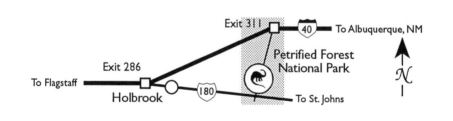

4.24 Museum of Northern Arizona Flagstaff, AZ

The recently remodeled geology section of this museum features dinosaurs found in the southwest.

Articulated Skeletons:

- *Scutellosaurus* (one of only two in the United States) and *Coelophysis*.
- The only three-dimensional mount of *Dilophosaurus* in the United States.

Exhibit Features:

- Material from *Pentaceratops*, *Coelophysis*, *Ornithomimus*, and duckbilled dinosaurs.
- Invertebrate fossil material and dinosaur tracks.
- *Tyrannosaurus* tooth material.
- Phytosaur and metoposaur skulls.
- An aetosaur foot.

Hours:

Daily 9:00 a.m.–5:00 p.m.
Closed: Thanksgiving, Christmas, New Year's Day.
Minimum time required to see exhibit: 45 minutes

Entrance Fees:

Adults $4.00
Seniors $3.00
Children (5–12) $2.00

Address:

Museum of Northern Arizona
3001 N. Fort Valley Road
Route 4, Box 720, Flagstaff, AZ 86001
Telephone: (602)774-5211

Directions:

The museum is three miles north of downtown Flagstaff on U.S. 180. Fort Valley Road becomes Highway 180 at the north end of Flagstaff.

Map to Museum of Northern Arizona and Dinosaur Tracksite

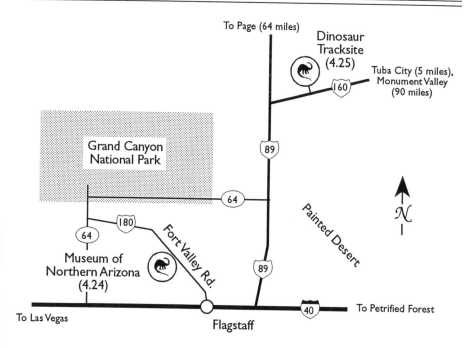

4.25 Dinosaur Tracksite
Tuba City, AZ

Early Jurassic dinosaur tracks are visible in the bright red rock of the Kayenta Formation. Look for two sizes of three-toed dinosaur tracks.

Hours: always open

Minimum time required to see exhibit: 15 minutes

Entrance Fees: free

Directions:

Tuba City is 65 miles north of Flagstaff. The tracks are located five miles west of Tuba City on the north side of Highway 160. A sign on Highway 160 marks a side road that leads a short distance to the tracksite.

4.26 Arizona Museum of Science and Technology, Phoenix, AZ

The museum has a small display of dinosaurs.

Exhibit Features:
- Skull casts of *Tyrannosaurus rex* and *Triceratops*.

Hours:
Monday–Saturday 9:00 a.m.–5:00 p.m.
Sunday Noon–5:00 p.m.
Closed: Thanksgiving, Christmas.
Minimum time required to see exhibit: 25 minutes

Entrance Fees:
Adults $4.50
Seniors $3.50
Children (4–12) $3.50

Address:
Arizona Museum of Science and Technology
147 East Adams, Phoenix, AZ 85004
Telephone: (602)256-9388

Directions:
The museum is located in downtown Phoenix at the southwest corner of 2nd and Adams Street.

4.27 Mesa Southwest Museum
Mesa, AZ

Exhibit Features:
- A small display of dinosaurs.

Hours:
Tuesday–Saturday 10:00 a.m.–5:00 p.m.
Sunday 1:00 p.m.–5:00 p.m.
Closed: Mondays.
Minimum time required to see exhibit: 20 minutes

Entrance Fees:
Adults $4.00
Children (3–12) $2.00

Address:
Mesa Southwest Museum
53 N. MacDonald Street, Mesa, AZ 85201
Telephone: (602)644-2230

Directions:
Mesa is in the southeastern corner of Phoenix. From I-10, exit at the Superstition Freeway headed east. From the freeway, take the Country Club exit and turn left. Continue on to Main Street and turn right. Turn left at MacDonald Street and go one block to the museum.

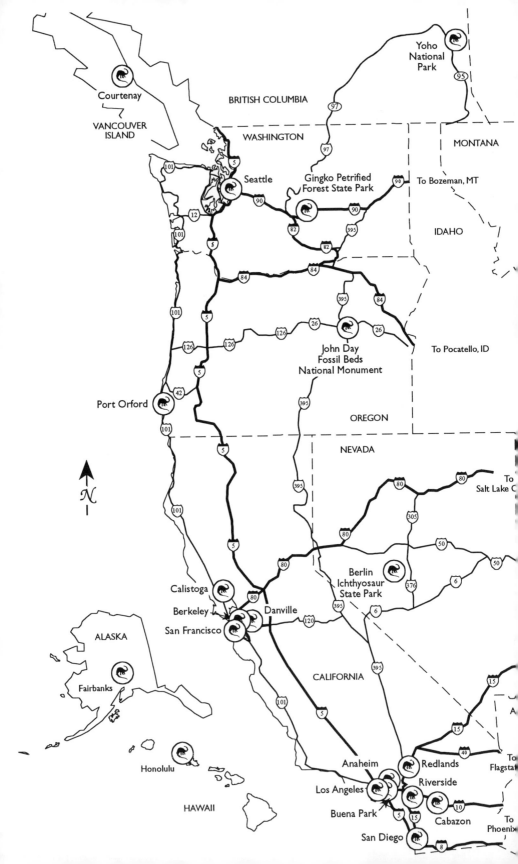

5.
The West Coast
Triassic Seas and Animated Dinosaurs

Most of the exposed Mesozoic rocks on the west coast of North America are not suitable for finding fossils of land animals. The majority of Mesozoic rock outcrops are metamorphic or igneous in origin. As a result, very few dinosaurs have been found here. However, spectacular finds of sea reptiles have been made in the Mesozoic marine sediments that occur in this area.

To make up for the dinosaur deficiency, animated dinosaur models are common here. Dinamation, the manufacturer of animated dinosaur exhibits that are displayed worldwide, has a dinosaur factory in California.

5.1 Berlin-Ichthyosaur State Park near Austin, NV

In 1810, Mary Anning, at the age of 11, was the first person to find fossil ichthyosaur remains along the coast of England. Over a century later, miners discovered ichthyosaur bones in the Shoshone Mountains of Central Nevada, almost 300 miles from the nearest ocean.

During the Triassic Period, 220 million years ago, this area was an inland bay of the ancient ocean Panthalassa. To the east was the coast of Pangaea. As sometimes happens to whales today, 37 ichthyosaurs (not dinosaurs but dolphin-shaped marine reptiles) became trapped in the bay. When the tides dropped, the ichthyosaurs were beached. When the tides returned, the creatures' remains were buried in the mudflats and fossilized. Millions of years later, the ocean subsided as the Shoshone Mountains rose to 7,000-foot elevation. Erosion eventually exposed the ichthyosaurs in their current location.

Articulated Skeletons:
- Ichthyosaurs *in situ*.

Exhibit Features:
- North America's most spectacular deposit of ichthyosaurs.
- A life-size frieze of the 56-foot-long ichthyosaur *Shonisaurus*.
- Camping is available at the park.

Hours:
(Entrance to the Quarry is limited to tours that last one hour.)

Memorial Day to Labor Day:
Tours daily 10:00 a.m., 2:00 p.m., and 4:00 p.m.

March 16 to Memorial Day:
Tours Saturday and Sunday only 10:00 a.m. and 4:00 p.m.

Labor Day to November 13:
Tours Saturday and Sunday only 10:00 a.m. and 4:00 p.m.

November 14 to March 16:
Tours by special request only.

Minimum time required to see exhibit: 30 minutes.

Entrance Fees:
$1.00 for the guided tour of the quarry.

Address:

Berlin-Ichthyosaur State Park
Route 1, Box 32, Austin, NV 89310
Telephone: (702)964-2440 or (702)867-3001

Directions:

Berlin-Ichthyosaur State Park is 150 miles southeast of Reno, 23 miles east of the town of Gabbs. From U.S. 50 between Fallon and Austin, turn south on Highway 361. Or, if you are coming from the south, follow U.S. 95 and turn north on Highway 361 between Hawthorne and Mina. Just north of Gabbs you will come to Highway 844. Follow Highway 844 east to Berlin-Ichthyosaur State Park. You will pass through the remains of the Berlin mining camp on the way to the quarry.

This part of Nevada is desolate. Although services are available in Gabbs, you should be prepared with plenty of gas and water.

Map to Berlin-Ichthyosaur State Park

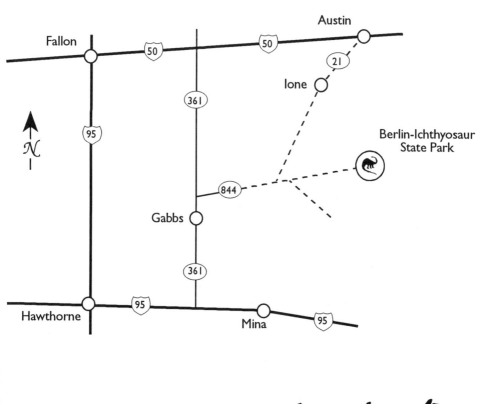

5.2 California Academy of Sciences San Francisco, CA

In 1990 the Academy of Sciences opened a permanent exhibit called "Life Through Time, The Evidence for Evolution." The exhibit traces the history of life on the earth from its origin to the present. Interactive video displays explain how the animals of the present descended from the animals of the past. To illustrate the role of evolution in our planet's history, the museum contrasts living animals with fossils.

Allow time for a walk through Golden Gate Park to see a small forest of giant tree ferns. Tree ferns were much more common during the Paleozoic and the Mesozoic than they are today. Possibly, ferns were the food of some of the great plant-eating dinosaurs.

Articulated Skeletons:

- *Tyrannosaurus rex* on display.
- *Allosaurus* in hot pursuit of *Camptosaurus*.
- A number of fossil pterosaur casts.
- *Dilophosaurus* and *Dimetrodon*.

Exhibit Features:

- The walls of the exhibit recreate fossil-bearing strata. Guests can hunt for fossils embedded in the wall.
- A spectacular diorama of three attacking *Deinonychus*.
- A juvenile *Quetzalcoatlus* replica.
- *Tyrannosaurus* skull (cast) and an *Ultrasaurus* leg bone.
- Sauropod leg fossils and a re-creation of a *Triceratops* excavation.
- Dioramas of Mesozoic ocean life and Paleozoic land life.

Hours:

(open on all holidays)
Daily 10:00 a.m.–5:00 p.m.
First Wednesday of the month 10:00 a.m.–9:00 p.m.
Summer hours (July 4 to Labor Day):
Daily 10:00 a.m.–7:00 p.m.
First Wednesday of the month 10:00 a.m.–9:00 p.m.
Minimum time required to see exhibit: 1 hour

Entrance Fees:
(free the first Wednesday of month)
Adults $7.00
Seniors $4.00
Ages 12–17 $4.00
Ages 6–11 $1.50
Under 6 free

Address:
California Academy of Sciences
Golden Gate Park, San Francisco, CA 94118
Telephone: (415)750-7145 or (415)750-7111

Directions:
The California Academy of Sciences is located in Golden Gate Park on the northwest side of San Francisco. To reach the park from U.S. 101, turn south on Highway 1 to the park. The major fern forests are indicated by the ferns on the map. If you explore the park you will discover many groves of ferns.

Map to California Academy of Sciences

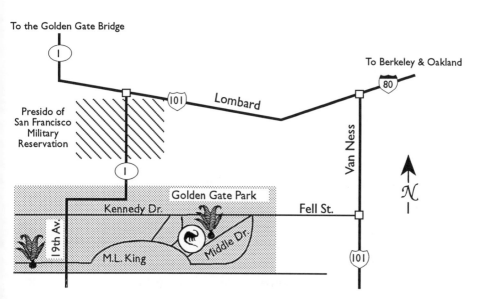

5.3 Museum of Paleontology
Berkeley, CA

Articulated Skeletons:
- *Parasaurolophus, Phytosaurus, Dilophosaurus, Heterodontosaurus,* and a juvenile *Maiasaura.*
- A plesiosaur, 2 ichthyosaurs, and the mosasaur, *Tylosaurus.*
- Four pterodactyls.

Exhibit Features:
- Skulls of *Tyrannosaurus rex, Anatosaurus,* and *Triceratops.*
- A comparison of the tails of an *Allosaurus,* a bird, a mammal, and a crocodile.
- Every year in March or April, the Paleontology Department hosts an open house. There are lectures for adults and hands-on activities for children.

Hours:
Monday–Friday 8:00 a.m.–5:00 p.m.
Saturday–Sunday 1:00 p.m.–5:00 p.m.
Closed: Martin Luther King Day, Presidents' Day, Memorial Day, Labor Day, Thanksgiving, Christmas, New Year's Day.
Summer hours:
Monday–Friday 8:00 a.m.–5:00 p.m.
Minimum time required to see exhibit: 40 minutes

Entrance Fees: free

Address:
Museum of Paleontology, University of California
7 Earth Sciences Building, Berkeley, CA 94720
Telephone: (510)642-1821

Directions:
The museum is located on the University of California at Berkeley campus. From I-80, take the University Avenue exit east (away from the bay). At the entrance to the University turn left (north) on Oxford Street. Then turn right (east) on Hearst. Try to park near the intersection of Euclid and Hearst.

Map to Museum of Paleontology

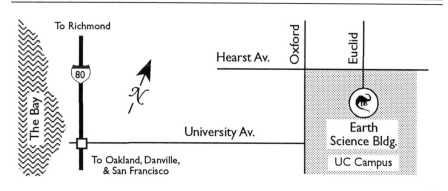

5.4 The Museums at Blackhawk Danville, CA

The museum has a modern paleontology exhibit entitled "In Pursuit of Ancient Life." Many of the fossils are of Cenozoic mammals from the Blackhawk area.

Articulated Skeletons:
- *Ichthyosaurus, Desmatosuchus,* and *Sphenacodon.*

Exhibit Features:
- *Dilophosaurus, Allosaurus,* and phytosaur skulls.
- Exhibits on human evolution and paleontology.

Hours:
Tuesday, Thursday, Saturday, and Sunday 10:00 a.m.–5:00 p.m.
Wednesday and Friday 10:00 a.m.–9:00 p.m.
Closed: Mondays; Easter, July 4, Thanksgiving, Christmas Eve, Christmas, New Year's Day.
Summer hours (June 1 to September 15):
Monday–Tuesday, Thursday, Saturday, and Sunday 10:00 a.m.–5:00 p.m.
Wednesday and Friday 10:00 a.m.–9:00 p.m.
Minimum time required to see exhibit: 20 minutes

Entrance Fees (includes entrance to auto museum, next door):
Adults $7.00
Students (under 18) $4.00
Seniors (65 and over) $2.00
Children under 6 free

Address:

The Museums at Blackhawk
3700 Blackhawk Plaza Circle, Danville, CA 94506
Telephone: (510)736-2277

Directions:

Danville is about 30 miles east of San Francisco, 12 miles south of Berkeley, and 30 miles north of San Jose. From I-680, take the Camino Tassajara exit east. Cross over Blackhawk Road and enter the shopping center to your right. The museum is in the Blackhawk Plaza near the movie theater.

Map to Museums at Blackhawk

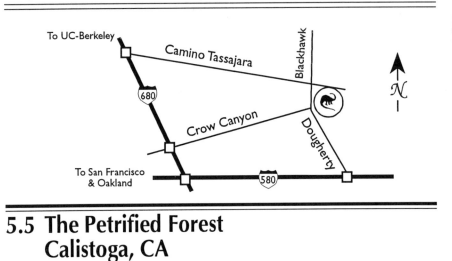

5.5 The Petrified Forest Calistoga, CA

This park has some excellent specimens of petrified trees. The trees were fossilized about three million years ago during the Pliocene Epoch.

Hours:

Daily 10:00 a.m.–5:00 p.m.
Summer hours (May 1 to September 30):
Daily 10:00 a.m.–6:00 p.m.
Minimum time required to see exhibit: 30 minutes

Entrance Fees:

Adults $3.00
Seniors $2.00
Children (4–11) $1.00

Address:

The Petrified Forest
4100 Petrified Forest Road, Calistoga, CA 94515
Telephone: (707)942-6667

Directions:

Calistoga is 60 miles north of San Francisco. Take Highway 29 to Calistoga. From Calistoga, take Petrified Forest Road to the park.

5.6 Natural History Museum of Los Angeles County, Los Angeles, CA

Founded in 1913, the Natural History Museum of Los Angeles County is the third-largest natural history museum in the United States. The museum is home to many spectacular dinosaur fossils. The museum's showpieces are articulated skeletons of *Allosaurus* and *Camptosaurus*.

Remains of the coelacanth, *Latimeria*, a lobe-finned fish, are displayed here. Lobe-finned fish are the ancestors of all tetrapods (the scientific name for land vertebrates). They are quite unusual because their fins look like paddles. The paddles evolved into the arms that allow you to hold this book.

Known only from fossils, coelacanths were thought to have become extinct along with the dinosaurs at the end of the Cretaceous. To the surprise of scientists, a living coelacanth was discovered in the Indian Ocean in 1938. Since then, several living coelacanths have been discovered. *Latimeria* is a true "Living Fossil." Who knows what we will find next?

Articulated Skeletons:

- *Allosaurus* attacking *Camptosaurus*.
- *Triceratops*, *Stegosaurus*, and *Dimetrodon* (a prehistoric reptile).
- *Corythosaurus*.
- The 72-foot-long *Mamenchisaurus*, a sauropod found in China. This dinosaur had the longest neck of any animal.
- Plesiosaur.

Exhibit Features:

- An excellent *Allosaurus* model.
- Skulls of *Tyrannosaurus rex* and *Triceratops*.
- A children's discovery area with plenty of hands-on activities.

Hours:

First Tuesday of the month 10:00 a.m.–5:00 p.m.

Wednesday–Sunday 10:00 a.m.–5:00 p.m.

Closed: Mondays; second, third, and fourth Tuesday of the month; Thanksgiving, Christmas, New Year's Day.

Minimum time required to see exhibit: 2 hours

Entrance Fees:

(free on the first Tuesday of the month)

Adults $5.00

Students & seniors $3.50

Children (5–12) $2.00

Address:

Natural History Museum of Los Angeles County

900 Exposition Boulevard, Los Angeles, CA 90007

Telephone: (213)744-DINO or (213)744-3466

Directions:

Take the Harbor Freeway (I-110) to the Exposition Park exit. The museum is located in Exposition Park across from the USC campus.

Map to the Los Angeles area prehistoric attractions

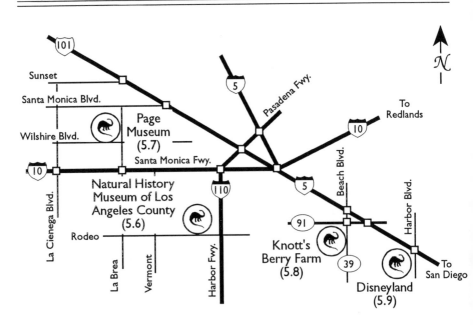

5.7 George C. Page Museum of La Brea Discoveries, Los Angeles, CA

Forty-thousand years ago, mammoths and sabertoothed cats inhabited what is now downtown Los Angeles. Underground, crude oil oozed upward through fissures in the earth's crust. The oil eventually evaporated and left pools of asphalt. Leaves and dust camouflaged the pools of sticky asphalt. Full-grown mammoths crossing the hidden pools became trapped in the asphalt like insects on flypaper. Looking for an easy meal, sabertoothed cats and dire wolves would respond to the cries of distress, only to be trapped by the unforgiving asphalt. Predator traps like these are great places to find the remains of carnivorous animals. Dire wolves are the most common fossils found at La Brea.

Articulated Skeletons:
- Ice Age mammals, sabertoothed cats, mammoths, and dire wolves.

Exhibit Features:
- You may walk through the park to view the "Tar Pits" (the "tar" actually is asphalt). Full-size models of a family of mammoths are placed around the "Tar Pits." One mammoth is depicted as trapped in the sticky asphalt.
- Outdoor bronze statues of Ice Age mammals.
- You can watch scientists prepare fossils in the laboratory.

Hours:
Tuesday–Sunday 10:00 a.m.–5:00 p.m.
Closed: Mondays; Thanksgiving, Christmas, New Year's Day.
Minimum time required to see exhibit: 1 hour

Entrance Fees:
(free on the first Tuesday of the month)
Adults $5.00
Students & seniors $3.50
Children (5–12) $2.00

Address:
George C. Page Museum of La Brea Discoveries
5801 Wilshire Boulevard, Los Angeles, CA 90036
Telephone: (213)857-6311 or (213)936-2230

Directions:
From I-10, exit at La Brea Boulevard north and follow it to Wilshire Boulevard. The museum is in Hancock Park next to the art museum.

5.8 Kingdom of the Dinosaurs, Knott's Berry Farm, Buena Park, CA

The Kingdom of the Dinosaurs is a $7-million special effects journey past animated dinosaurs and an erupting volcano. The park also has a fossil exhibit and employs a full-time paleontologist.

Hours:
Monday–Friday 10:00 a.m.–6:00 p.m.
Saturday 10:00 a.m.–10:00 p.m.
Sunday 10:00 a.m.–7:00 p.m.
Closed: Christmas.
Summer hours (June 19 to September 5):
Monday–Friday 9:00 a.m.–11:00 p.m.
Saturday 9:00 a.m.–Midnight
Sunday 9:00 a.m.–11:00 p.m.
Minimum time required to see exhibit: 1 day

Entrance Fees:
Adults $25.90
Seniors $17.95
Children (3–11) $15.95

Address:
Kingdom of the Dinosaurs, Knott's Berry Farm
8039 Beach Boulevard, Buena Park, CA 90620
Telephone: (714)220-5200

Directions:
Buena Park is just west of Anaheim. From I-5, take the Beach Boulevard (Route 39) exit south. After you cross over Highway 91, the park will be to your right.

5.9 Disneyland
Anaheim, CA

The train ride that circles the park passes by dioramas of Mesozoic life. The scenes are based on the movie "Fantasia."

Hours: vary; open past midnight in the summer
Minimum time required to see exhibit: 1 day

Entrance Fees:
Adults $30.00
Seniors $24.00
Children (3–11) $24.00
Children under 3 free

Address:
Disneyland
1313 Harbor Boulevard, Anaheim, CA 92803
Telephone: (714)999-4000

Directions:
From I-5, take the Harbor Boulevard exit south.

5.10 Jurupa Mountains Cultural Center Riverside, CA

The Cultural Center has some large concrete dinosaur statues. Although the statues are not technically accurate, they delight most children.

Hours:

Tuesday–Saturday 8:00 a.m.–5:00 p.m.
Closed: Sundays, Mondays; July 4, Thanksgiving, Christmas, New Year's Day.

Entrance Fees:

(museum only)
Adults $3.00
Children $2.00

Address:

Jurupa Mountains Cultural Center
7621 Granite Hill Drive, Riverside, CA 92509
Telephone: (909)685-5818

Directions:

Riverside, California, is east of Los Angeles. Jurupa Mountains Cultural Center is off Highway 60 between I-15 and I-215. Freeway off-ramp signs mark the Cultural Center.

Map to Cabazon, Redlands, and Jurupa

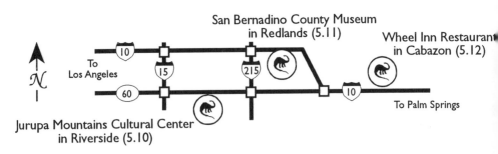

San Bernadino County Museum in Redlands (5.11)

Wheel Inn Restaurant in Cabazon (5.12)

To Los Angeles

To Palm Springs

Jurupa Mountains Cultural Center in Riverside (5.10)

5.11 San Bernardino County Museum Redlands, CA

Exhibit Features:
- The only dinosaur tracks ever found in California.

Hours:
Tuesday–Saturday 9:00 a.m.–5:00 p.m.
Sunday 11:00 a.m.–5:00 p.m.
Closed: Mondays; Thanksgiving, Christmas, New Year's Day.
Minimum time required to see exhibit: 10 minutes

Entrance Fees:
Adults: $3.00
Seniors: $2.00
Students (13–17 or older with I.D.): $2.00
Children (2–12) $1.00
Members of Museum and children under 2: free

Address:
San Bernardino County Museum
2024 Orange Tree Lane, Redlands, CA 92374
Telephone: (909)798-8570

Directions:
The museum is east of Los Angeles and west of Palm Springs in Redlands. From I-10 in Redlands, exit at California Street north. Take the first right onto Orange Tree Lane. The museum is about three or four blocks up Orange Tree.

5.12 Wheel Inn Restaurant Cabazon, CA

The restaurant has bigger-than-life *Tyrannosaurus rex* and *Apatosaurus* statues. There's a children's gift store inside the *Apatosaurus*.

Hours: always open (gift shop is open 10:00 a.m.–8:00 p.m.)
Minimum time required to see exhibit: 10 minutes

Entrance Fees: free; donations appreciated

Address:
Wheel Inn Restaurant
50800 Seminole Drive, Cabazon, CA 92230
Telephone: (909)849-8309

Directions:
Cabazon, California, is about 10 miles west of Palm Springs and 80 miles east of Los Angeles. The statues are located on the north side of Cabazon; you can see them from I-10.

5.13 San Diego Natural History Museum San Diego, CA

The San Diego Natural History Museum is the second-oldest scientific institution in the western United States. The museum displays some of the few dinosaur remains ever discovered in California.

Articulated Skeletons:
- *Allosaurus* and a mosasaur.

Exhibit Features:
- The only nodosaur found west of the Rockies was found in San Diego County. The museum displays the remains of this armored Cretaceous dinosaur.

Hours:
Daily 10:00 a.m.–5:00 p.m.
Summer hours:
Daily 9:30 a.m.–6:30 p.m.
Closed: Thanksgiving, Christmas, New Year's Day.
Minimum time required to see exhibit: 45 minutes

Entrance Fees:
Adults $6.00
Seniors $5.00
Military $4.00
Children (6–17) $2.00
(Half price Thursdays from 6:00 p.m.–9:00 p.m.)

Address:

San Diego Natural History Museum
Balboa Park, P.O. Box 1390, San Diego, CA 92112
Telephone: (619)232-3821

Directions:

The museum is located in Balboa Park near the San Diego Zoo. From I-5, take President's Way/Park Boulevard north. Turn left on Village Place and continue to the museum.

Nearby:

Also in Balboa Park is an excellent Botanical Garden with huge tree ferns and cycads on display. Admission to the Botanical Garden is free, and it is open Tuesday–Sunday 10 a.m.–4 p.m. (closed on Mondays).

San Diego State University's Allison Center for the Study of Paleontology has a few displays on paleontology and a theropod footprint. Located in the Geology and Chemistry Building, San Diego State University, Geology Department, San Diego, CA 92182. Telephone: (619) 594-5586.

Directions:

The Allison Center for the Study of Paleontology is on the San Diego State University campus. From I-8, exit onto College Avenue South. Park as close to campus as possible and then walk to the Geology and Chemistry Building.

Map to San Diego Natural History Museum and Allison Center for Paleontology

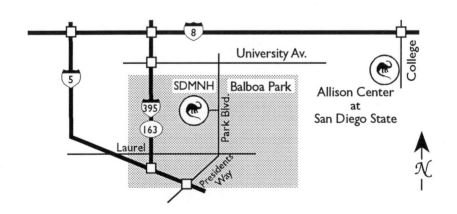

5.14 Paradise Park
Honolulu, HI

You will find three Dinamation dinosaurs in the lush tropical forest.

Exhibit Features:
- *Tyrannosaurus, Triceratops, Pteranodon.*

Hours:
Monday–Friday 8:00 a.m.–4:00 p.m.
Saturday–Sunday 8:00 a.m.–5:00 p.m.
Summer hours (June 1 to Labor Day):
Daily 8:00 a.m.–5:00 p.m.
Closed: Christmas.
Minimum time required to see exhibit: 20 minutes

Entrance Fees:
Adults $14.95
Seniors $8.95
Children (3–12) $7.95

Address:
Paradise Park
3737 Manoa Road, Honolulu, HI 96822
Telephone: (808)988-0200

Directions:
Paradise Park is 30 minutes from Waikiki.

5.15 Prehistoric Gardens
Port Orford, OR

The Prehistoric Gardens have existed in this protected coastal valley since 1953. Surrounded by the lush rainforest vegetation of coastal Oregon are 22 full-size statues of prehistoric animals. The life-size *Brachiosaurus* model is enormous.

Hours:
Daily 8:00 a.m.–dusk
Minimum time required to see exhibit: 30 minutes

Entrance Fees:
Adults $5.00
Students (12–18) and seniors $4.00
Children (5–11) $3.00

Address:
Prehistoric Gardens
3648 Highway 101 South, Port Orford, OR 97465
Telephone: (503)332-4463

Directions:
Port Orford is in southwest Oregon. The park is on the west side of U.S. 101 between Ophir and Port Orford, 14 miles north of Gold Beach, Oregon.

5.16 John Day Fossil Beds National Monument John Day, OR

The fossil record here is from the Cenozoic Era. The fossils provide a continuous record of life from 50 million to 5 million years ago. This gives scientists the opportunity to "watch" animals evolve in a particular geographical area over a period of 45 million years.

The park is spread out over four locations: Clarno, Painted Hills, Sheep Rock, and John Day.

Hours:
(Visitor Center in the town of John Day)
Daily 8:30 a.m.–5:00 p.m.
Summer hours (End of May to End of October):
Daily 8:30 a.m.–6:00 p.m.
Closed: weekends during December, January, and February; Thanksgiving, Christmas, New Year's Day.
Minimum time required to see exhibit: It takes several hours to travel between the four locations.

Entrance Fees: free

Address:
John Day Fossil Beds National Monument
420 West Main, John Day, OR 97845

Telephone: (503)987-2333

Directions:

The main Visitor Center for the John Day Fossil Beds National Monument is located in the town of John Day in eastern Oregon. The town is located at the intersection of U.S. 26 and U.S. 395. The Sheep Rock site is 35 miles west of John Day on U.S. 26. The Painted Hills site is 25 miles west of Sheep Rock on U.S. 26.

To reach Clarno, take Highway 19 about 65 miles north from Sheep Rock to Fossil. Then take Highway 218 southwest to Clarno.

Map to John Day Fossil Beds National Monument

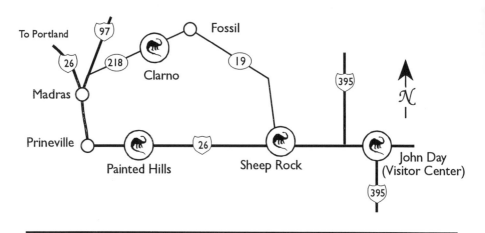

5.17 Ginkgo Petrified Forest State Park Vantage, WA

Although the park is named for the Ginkgo tree, the petrified wood is of the Cenozoic Age and thus petrified Gingko trees are relatively rare here. The museum in Vantage displays petrified wood. A three-quarter-mile interpretive trail leads you past several petrified logs encased in cages to prevent vandalism and theft.

Hours:

Daily 8:00 a.m.–5:00 p.m.

Minimum time required to see exhibit: 30 minutes

Entrance Fees: free

Address:

Ginkgo Petrified Forest State Park
Vantage, WA 98950
Telephone: (509)856-2710

Directions:

The park is near Vantage, along the Columbia River in central Washington. Vantage is 27 miles east of Ellensburg on I-90. From the interstate, take the Vantage exit (Exit 136). To reach the interpretive center and the Petrified Log Trail, turn north toward Vantage on Old Vantage Highway. The interpretive center is just past the KOA campground on Old Vantage Highway. The Petrified Log Trail is two miles farther down the highway. Watch for the signs.

Map to Ginkgo Petrified Forest State Park

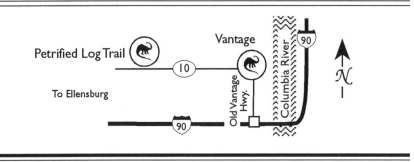

5.18 Burke Museum
Seattle, WA

Much of this extensive fossil mammal and invertebrate collection is used for teaching and research. This museum has the only dinosaur display in the state of Washington.

Articulated Skeletons:

- *Allosaurus.*
- *Megalonyx* (Ice Age ground sloth).
- *Hoplophoneus* (sabertoothed cat).

Exhibit Features:

- Models of *Deinonychus* and *Ornitholestes.*
- *Tylosaurus* skulls.
- Dinosaur footprints, octopuslike ammonites, Paleozoic fish fossils, and Cenozoic vertebrate fossils.

Hours:

Daily 10:00 a.m.–5:00 p.m.

Closed: July 4, Thanksgiving, Christmas.

Minimum time required to see exhibit: 30 minutes

Entrance Fees:

Adults $3.00

Students and seniors $2.00

Children (6–18) $1.50

Address:

Burke Museum

University of Washington, DB-10, Seattle, WA 98195

Telephone: (206)543-5590

Directions:

From I-5, exit east on NE 45th Street. The museum is on your right, on the 17th Avenue Northeast entrance to the University campus.

Map to Burke Museum

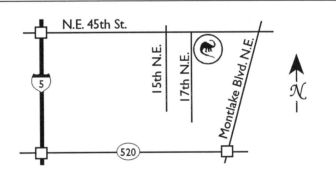

5.19 Courtenay & District Museum Courtenay, BC

Eighty million years ago, Vancouver Island was covered by a warm shallow sea. We know this because of the Cretaceous marine fossils found here. In 1988, an elasmosaur, a long-necked marine reptile, was discovered along the Puntledge River. This elasmosaur is the centerpiece of the museum's new paleontology display, which opened in June of 1993.

Articulated Skeletons:

- An elasmosaur.

Exhibit Features:
- A mural of Cretaceous sea life.
- A mosasaur, *Desmatochelys,* and marine invertebrates.

Hours:
Tuesday–Saturday 10:00 a.m.–4:30 p.m.
Summer hours (May to August):
Daily 10:00 a.m.–4:30 p.m.
Closed: Easter, Christmas, Statutory Holiday, New Year's Day.
Minimum time required to see exhibit: 35 minutes

Entrance Fees: $1.00 recommended donation

Address:
Courtenay & District Museum
360 Cliffe Avenue, Courtenay, BC Canada V9N 2H9
Telephone: (604)334-3611

Directions:
Courtenay is located on Vancouver Island, 240 kilometers (150 miles) northwest of Victoria along the Island Highway (19). The Island Highway becomes Cliffe Avenue as you enter the town of Courtenay. The museum is located between 3rd and 2nd streets. It is in the largest free-span log building in Canada.

5.20 Yoho National Park near Field, BC

In 1909, Charles Walcott discovered some fossils near Burgess Pass. The fossils were of ancient animals that lived more than a half-billion years ago. The famous Burgess Shale fossil beds in Yoho National Park contain rare fossils of soft-bodied invertebrates from the Cambrian Period (570 million years ago). The animals found here were so strange that they have names such as *Hallucigenia*. Some scientists feel that these animals represent a diversity of life far greater than what exists today.

There is an exhibit of Burgess Shale fossils at the Travel Information Center at Field, in Yoho Park. The only access to the fossil beds is through guided tours on Tuesdays and Saturdays at 9:00 a.m. Advance reservations are recommended. The tours are limited to 15 people and require a strenuous and steep 20-kilometer (12-mile) hike. Snow covers the fossil beds from October until the end of June.

Entrance Fees:
Per vehicle $4.00
4-day pass $9.00

Address:
Yoho National Park
Box 99, Field, BC, Canada V0A 1G0
Telephone: (604)343-6324

Directions:
Yoho National Park is 183 kilometers (110 miles) west of Calgary, on TransCanada 1, just over the Great Divide.

5.21 University of Alaska Museum Fairbanks, AK

Many people think dinosaurs lived only in tropical environments. The work of William Clemens on the Alaskan North Slope has changed that picture dramatically. Clemens recovered dinosaurs in an area that had an arctic climate during the Late Cretaceous. While pinpointing paleo-climates is a difficult task, we know that the environment clearly was too cold for cold-blooded turtles and crocodiles; yet dinosaurs appear to have flourished.

Although many of the bones are fragmentary, they show little sign of permineralization and look more like Ice Age fossils than 65-million-year-old dinosaurs. The museum specializes in retaining DNA from Ice Age and rare arctic mammals.

Exhibit Features:
- Ice Age mammals (including frozen mammals whose tissue has been preserved for thousands of years).
- Dinosaur remains from the North Slope near the Colville River.

Hours:
October to April:
Daily Noon–5:00 p.m.
May and September:
Daily 9:00 a.m.–5:00 p.m.
June, July, and August:
Daily 9:00 a.m.–7:00 p.m.
Closed: Thanksgiving, Christmas, New Year's Day.
Minimum time required to see exhibit: 30 minutes

Entrance Fees:
(free Fridays October 1 to April 30)
Adults $4.00
Children (12–18), seniors, and students $3.00
Families $12.50

Address:
University of Alaska Museum
907 Yukon Drive, Fairbanks, AK 99775-1200
Telephone: (907)474-7505

Directions:
From Fairbanks, follow Airport Way to University Avenue. Turn right and follow University to Farmers Loop. Turn left into the campus. At the top of the hill, turn right and then take the immediate left onto Yukon Drive. The museum is about a half-mile up Yukon. Watch for the signs.

Map to University of Alaska Museum

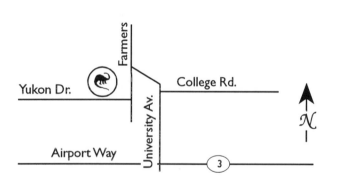

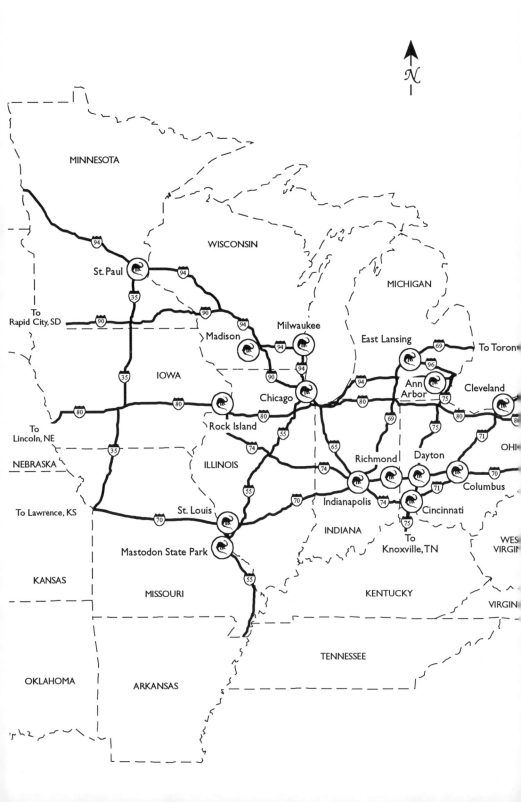

6.
The Great Lakes Region
Museum Collections

The rocks in this area are principally Paleozoic. Very few dinosaurs have been discovered in the Great Lakes Region. However, plenty of dinosaurs can be spotted at the museums in this area. The museums have sent scientists and adventurers to all corners of the earth, hunting for dinosaurs. These dinosaurs have been mounted and are on display.

6.1 The Cleveland Museum of Natural History Cleveland, OH

The dramatic focal point of this museum is a *Haplocanthosaurus*, an enormous sauropod that scientists from the Cleveland Museum of Natural History unearthed near Canon City, Colorado.

The museum's active research program continues to expand both the museum's collection and our understanding of dinosaurs.

Articulated Skeletons:
- *Haplocanthosaurus*, a 70-foot-long sauropod.
- The duckbilled dinosaur *Anatosaurus*, the mosasaur *Platecarpus*, and an *Allosaurus*.
- Cleveland Shale marine fossils from the Devonian age (408 to 360 million years ago) including sharks and several *Dunkleosteus*.
- Sabertoothed cats, a giant elk cast, a mammoth, and a mastodon.

Exhibit Features:
- Life-sized *Stegosaurus* statue and a reconstruction of *Pteranodon*.
- The only known *Nanotyrannus* skull. *Nanotyrannus* was a small but advanced tyrannosaurid. It was once thought to be a juvenile *Tyrannosaur*, but CAT-scans of the skull have verified that it is an adult.
- Skulls of *Parasaurolophus* and *Triceratops*.
- The Hall of Man presents the story of human evolution with casts of "Lucy," our three-million-year-old ancestor.

Volunteer Opportunities:
The museum welcomes volunteers to help with field work and to prepare fossils. Contact the Coordinator of Volunteers at the museum.

Hours:
Monday–Saturday 10:00 a.m.–5:00 p.m.
Wednesday (September to May only) 10:00 a.m.–10:00 p.m.
Sunday 1:00 p.m.–5:30 p.m.
Closed: Memorial Day, Labor Day, Thanksgiving, Christmas Eve, Christmas, New Year's Eve, New Year's Day.
Minimum time required to see exhibit: 1 hour

Entrance Fees:
Adults $5.00
Seniors and students $3.00
Children (5–17) $3.00

Address:

Cleveland Museum of Natural History
One Wade Oval Drive, University Circle, Cleveland, OH 44106-1767
Telephone: (216)231-4600

Directions:

Located near Cleveland Heights and Wade Park, the museum is at the junction of Martin Luther King and East Boulevard, near Euclid Avenue.

Map to Cleveland Museum of Natural History

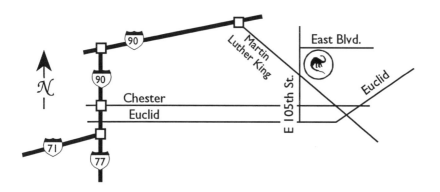

6.2 Orton Geological Museum
Columbus, OH

Many of this building's walls are built from fossiliferous stone, and the gargoyles on the roof have the faces of prehistoric animals.

Articulated Skeletons:

- Examples of Jurassic pterosaur and *Archaeopteryx* fossils from the lithographic limestone of Solnhoffen, Germany.
- A giant ground sloth and a *Glyptodon*.

Exhibit Features:

- Reproduction of a *Tyrannosaurus rex* skull.
- *Dunkleosteus* skull.
- Paleozoic and Mesozoic invertebrate fossils.

Hours:

Monday–Friday 8:00 a.m.–5:00 p.m.
Closed: Thanksgiving, Christmas, New Year's Day; University holidays.
Minimum time required to see exhibit: 30 minutes

Entrance Fees: free

Address:
Orton Geological Museum, Ohio State University
155 S. Oval, Columbus, OH 43210
Telephone: (614)292-6896

Directions:
From I-71, take exit 110B west. The museum is on the Ohio State University campus at the end of Haggerty Street.

6.3 Cincinnati Museum of Natural History Cincinnati, OH

Exhibit Features:
- An Ice Age exhibit displays sabertoothed cats and giant ground sloths.

Hours:
Monday–Saturday 9:00 a.m.–5:00 p.m.
Sunday 11:00 a.m.–6:00 p.m.
Minimum time required to see exhibit: 30 minutes

Entrance Fees:
Adults $4.95
Children (3–12) $2.95

Address:
Cincinnati Museum of Natural History
1301 Western Avenue, Cincinnati, OH 45203
Telephone: (513)287-7000, 800-733-2077

Directions:
From I-75 heading south, take exit 2A and turn left onto Western Avenue. The museum is about one mile down Western on the right.

6.4 Dayton Museum of Natural History Dayton, OH

The museum displays local Paleozoic marine fauna. Skeletons of a mammoth and a giant ground sloth from the Pleistocene are also on exhibit.

Articulated Skeletons:
- *Mammut* and *Megalonyx*.

Hours:
Wednesday, Thursday, and Saturday 9:00 a.m.–5:00 p.m.
Tuesday and Friday 9:00 a.m.–9:00 p.m.
Sunday 1:00 p.m.–5:00 p.m.
Closed: Thanksgiving, Christmas.
Minimum time required to see exhibit: 20 minutes

Entrance Fees:
Adults $3.00
Seniors $2.50
Children (3–16) $1.50

Address:
Dayton Museum of Natural History
2600 DeWeese Parkway, Dayton, OH 45414
Telephone: (513)275-7431

Directions:
The museum is just north of downtown Dayton. From I-75, take the 57B exit and follow the signs.

6.5 Michigan State University Museum East Lansing, MI

This dinosaur exhibit emphasizes evolution and the history of life. The "Send a Dinosaur to College" fund-raising program paid for the two dinosaur skeletons exhibited here.

Articulated Skeletons:
- *Allosaurus* and *Stegosaurus*, and a cast of *Archaeopteryx*.

Exhibit Features:
- Skulls from *Triceratops* and *Parasaurolophus*.
- A hall of evolution that traces life from its origin to the present.

Hours:
(hours vary on home-football Saturdays)
Monday–Wednesday and Friday 9:00 a.m.–5:00 p.m.
Thursday 9:00 a.m.–9:00 p.m.
Saturday 10:00 a.m.–5:00 p.m.
Sunday 1:00 p.m.–5:00 p.m.
Closed: July 4, Thanksgiving, Christmas, New Year's Day; all university holidays.
Minimum time required to see exhibit: 30 minutes

Entrance Fees: free ($2.00 donation suggested)

Address:
Michigan State University Museum
West Circle Drive, East Lansing, MI 48824-1045
Telephone: (517)355-2370

Directions:
East Lansing is east of Lansing, Michigan, and about 70 miles northwest of Detroit. Heading east on Grand River Avenue in East Lansing, turn right onto Abbot. Abbot ends at West Circle Drive. Turn right onto West Circle and follow the loop to the museum, which will be to your right.

Map to Michigan State University Museum

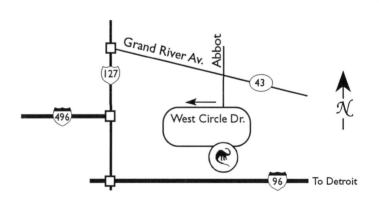

6.6 University of Michigan Exhibit Museum Ann Arbor, MI

The museum has an entire floor devoted to paleontology. Specimens from most of the geological periods are on exhibit.

Articulated Skeletons:

- *Allosaurus, Anatosaurus, Stegosaurus, Coelophysis.*

Exhibit Features:

- *Tyrannosaurus rex* skull.
- Fossilized eggs of *Protoceratops* and *Hypselosaurus.*
- Leg bones of *Apatosaurus.*

Hours:

Monday–Saturday 9:00 a.m.–5:00 p.m.
Sunday 1:00 p.m.–5:00 p.m.
Closed: Easter, Memorial Day, July 4, Labor Day, Thanksgiving, Christmas Eve, Christmas, New Year's Day.
Minimum time required to see exhibit: 30 minutes

Entrance Fees: free (groups of more than 10 should call ahead)

Address:

University of Michigan Exhibit Museum
Alexander G. Ruthven Museum Building
1109 Geddes Avenue, Ann Arbor, MI 48109-1079
Telephone: (313)763-6085 or (313)764-0478

Directions:

Ann Arbor is about 30 miles west of Detroit. Take exit 37B from U.S. 23 and head west on Washtenaw to the University of Michigan campus.

Map to University of Michigan Exhibit Museum

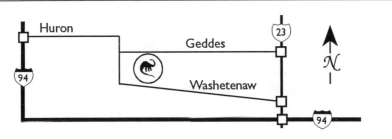

6.7 Children's Museum of Indianapolis Indianapolis, IN

Founded in 1925, the Children's Museum of Indianapolis is the largest children's museum in the world. The exhibits provide even the youngest visitors with an excellent educational experience. The museum makes learning fun; many of the signs on exhibits read "please touch." You can get your hands dirty at the dinosaur excavation hunting for the remains of a duckbilled dinosaur.

Articulated Skeletons:
- *Chasmosaurus* and *Coelophysis.*

Exhibit Features:
- A children's dinosaur excavation.
- The "What if . . . " Gallery, where puzzles and interactive computer games explain the science of paleontology.

Hours:
Tuesday, Wednesday, Friday, Saturday 10:00 a.m.–5:00 p.m.
Thursday 10:00 a.m.–8:00 p.m.
Sunday Noon–5:00 p.m.
Closed: Mondays from Labor Day to Memorial Day; Thanksgiving, Christmas.
Minimum time required to see exhibit: 1 hour

Entrance Fees:
(free Thursdays from 5:00 p.m. to 8:00 p.m.)
Adults $6.00
Seniors (60+) $5.00
Children (2–17) $3.00

Mailing Address:
Children's Museum of Indianapolis
P.O. Box 3000, Indianapolis, IN 46208
Telephone: (317)924-KIDS or (317)924-5431

Location Address:
Children's Museum of Indianapolis
3000 N. Meridian Street, Indianapolis, IN 46208

Directions:

From I-65, take the 30th Street exit and head east on 29th Street. Turn left (north) on Meridian. The museum is one block up on the corner of 30th and Meridian streets.

Map to Children's Museum of Indianapolis

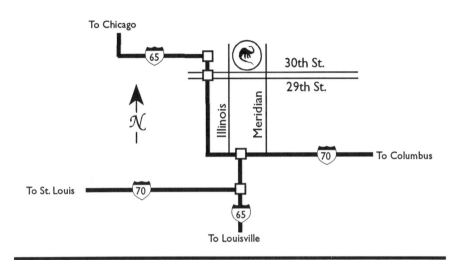

6.8 Joseph Moore Museum Richmond, IN

Exhibit Features:

- A small paleontology exhibit displaying a beaver fossil and mastodon.

Hours:

Monday, Wednesday, Friday 1:00 p.m.–4:00 p.m.

Sunday 1:00 p.m.–5:00 p.m.

Closed: Tuesdays, Thursdays; July 4, Thanksgiving, Christmas Eve, Christmas, New Year's Day.

Summer hours (June 12 to September 5):

Sunday 1:00 p.m.–5:00 p.m.

Minimum time required to see exhibit: 15 minutes

Entrance Fees: free

Address:

Joseph Moore Museum
Earlham College, Richmond, IN 47374
Telephone: (317)983-1302

Directions:

Richmond is on the Ohio-Indiana border, 75 miles east of Indianapolis.
The museum is off U.S. 40 on the Earlham College campus in Richmond.

6.9 St. Louis Science Center
St. Louis, MO

The highlight of this museum is a life-size diorama of *Triceratops* being attacked by *Tyrannosaurus*.

Exhibit Features:

- Life-size robotic models of *Triceratops*, *Tyrannosaurus*, and *Pteranodon*.
- Many smaller fossils.
- Outdoor exhibit of fiberglass models, including *Tyrannosaurus rex*.

Hours:

Monday–Thursday 9:30 a.m.–5:00 p.m.
Friday–Saturday 9:30 a.m.–9:00 p.m.
Sunday 9:30 a.m.–5:00 p.m.
Summer hours (Memorial Day to Labor Day):
Monday–Thursday 9:30 a.m.–5:00 p.m.
Friday–Saturday 9:30 a.m.–9:00 p.m.
Sunday 9:30 a.m.–5:00 p.m.
Closed: Thanksgiving, Christmas, New Year's Day.
Minimum time required to see exhibit: 45 minutes

Entrance Fees: free

Address:

St. Louis Science Center
5050 Oakland Avenue, St. Louis, MO 63110
Telephone: (800)456-7572

Directions:

From U.S. 40 westbound, exit at Kingshighway south. At the first stoplight, turn right onto Oakland Avenue. The museum is in Forest Park, about two blocks up.

Map to St. Louis Science Center

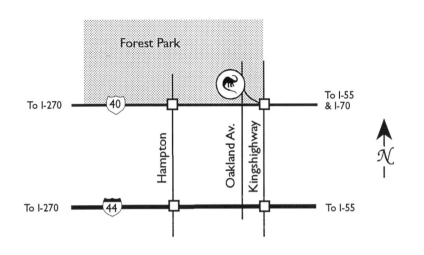

6.10 Mastodon State Park
near Imperial, MO

During the Pleistocene, the area near Imperial, Missouri, was often swampy and contained a mineral spring. Large mammals would sometimes became trapped in the mud. Bones from more than 60 mastodons (elephantlike animals from the Miocene and Pleistocene) have been removed from the pit. In 1979, archaeologists discovered a Clovis Period (10,000 to 14,000 years ago) spear point associated with the bones. The spear point verified that the first human inhabitants of North America hunted the mastodon and possibly contributed to their extinction.

Articulated Skeletons:

- Mastodon.

Hours:

Museum/Bone Bed:
Monday–Saturday 9:00 a.m.–4:30 p.m.
Sunday Noon–4:30 p.m.
Park:
Monday–Saturday 8:00 a.m.–Dusk
Closed: Easter, Thanksgiving, Christmas, New Year's Day.
Minimum time required to see exhibit: 45 minutes

Entrance Fees:

Adults (over 14 years old) $2.00

Families $10.00

Address:

Mastodon State Park

1551 Seckman Road, Imperial, MO 63052

Telephone: (314)464-2976

Directions:

The park is about 12 miles south of St. Louis. Take the Imperial exit off of I-55 and follow the signs to the park.

Map to Mastodon State Park

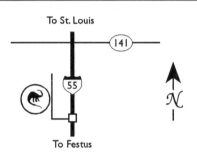

6.11 Fryxell Geology Museum
Rock Island, IL

The museum displays fossils from all over the world. The fossils range from plants and invertebrates to several dinosaur skulls.

Exhibit Features:

- *Triceratops* and *Tyrannosaurus* skulls.
- A wall-mounted mosasaur.
- Dinosaur eggs.
- Mastodon skull.
- *Allosaurus* skull.

Hours:

Monday–Friday 8:00 a.m.–5:00 p.m.

Saturday–Sunday 1:00 p.m.–4:00 p.m.

Closed: when Augustana College is not in session; all holidays, during fall and spring breaks, Good Friday, and for two weeks over Christmas. Summer hours are limited. Call for information.

Minimum time required to see exhibit: 30 minutes

Entrance Fees: free

Address:
Augustana College
820 38th Street, Rock Island, IL 61201
Telephone: (309)794-7318

Directions:
Rock Island is in the Quad Cities area along the Mississippi River, 175 miles west of Chicago. The museum is located in the New Science Building at 38th Street and 9th Avenue on the Augusta College campus.

6.12 Field Museum of Natural History Chicago, IL

In 1926, the Field Museum commissioned Charles Knight to paint 28 giant murals depicting 4.5 billion years of earth history. At the time, Knight was the acknowledged master of prehistoric art and was paid $150,000 to paint the murals, which took four years to complete The paintings are masterpieces in composition and form. They provide a dramatic background for this museum's excellent collection of dinosaur skeletons.

Articulated Skeletons:
- *Albertosaurus, Lambeosaurus, Apatosaurus, Diplodocus, Protoceratops.*
- *Pteranodon* and *Nyctosaurus.*
- *Brachiosaurus* bones found near Grand Junction, Colorado.

Exhibit Features:
- 28 murals by Charles Knight.
- 34 fossil dinosaurs and reptiles.

Hours:
Daily 9:00 a.m.–5:00 p.m.
Closed: Christmas.
Minimum time required to see exhibit: 3 hours

Entrance Fees:
(free on Thursdays)
Adults $5.00
Students and seniors $3.00
Children (2–17) $3.00

Address:
Field Museum of Natural History
Lake Shore Drive at Roosevelt Road, Chicago, IL 60605
Telephone: (312)922-9410

Directions:
Located on the lake front in Grant Park, the museum is next to Soldier
Field and the Burnham Park Harbor.

Map to Field Museum and the Chicago Academy of Sciences

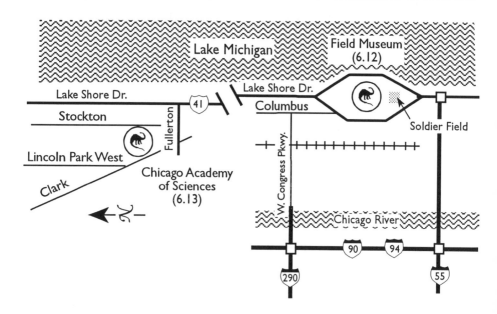

6.13 Chicago Academy of Sciences Chicago, IL

The Academy presents the natural history of the region around Chicago.

Exhibit Features:

- A walk-through Paleozoic coal forest.
- Displays on life through the ages.

Hours:

Daily 10:00 a.m.–5:00 p.m.
Closed: Christmas.
Minimum time required to see exhibit: 15 minutes

Entrance Fees:

Adults $1.00
Seniors $.50
Children (3–17) $.50

Address:

Chicago Academy of Sciences
2001 N. Clark Street, Chicago, IL 60614
Telephone: (312)871-2668

Directions:

From Lake Shore Drive exit at Fullerton going west. Take Fullerton to Clark. The museum will be on your right.

6.14 Milwaukee Public Museum Milwaukee, WI

The museum is continually adding to its collection of dinosaurs.

Articulated Skeletons:

- The world's most complete *Torosaurus* skeleton.

Exhibit Features:

- A diorama of *Tyrannosaurus* and *Triceratops*.
- Stegosaurs and other exhibits showing ancient life in Wisconsin.
- *Pachycephalosaurus* skulls.
- Reconstructions of *Archaeopteryx*.

Volunteer Opportunities:

The museum accepts volunteers to help with field work and the preparation and repair of exhibits and fossils.

Hours:

Daily 9:00 a.m.–5:00 p.m.
Closed: Thanksgiving, Christmas, New Year's Day.
Minimum time required to see exhibit: 45 minutes

Entrance Fees:

Adults $4.00
Seniors $2.00
Children (4–17) $2.00

Address:

Milwaukee Public Museum
800 West Wells Street, Milwaukee, WI 53233
Telephone: (414)278-2702

Directions:

The museum is located near the Civic Center in downtown Milwaukee. From I-43, take the Civic Center exit and follow the signs.

Map to Milwaukee Public Museum

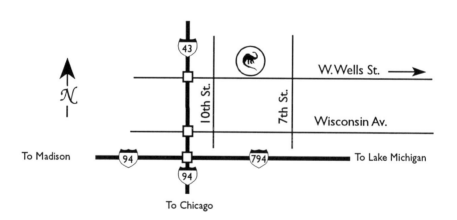

6.15 University of Wisconsin Geology Museum, Madison, WI

In 1985, the University of Wisconsin completed excavation of the duckbilled dinosaur, *Edmontosaurus*. The dinosaur was found in South Dakota. The museum is working to expand its fossil collection and is now excavating a *Triceratops* in Montana.

Articulated Skeletons:
- A 33-foot *Edmontosaurus* and an 18-foot mosasaur.
- Mastodon, sabertoothed cat, and *Mesohippus* (an ancestral horse).
- *Hesperornis* (a wingless, diving marine bird with teeth).

Exhibit Features:
- The ferocious looking skull of a 12-foot bulldog fish.
- A large collection of fossil invertebrates including a 13-inch trilobite.
- Museum visitors can watch scientists prepare and study fossil specimens.

Volunteer Opportunities:
The museum accepts volunteers to help with preparation and repair of exhibits, fossil preparation, and field work.

Hours:
Monday–Friday 8:30 a.m.–4:30 p.m.
Saturday 9:00 a.m.–1:00 p.m.
Closed: Sundays; Martin Luther King Day, Thanksgiving, Christmas Eve, Christmas, New Year's Day.
Minimum time required to see exhibit: 1 hour

Entrance Fees: free

Address:
University of Wisconsin Geology Museum
1215 West Dayton Street, Madison, WI 53706
Telephone: (608)262-2399

Directions:
The museum is at the corner of Charter and West Dayton streets, two blocks east of Camp Randall Stadium, on the University of Wisconsin campus. There is very little parking close to the museum. Public transportation is your best bet.

6.16 Science Museum of Minnesota Saint Paul, MN

The *Diplodocus* displayed at the Science Museum of Minnesota reflects the very latest in scientific theory. Many older restorations of the large sauropods show them as swampbound, tail-dragging behemoths. While *Diplodocus* may have been big, it is now known that they stayed mainly on dry land and they normally held their tail straight out. The *Diplodocus* at the Science Museum of Minnesota holds his tail high. The museum is in the process of remodeling, and the work is expected to be completed in 1994.

Articulated Skeletons:
- *Allosaurus, Camptosaurus, Diplodocus.*

Exhibit Features:
- Fossil preparation laboratory.
- *Tyrannosaurus rex* skull.
- Plant and invertebrate fossils.

Hours:
Monday–Saturday 9:30 a.m.–5:00 p.m.
Sunday 11:00 a.m.–5:00 p.m.
Closed: Thanksgiving, Christmas, New Year's Day.
Minimum time required to see exhibit: 2 hours

Entrance Fees:
Adults $3.50
Seniors $2.50
Children (4–12) $2.50

Address:
Science Museum of Minnesota
30 East Tenth Street, St. Paul, MN 55101
Telephone: (612)221-9488

Directions:
The museum is located in downtown St. Paul near the intersection of I-94 and I-35E.

Map to Science Museum of Minnesota

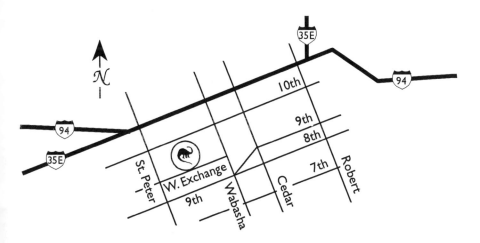

7.
The Southeast
Cretaceous and Paleozoic Marine Fossils

Dinosaurs are extremely rare in the South. During the Cretaceous Period, the Gulf of Mexico connected to the Mid-Continental Seaway. The Gulf covered the southern states during the Cenozoic Era as well. Most of the vertebrate fossils found in the South are marine and most are from the Cenozoic Era.

7.1 Calvert Marine Museum Solomons, MD

The Calvert Cliffs, about two miles north of Solomons, contain vast amounts of marine fossils from the Miocene Epoch of the Cenozoic Era (17 million years ago). There are fossils of sharks, sea mammals, and shells. The museum is opening a new paleontology exhibit to display the finds. You might want to walk along the beach to see what you can find in the cliffs.

Articulated Skeletons:
- *Pelagornis*, a bird with an 18-foot wingspan.

Exhibit Features:
- A shark with 7-foot jaws.

Hours:
Daily 10:00 a.m.–5:00 p.m.
Closed: July 4, Thanksgiving, Christmas Eve, Christmas, New Year's Day.
Minimum time required to see exhibit: 20 minutes

Entrance Fees:
Adults $3.00
Seniors $2.00
Children (13 and older) $2.00
Children under 13 free

Address:
Calvert Marine Museum
P.O. Box 97, Solomons, MD 20688
Telephone: (410)326-2042

Directions:
The museum is about 45 miles south of Washington, D.C., on Route 2/4 along the Chesapeake Bay. The fossil-bearing cliffs are a few miles north of the museum along the beach.

7.2 Virginia Museum of Natural History Martinsville, VA

The "Age of Reptiles" exhibit includes animated dinosaurs and models of prehistoric animals. The museum sponsors a guided tour to the Culpeper Stone Quarry, near Stevensburg, Virginia, where dinosaur footprints have been found.

Exhibit Features:
- Dinosaur tracks from Virginia and samples of petrified wood.
- An animated *Triceratops* and a phytosaur model and skull.
- A fossil whale skeleton.

Hours:
Tuesday–Saturday 10:00 a.m.–5:00 p.m.
Sunday 1:00 p.m.–5:00 p.m.
Closed: Mondays; Thanksgiving, Christmas, New Year's Day.
Minimum time required to see exhibit: 20 minutes

Entrance Fees: free (donations welcomed)

Address:
Virginia Museum of Natural History
1001 Douglas Avenue, Martinsville, VA 24112
Telephone: (703)666-8600

Directions:
Martinsville is near the Virginia–North Carolina border, about 140 miles southwest of Richmond, near Danville.

7.3 Virginia Living Museum
Newport News, VA

The Virginia Living Museum is part museum, part zoo.

Exhibit Features:
- Dinosaur footprints from Virginia.

Hours:
Monday–Saturday 9:00 a.m.–5:00 p.m.
Sunday 1:00 p.m.–5:00 p.m.
Summer hours (Memorial Day to Labor Day):
Daily 9:00 a.m.–6:00 p.m.
Sunday 10:00 a.m.–6:00 p.m.
Closed: Thanksgiving, Christmas, New Year's Day.
Minimum time required to see exhibit: 10 minutes

Entrance Fees:
Adults $5.00
Children (3–12) $3.25

Address:
Virginia Living Museum
524 Clyde Morris Boulevard, Newport News, VA 23601
Telephone: (804)595-1900

Directions:
Newport News is in southeastern Virginia near Norfolk. From I-64, take exit 258A to J. Clyde Morris and head west. After you cross Jefferson Avenue the museum is on your left.

Map to Virginia Living Museum

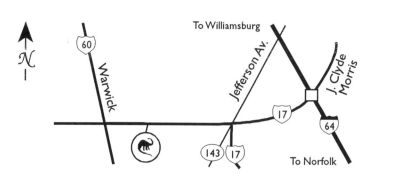

7.4 McClung Museum of Natural History Knoxville, TN

The museum displays the remains of the only dinosaur ever found in Tennessee.

Exhibit Features:
- A few hadrosaur bones.
- Cast of a *Tyrannosaurus rex* skull.
- Plant and invertebrate fossils.

Hours:
Monday–Friday 9:00 a.m.–5:00 p.m.
Saturday 10:00 a.m.–3:00 p.m.
Sunday 2:00 p.m.–5:00 p.m.
Closed: July 4, Labor Day, Thanksgiving, Christmas, New Year's Day.
Minimum time required to see exhibit: 20 minutes

Entrance Fees: free

Address:
Frank H. McClung Museum
1327 Circle Park Drive, University of Tennessee, Knoxville, TN 37919
Telephone: (615)974-2144

Directions:
From I-75/40, take exit 386 south on to the Alcoa Highway. From the Alcoa Highway exit east to the Kingston Pike. The museum is located on the campus of the University of Tennessee, southwest of the Torchbearer Statue and Neyland Stadium.

7.5 The Memphis Pink Palace Museum Memphis, TN

Exhibit Features:
- Local fossils, a mosasaur, and dinosaur tracks.

Hours:
Daily 10:00 a.m.–5:00 p.m.
Closed: Thanksgiving, Christmas Eve, Christmas, New Year's Day.
Minimum time required to see exhibit: 20 minutes

Entrance Fees:

Adults $3.00

Children, students, & seniors $2.00

Address:

Memphis Museum System

3050 Central Avenue, Memphis, TN 38111-3399

Telephone: (901)320-6363 or (901)320-6320

Directions:

From I-40 heading west, exit to Highland Street and head south. Turn right onto Central and head west to the museum.

Or, from I-40 heading east, exit to I-240 and head south. Exit southeast on U.S. 78/Lamar Avenue. At Central bear left and head east.

Nearby:

The Coon Creek Science Center takes its name from the Cretaceous marine deposits of the Coon Creek Formation. The Center provides educational classes on the 240-acre site. Information on paleontology classes is available from the Memphis Pink Palace Museum.

7.6 North Carolina State Museum of Natural Science, Raleigh, NC

The museum has recently acquired fossils from an expedition to Wyoming.

Exhibit Features:

- Casts of *Triceratops* and *Tyrannosaurus* skulls.
- Casts of *Archaeopteryx*.

Hours:

Monday–Saturday 9:00 a.m.–5:00 p.m.

Sunday 1:00 p.m.–5:00 p.m.

Closed: Martin Luther King Day, Memorial Day, Good Friday, Veterans Day, Labor Day, Thanksgiving, Christmas, New Year's Day; all other state holidays.

Minimum time required to see exhibit: 20 minutes

Entrance Fees: free

Address:
North Carolina State Museum of Natural Science
P.O. Box 27647, Raleigh, NC 27647
Telephone: (919)733-7450

Directions:
The museum is on Bicentennial Plaza in downtown Raleigh, between the
State Capitol and the Legislative building.

7.7 South Carolina State Museum
Columbia, SC

The display focuses on Cenozoic fossils.

Exhibit Features:
- Models of a mastodon, a glyptodont, and a 40-foot shark.
- Miocene shark teeth, commonly found in South Carolina.

Hours:
Monday–Saturday 10:00 a.m.–5:00 p.m.
Sunday 1:00 p.m.–5:00 p.m.
Closed: Thanksgiving, Christmas.
Minimum time required to see exhibit: 20 minutes

Entrance Fees:
Adults $4.00
Seniors, military, and college students with ID $3.00
Children (6–17) $1.50

Address:
South Carolina State Museum
301 Gervais Street, P.O. Box 100107, Columbia, SC 29202
Telephone: (803)737-4921

Directions:
From I-26, take the U.S. 1 exit. U.S. 1 turns into Gervais Street in downtown Columbia. The museum is on Gervais Street to your left as you
cross the river.

7.8 West Georgia Museum of Tallapoosa Tallapoosa, GA

Exhibit Features:
- Full-size replica of a *Hadrosaurus*.

Hours:
Tuesday–Friday 9:00 a.m.–3:00 p.m.
Saturday 9:00 a.m.–5:00 p.m.
Sunday 2:00 p.m.–4:00 p.m.
Closed: Mondays; all holidays.
Minimum time required to see exhibit: 15 minutes

Entrance Fees:
Adults $1.00
Children (4–12) $.50
Children under 4 free

Address:
West Georgia Museum of Tallapoosa
8 Lyon Street, P.O. Box 725, Tallapoosa, GA 30176
Telephone: (404)574-3125

Directions:
Tallapoosa is on the Alabama-Georgia border, 40 miles west of Atlanta. Take exit 1 from I-20 and head north on 100 N. Cross over Highway 78 and continue to Lyon Street. Turn left on Lyon; the museum will be on your right.

7.9 Anniston Museum of Natural History Anniston, AL

The theme of this paleontology exhibit is "Adaptation to the Environment."

Articulated Skeletons:
- An ichthyosaur.

Exhibit Features:
- Full-size replicas of *Albertosaurus* and *Pteranodon*.
- Mastodon bone.
- Fiberglass cast of *Triceratops* skull.
- Fossil displays.

Hours:
Tuesday–Friday 9:00 a.m.–5:00 p.m.
Saturday 10:00 a.m.–5:00 p.m.
Sunday 1:00 p.m.–5:00 p.m.
Closed: Mondays; Thanksgiving, Christmas Eve, Christmas, New Year's Day.
Minimum time required to see exhibit: 45 minutes

Entrance Fees:
Adults $3.00
Seniors $2.50
Children (4–17) $2.00

Mailing Address:
Anniston Museum of Natural History
P.O. Box 1587, Anniston, AL 36202
Telephone: (205)237-6766

Location Address:
Anniston Museum of Natural History
800 Museum Drive, Anniston, AL 36201

Directions:
Anniston is located 55 miles east of Birmingham. Take exit 185 from I-20 and head north about 6 miles to Langarde Park. The museum is inside the park.

7.10 Red Mountain Museum
Birmingham, AL

The museum displays Cretaceous marine specimens found in Alabama.

Articulated Skeletons:

- A mosasaur.

Exhibit Features:

- An *Allosaurus* skull, and a scaled-down dinosaur model.

Hours:

Tuesday–Friday 9:00 a.m.–4:00 p.m.
Saturday 10:00 a.m.–3:00 p.m.
Sunday 1:00 p.m.–4:00 p.m.
Closed: Mondays; the month of September; major holidays.
Minimum time required to see exhibit: 20 minutes

Entrance Fees:

Adults $2.00
Children (1–15) $1.50

Address:

Red Mountain Museum Discovery 2000
1421 22nd Street South, Birmingham, AL 35205
Telephone: (205)939-1176

Directions:

From Highway 31N, exit at Highland/Arlington Avenue. When the exit
ramp forks, veer right. Follow signs.

7.11 Alabama Museum of Natural History
Tuscaloosa, AL

Exhibit Features:

- Cretaceous marine specimens.

Hours:

Monday–Friday 8:00 a.m.–4:30 p.m.
Saturday 1:00 p.m.–4:00 p.m.
Closed: Sundays.
Minimum time required to see exhibit: 20 minutes

Entrance Fees: free

Address:
Alabama Museum of Natural History
Box 870340, Tuscaloosa, AL 35487-0340
Telephone: (205)348-2040

Directions:
Tuscaloosa is 60 miles southwest of Birmingham. The museum is on Sixth
Avenue on the University of Alabama campus.

7.12 Mississippi Museum of Natural Science Jackson, MS

Eocene whale fossils are common in the Mississippi-Alabama area.

Exhibit Features:
- A mounted fossil of an ancient whale, *Zygorhiza*.

Hours:
Monday–Friday 9:00 a.m.–5:00 p.m.
Closed: weekends; Thanksgiving, Christmas Eve, Christmas, New Year's
Day.
Minimum time required to see exhibit: 10 minutes

Entrance Fees: free

Address:
Mississippi Museum of Natural Science
Mississippi State University
111 N. Jefferson Street, P.O. Box 5167, Jackson, MS 39202
Telephone: (601)325-3915

Directions:
The museum is near the Jackson fairgrounds. From I-55 take the Pearl
Street exit.

7.13 Mississippi Petrified Forest near Flora, MS

You can explore this 50-million-year-old petrified forest.

Hours:
Memorial Day to Labor Day:
Daily 9:00 a.m.–6:00 p.m.
Labor Day to Memorial Day:
Daily 9:00 a.m.–5:00 p.m.
Closed: Christmas.
Minimum time required to see exhibit: 25 minutes

Entrance Fees:
Adults $3.00
Seniors $2.00
Children (Grades 1–12) $2.00

Address:
Mississippi Petrified Forest
P.O. Box 98, Flora, MS 39071
Telephone: (601)879-8189

Directions:
Flora is about 17 miles northwest of Jackson, Mississippi, on Highway 49. At Flora, take Highway 22 west about one mile to the Petrified Forest.

7.14 Dunn-Seiler Museum State College, MS

Exhibit Features:
- Turtle fossils and a phytosaur.

Hours:
Monday–Friday 8:00 a.m.–5:00 p.m.
Closed: weekends; July 4, Thanksgiving, Christmas, New Year's Day; and between academic semesters.
Minimum time required to see exhibit: 15 minutes

Entrance Fees: free

Address:

Dunn-Seiler Museum

Mississippi State University, Department of Geology

P.O. Drawer 5167, Mississippi State, MS 39762

Telephone: (601)325-3915

Directions:

State College is 20 miles west of Columbus, Mississippi, on U.S. 82. The museum is on the campus of Mississippi State University.

7.15 Dinosaur World
near Eureka Springs, AR

This park features life-size re-creations of dinosaurs.

Hours:

March 1 to December 15:

Daily: 8:30 a.m.–7:00 p.m.

Minimum time required to see exhibit: 15 minutes

Entrance Fees:

Camping $10.50 RVs, $7.50 tents

Adults $4.00

Seniors $3.50

Children (4–12) $2.50

Address:

Dinosaur World

Route 2, Box 408, Eureka Springs, AR 72632

Telephone: (501)253-8113

Directions:

Eureka Springs is 30 miles northeast of Fayetteville and 140 miles northwest of Little Rock on U.S. 65. The park is 8 miles west of Eureka Springs on Highway 187.

7.16 Florida Museum of Natural History Gainesville, FL

Exhibit Features:

- The jaws of a prehistoric shark with six-inch teeth.

Hours:

Tuesday–Saturday 10:00 a.m.–5:00 p.m.
Sunday 1:00 p.m.–5:00 p.m.
Closed: Mondays; Christmas.
Minimum time required to see exhibit: 10 minutes

Entrance Fees: free

Address:

Florida Museum of Natural History
Museum Road, University of Florida, Gainesville, FL 32611
Telephone: (904)392-1721

Directions:

Gainesville is in north-central Florida. From I-75, exit at W. University Avenue and head east. Turn right at Newell Drive and head south. The museum is at the intersection of Newell and Museum Road.

7.17 Epcot Center
Orlando, FL

Epcot Center has one of the most dazzling displays of dinosaur special effects in the world. The display is based on the Disney movie *Fantasia*.

Hours: vary; open past midnight in the summer
Minimum time required to see exhibit: 1 day

Entrance Fees:
Adults $36.95
Children (3–9) $29.55

Address:
Walt Disney World, Epcot Center
P.O. Box 10000, Lake Buena Vista, FL 32830-1000
Telephone: (407)824-4321

Directions:
The ride is located in the Exxon Pavilion at Epcot Center.

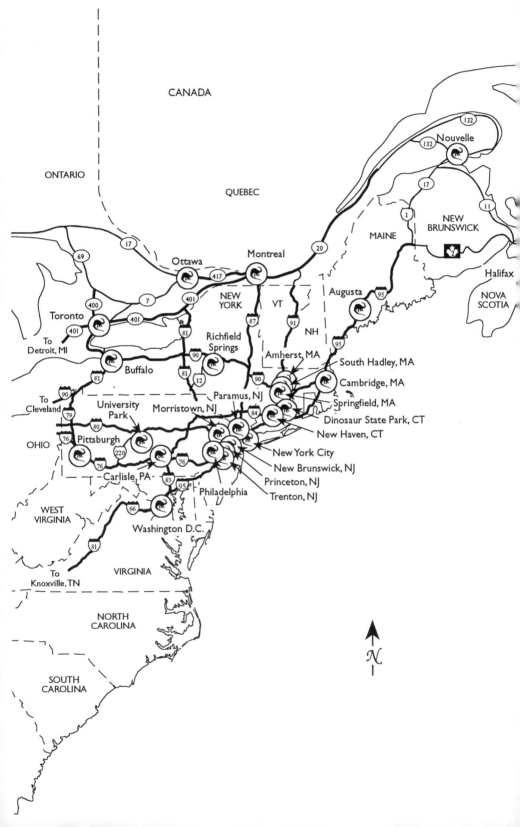

8.
The Northeast
The Great Museums

The dinosaur tracks of the Connecticut River valley and the vast collections of the great museums of the East attract dinosaur lovers from all over the world. For over a century, these museums have sent professional fossil hunters to every corner of the globe, from the Far East of Mongolia to the American West. Although they were scientists, they often carried rifles into the field, never knowing when Indian or Mongolian bandits might attack. These men braved the dangers of unexplored territories to bring back dinosaurs that would be exhibited in the great museums of the Northeast.

Rivalries were common, though usually friendly, among the fossil hunters. But for Edward Drinker Cope and Othniel Charles Marsh, it was war. Both Cope and Marsh were well financed and obsessed with dinosaurs. Both desired to posses every fossil in existence. Their intense competition led to the excavation of hundreds of prehistoric animals. The results of their battle fill the Yale Peabody and the Smithsonian Institution. If you hunted for fossils in the late 1800s, you worked either for Cope or for Marsh.

The flamboyant Roy Chapman Andrews was a role model for Hollywood's Indiana Jones. Andrews organized the Central Asiatic Expedition, an overland adventure through the Gobi Desert of Mongolia in the 1920s. The Chinese often suspected that he was not a scientist, but a spy. Along the Flaming Cliffs of the Gobi, his expedition was the first to discover dinosaur eggs. These priceless fossils were brought back to the American Museum of Natural History in New York City.

Also employed by the American Museum of Natural History was Barnum Brown, who probably dug up more dinosaurs than any man who walked the earth. People who knew him said that he could smell fossils buried in the ground.

8.1 The National Museum of Natural History Washington, D.C.

The Smithsonian Institution's National Museum of Natural History houses one of the finest paleontology collections in the world. The collection spans the history of the earth from 3.5-billion-year-old algae to the origin of humans. Many of the fossils collected by Cope are on display here.

Visit the United States Botanical Garden and see their excellent collection of cycads—the food of choice for many Jurassic-period dinosaurs.

Articulated Skeletons:

- *Diplodocus, Stegosaurus* (upright and death mount), *Edmontosaurus, Brachyceratops, Camarasaurus, Camptosaurus* (adult and juvenile), *Coelo-physis, Thescelosaurus, Allosaurus, Triceratops, Ceratosaurus, Albertosaurus, Heterodontosaurus, Maiasaura, Dinichthys, Pteranodon, Rhamphorhynchus,* and Cenozoic mammals.
- "Life in the Ancient Seas" includes three different ichthyosaurs, plesiosaurs, mosasaurs, *Nothosaurus, Hesperornis,* Paleozoic fish and Cenozoic sea mammals displayed with a giant mural of the prehistoric ocean as a backdrop.

Exhibit Features:

- An excellent film on the origin of life.
- Dinosaur tracks and fossils of early reptiles.
- The evolution of horses in response to their changing environment is explained with a fossil and video display.
- Displays on the evolutionary adaptations to life on land and in the air.
- Full-size models of *Stegosaurus* and *Quetzalcoatlus.*
- Skulls of *Tyrannosaurus rex* and *Monoclonius,* and duckbill jaws.
- Paleozoic invertebrates including the Burgess Shale Fauna and the giant trilobite *Isotelus* which grew over one foot long.
- Ammonites with mosasaur tooth marks, and a video on mosasaurs.
- An excellent paleobotany display.
- Visitors may watch scientists prepare fossils in the laboratory.

Hours:

Daily 10:00 a.m.–5:30 p.m.
Summer hours (June 14 to Labor Day):
Daily 10:00 a.m.–6:00 p.m.
Closed: Christmas.
Minimum time required to see exhibit: 4 hours

Entrance Fees: free

Address:

The Smithsonian Institution
National Museum of Natural History
Tenth Street and Constitution Avenue NW, Washington, D.C. 20560
Telephone: (202)357-2020

Directions:

The museum is at the corner of Constitution Avenue and 10th Street.
Parking is difficult; your best bet is to take the Yellow or Orange line
Metrorail to the Smithsonian station.

Map to National Museum of Natural History

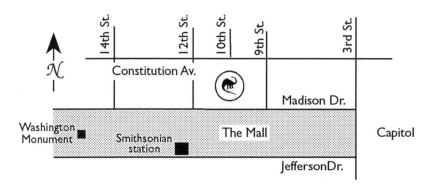

8.2 The Academy of Natural Sciences Philadelphia, PA

Founded in 1812, the Academy of Natural Sciences is the oldest continually operating scientific research and exhibition institution in the western hemisphere. In 1868 the Academy displayed the world's first mounted dinosaur skeleton, *Hadrosaurus foulkii*.

Walk into the dinosaur gallery and you will be staring into the jaws of *Tyrannosaurus rex*. This magnificent animal is reconstructed as an agile hunter ready to chase down its next meal.

Articulated Skeletons:

- *Tyrannosaurus rex, Tenontosaurus* (four), *Deinonychus, Pteranodon* (two), *Chasmosaurus, Hadrosaurus,* and *Corythosaurus*.
- The marine reptiles *Elasmosaurus* (a very long-necked plesiosaur), *Platecarpus* (a mosasaur), and several other sea reptiles.

Exhibit Features:

- *Deinonychus* is shown attacking a family of Tenontosaurs.
- A *Torosaurus* skull.
- Simulated dinosaur skin you can touch.
- A wall mural of Cretaceous life.
- The enormous leg bones of *Ultrasaurus* and *Diplodocus* are compared with those of an elephant.
- *Hadrosaurus foulkii*, the world's first complete dinosaur.
- Casts of the first dinosaur remains to be scientifically described, *Megalosaurus*, described by Buckland in 1818 and classified in 1841.
- A reconstruction of a *Maiasaura* nesting colony.
- Models of *Apatosaurus* and *Stenonychosaurus* inequalis.
- An exhibit on dinosaurs in the movies.
- Outdoor bronze sculpture of *Deinonychus*.

Hours:

Monday–Friday 10:00 a.m.–4:30 p.m.
Saturday–Sunday 10:00 a.m.–5:00 p.m.
Summer hours (June 30 to September 15):
Daily 10:00 a.m.–5:00 p.m.
Closed: Thanksgiving, Christmas, New Year's Day.
Minimum time required to see exhibit: 2 hours

Entrance Fees:
Adults $6.00
Seniors and military $5.50
Children (3–12) $5.00
Members of the Academy and children under 3: free

Address:
The Academy of Natural Sciences
1900 Ben Franklin Parkway, Philadelphia, PA 19103
Telephone: (215)299-1000 or (215)299-1020 or (215)299-1027

Directions:
From I-676, exit at Ben Franklin Parkway and head towards Logan Circle.
The museum is on Logan Circle at the corner of 19th and Race.

Map to the Academy of Natural Sciences Museum

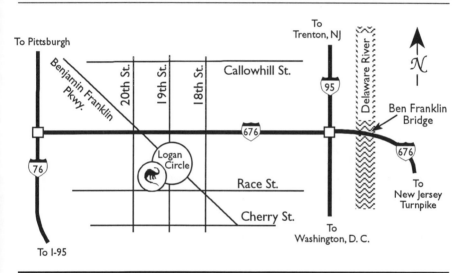

8.3 Rennie Geology Museum
Carlisle, PA

Exhibit Features:
- An exceptional trilobite collection.

Hours:
Monday–Friday 8:00 a.m.–5:00 p.m.
Closed: weekends; July 4, Thanksgiving, December 24 to January 1.
Minimum time required to see exhibit: 20 minutes

Entrance Fees: free

Address:

Rennie Geology Museum Department of Geology
Dickinson College, Carlisle, PA 17013-2896
Telephone: (717)245-1448

Directions:

Carlisle is just west of Harrisburg, Pennsylvania, off of I-81. The museum
is on the first floor of the James Center, on the northwest corner of College and Louther streets.

8.4 Earth & Mineral Science Museum University Park, PA

The emphasis at the Earth & Mineral Science Museum is on local fossils.

Exhibit Features:

- A good collection of Pennsylvania fossil ferns and trees.
- Dinosaur models and some large footprints.
- An exceptionally large *Diplodocus* leg bone and some mastodon tusks.

Hours:

Monday–Friday 9:00 a.m.–4:30 p.m.
Closed: weekends; July 4, Thanksgiving, Christmas, New Year's Day; all
University holidays.
Minimum time required to see exhibit: 20 minutes

Entrance Fees: free

Address:

Earth & Mineral Science Museum
Pennsylvania State University
112 Steidle Building, University Park, PA 16802
Telephone: (814)865-6427

Directions:

University Park is about 137 miles northeast of Pittsburgh and about 90
miles northwest of Harrisburg. The museum is on the Pennsylvania State
University campus.

8.5 Carnegie Museum of Natural History Pittsburgh, PA

The wealthy industrialist Andrew Carnegie wanted something really big for his museum in Pittsburgh. In 1898 he read a newspaper article about the discovery of a huge dinosaur in the western United States. A year later, two Carnegie Museum paleontologists presented their benefactor with the bones of a *Diplodocus*, the museum's first dinosaur, discovered at Sheep Creek, Wyoming. Carnegie was so fond of *Diplodocus* that he had full-sized casts made of the skeleton and gave them to museums around the world.

In 1909, Carnegie Museum paleontologist Earl Douglass found a spectacular deposit of dinosaur bones near Vernal, Utah. The quarry yielded so many well preserved dinosaurs that an 80-acre parcel around the quarry was made a national monument—Dinosaur National Monument. Many of the dinosaurs excavated here are displayed at the Carnegie Museum.

The *Tyrannosaurus rex* displayed here was found by Barnum Brown in Hell Creek, Montana, and was originally displayed at the American Museum of Natural History. The skeleton was sold to the Carnegie Museum in 1941. It is one of only six such skeletons ever found.

Articulated Skeletons:
- *Tyrannosaurus rex*, *Corythosaurus*, *Triceratops*, *Protoceratops*, *Camarasaurus*, *Allosaurus*, *Camptosaurus*, *Dryosaurus*, *Stegosaurus*, *Coelophysis*.
- The two giant sauropod dinosaurs *Diplodocus* and *Apatosaurus* mounted side by side.
- A collection of Mesozoic fossils including pterosaurs and ichthyosaurs bought from the Baron Bayet of Brussels.

Exhibit Features:
- Life-size mural of *Tyrannosaurus rex* in the late Cretaceous.
- The dinosaurs are displayed so you can see them close up.

Hours:
Tuesday–Saturday 10:00 a.m.–5:00 p.m.
Sunday 1:00 p.m.–5:00 p.m.
Summer hours (July and August):
Monday–Saturday 10:00 a.m.–5:00 p.m.
Sunday 1:00 p.m.–5:00 p.m.
Closed: July 4, Thanksgiving, Christmas, New Year's Day.
Minimum time required to see exhibit: 1 day

Entrance Fees:

Adults $5.00

Seniors $4.00

Children (3–18) $3.00

Address:

The Carnegie Museum of Natural History

4400 Forbes Avenue, Pittsburgh, PA 15213-4080

Telephone: (412)622-3283 or (412)622-3131

Directions:

The Carnegie Museum is on Forbes Avenue in Oakland. From I-376 take Exit 6.

Map to Carnegie Museum of Natural History

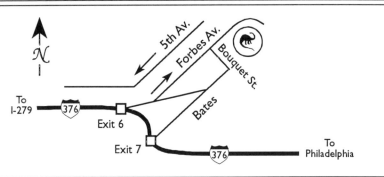

8.6 New Jersey State Museum Trenton, NJ

Discovered at Haddonfield, New Jersey, in 1858, *Hadrosaurus foulkii* was the first dinosaur found in North America. The group of dinosaurs known as the hadrosaurs were named for the town of Haddonfield.

The New Jersey State Museum places a strong emphasis on New Jersey dinosaur specimens. The museum also runs a wide range of children's classes on dinosaurs and paleontology.

Articulated Skeletons:

- A skeletal cast of *Monoclonius*.
- Mounted mastodons.

Exhibit Features:
- Local dinosaur finds.
- A representation of *Hadrosaurus foulkii*.

Hours:
Tuesday–Saturday 9:00 a.m.–4:45pm
Sunday noon–5:00 p.m.
Closed: Mondays; all official state holidays.
Minimum time required to see exhibit: 1 hour

Entrance Fees: free

Address:
Bureau of Natural History
New Jersey State Museum, CN-530
205 West State Street, Trenton, NJ 08625-0530
Telephone: (609)292-6330

Directions:
Located in downtown Trenton, the museum is near the State House and the Old Barracks Museum, overlooking the Delaware River.

8.7 Princeton Natural History Museum Princeton, NJ

John Horner was employed as a preparator for the Princeton Natural History Museum when he discovered dinosaur nests in Montana. The paleontology operations at this museum have been greatly reduced in recent years.

Articulated Skeletons:
- *Allosaurus*.
- Juvenile *Maiasaura*.

Exhibit Features:
- *Apatosaurus* femur.
- *Tyrannosaurus* skull.

Hours:
Daily 9:00 a.m.–5:00 p.m.
Closed: all University holidays.
Minimum time required to see exhibit: 15 minutes

Entrance Fees: free

Address:

> Princeton Natural History Museum
> Guyot Hall, Washington Street, Princeton, NJ 08544
> Telephone: (609)258-1322

Directions:

> Princeton is just northeast of Trenton, New Jersey. The museum is at the Princeton University campus on Washington Street. From U.S. 1, take Highway 571 northwest at Penns Neck.

8.8 Rutgers University Geology Museum New Brunswick, NJ

The geology department at Rutgers University maintains a museum that displays fossils found in New Jersey.

Articulated Skeletons:

- Juvenile *Maiasaura*.
- Mastodon.

Exhibit Features:

- An 18-by-9-foot Jurassic dinosaur track from Towaco, New Jersey.
- Skull casts of *Allosaurus* and *Styracosaurus*.
- A *Megalosaurus* footprint and a *Diplodocus* leg bone.

Hours:

> Monday 1:00 p.m.–4:00 p.m.
> Tuesday–Friday 9:00 a.m.–12:00 a.m.
> **Closed:** weekends; July 4, Thanksgiving, Christmas, New Year's Day.
> **Minimum time required to see exhibit:** 20 minutes

Entrance Fees: free

Address:

> Rutgers University Geology Museum, Geology Hall C. A. C.
> Rutgers University, New Brunswick, NJ 08903
> Telephone: (908)932-7243

Directions:

> New Brunswick is south of Newark, New Jersey. The museum is on the Rutgers University campus. From I-95/New Jersey Turnpike, take exit 9 and follow Route 18 north, which becomes Albany street. Turn right on George Street and park near the intersection of George and Hamilton.

8.9 Bergen Museum of Art and Science Paramus, NJ

Exhibit Features:
- The remains of two mastodons.

Hours:
Daily 10:00 a.m.–5:00 p.m.

Closed: July 4, Thanksgiving, Christmas Eve, Christmas, New Year's Day.

Minimum time required to see exhibit: 10 minutes

Entrance Fees: donation requested

Address:
Bergen Museum of Art and Science

Ridgewood and Farview, Paramus, NJ 07652

Telephone: (201)265-1248

Directions:
Paramus is about 14 miles north of Newark, New Jersey. To reach the museum from I-80 take the Garden State Parkway North to exit 165. From Route 17 take the Ridgewood-Oradell exit.

8.10 Morris Museum Morristown, NJ

Exhibit Features:
- Models of *Pteranodon* and *Stegosaurus*.

Hours:
Monday–Saturday 10:00 a.m.–5:00 p.m.

Sunday 1:00 p.m.–5:00 p.m.

Closed: Thanksgiving, Christmas, New Year's Day.

Minimum time required to see exhibit: 15 minutes

Entrance Fees:
Adults $2.00

Students & children $1.00

Address:

The Morris Museum
6 Normandy Heights Road, Morristown, NJ 07960
Telephone: (201)538-0454

Directions:

Morristown is about 20 miles west of Newark, New Jersey. From I-287, take exit 31 west (Highway 24) to Morristown.

8.11 American Museum of Natural History New York, NY

In 1897, the American Museum of Natural History did not have a single dinosaur bone in their collection. That year they hired paleontologist Barnum Brown. The museum now claims the largest collection of dinosaur fossils in the world.

The museum is currently undergoing extensive renovation. When completed the museum will be on the cutting edge of dinosaur science (completion is expected in 1995). In the interim, you will be able to see only part of the collection.

Articulated Skeletons:

- Perhaps the most fantastic dinosaur reconstruction ever, a mother *Barosaurus* rearing up on her hind legs to defend her baby from an attacking *Allosaurus*. The *Barosaurus* fossils were found at Howe quarry. Because the original rock is too heavy to be mounted in such an active pose, the display is made from fiberglass casts of the bones. Just one of the neck vertebrae weighs 200 pounds.
- *Albertosaurus, Allosaurus, Anatosaurus, Apatosaurus, Camptosaurus, Coelophysis, Corythosaurus, Lambeosaurus, Montanoceratops, Monoclonius, Ornitholestes, Panoplosaurus, Plateosaurus, Protoceratops, Psittacosaurus, Saurolophus, Stegosaurus, Styracosaurus, Triceratops, Tyrannosaurus rex.*
- Fossils of at least seven pterosaurs.
- The fossil remains of a mummified duckbilled dinosaur that the great fossil hunter Charles Sternberg called "the crowning specimen of my life's work."

Exhibit Features:

- Complete growth sequence of *Protoceratops*, including eggs and nests brought back from the Mongolian Gobi desert during the Central Asiatic Expedition in the 1920s. This was the first evidence of dinosaurs laying eggs.

Hours:

Monday–Thursday & Sunday 10:00 a.m.–5:45 p.m.
Friday and Saturday 10:00 a.m.–8:45 p.m.
Closed: Thanksgiving, Christmas.
Minimum time required to see exhibit: 1 day

Entrance Fees:

(free Friday and Saturday after 5:00 p.m.)
Adults $5.00
Children $2.50

Address:

American Museum of Natural History
Central Park West at 79th Street, New York, NY 10024
Telephone: (212)769-5000 or (212)769-5100

Directions:

The museum is on the west side of Central Park in Manhattan between 77th and 81st streets. For $12.00 you can park in the museum lot on the 81st Street side of the museum.

Map to American Museum of Natural History

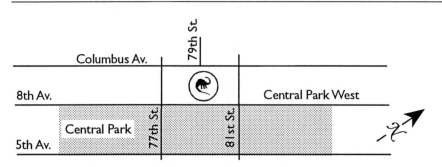

8.12 Petrified Creatures Museum Richfield Springs, NY

This privately run museum has a special attraction for young paleontologists. The museum grounds contain the remains of Paleozoic sea creatures. Here everyone can experience the excitement of discovering fossils. The reef left behind so many fossils that everyone can easily find their own. You are allowed to keep what you find in the fossil discovery area.

Exhibit Features:

- Dig for your own fossils in the remains of a Paleozoic reef over 300 million years old.
- Life-size replicas of 47 dinosaur species.

Hours:

May 15 to June 23:
Thursday–Monday 10:00 a.m.–5:00 p.m.
June 24 to September 10:
Daily 9:00 a.m.–dark
September 16 to October 15:
Thursday–Monday 10:00 a.m.–5:00 p.m.
Minimum time required to see exhibit: 1 hour

Entrance Fees:

Adults $7.00
Children (6–11) $4.00
Children 5 and under free

Address:

Petrified Creatures Museum
P.O. Box 751, U.S. 20, Richfield Springs, NY 13439
Telephone: (315)858-2868

Directions:

Richfield Springs is midway between Albany and Syracuse, New York. The museum is four miles east of Richfield Springs on U.S. 20.

8.13 Buffalo Museum of Science Buffalo, NY

This area was under an ocean during the Paleozoic Era. The Museum of Science has an excellent collection of Paleozoic marine invertebrates.

Articulated Skeletons:

- *Triceratops, Allosaurus, Psittacosaurus, Nanosaurus.*

Exhibit Features:

- *Tyrannosaurus rex* skull.
- An excellent collection of eurypterids (scorpionlike denizens of the Paleozoic oceans).
- Several casts of small pterosaurs and *Archaeopteryx* fossils.
- An *Archaeopteryx* model, and a bat fossil.
- A tail club from an ankylosaur.

Hours:

Tuesday–Sunday 10:00 a.m.–5:00 p.m.
Friday 10:00 a.m.–10:00 p.m.
Closed: Mondays; July 4, Thanksgiving, Christmas, New Year's Day.
Minimum time required to see exhibit: 1 hour

Entrance Fees:

Adults $5.00
Seniors $3.25
Children (4–17) $3.25

Address:

Buffalo Museum of Science
1020 Humboldt Parkway, Buffalo, NY 14211-1293
Telephone: (716)896-5200

Directions:

Take the Best Street exit off Route 33. The museum is just east of the freeway on Best Street.

8.14 Peabody Museum of Natural History New Haven, CT

The Peabody Museum was built in 1866 with an endowment by George Peabody, the uncle of O. C. Marsh. The Peabody Museum became Marsh's headquarters during the Cope-Marsh bone wars. Marsh applied his influence and the financial resources of his inheritance to launch fossil expeditions on a scale never before imagined. The Peabody Museum's vast dinosaur collection is a legacy of that "war."

Scientists from the Peabody Museum have continued to ignite controversy. In August of 1964, John Ostrom uncovered the remains of *Deinonychus* near the small town of Bridger, Montana. The well-preserved remains revealed an agile predator with the tail held high and stiff. This discovery catapulted the perception of dinosaurs from sluggish, tail dragging reptiles to energetic, birdlike terrors.

Articulated Skeletons:

- 60-foot long *Apatosaurus*, *Stegosaurus*, *Camptosaurus*, *Edmontosaurus*, *Camarasaurus*, *Archelon* (largest turtle known), *Edaphosaurus*, and a pair of *Deinonychus*.
- At least six pterosaurs.

Exhibit Features:

- A 110-foot-long mural, "The Age of Reptiles," by Rudolph F. Zallinger.
- Skulls from *Torosaurus*, *Triceratops*, *Monoclonius*, and a cast of *Tyrannosaurus rex*.
- Model of *Deinonychus*.

Hours:

Monday–Saturday 10:00 a.m.–5:00 p.m.

Sunday Noon–5:00 p.m.

The museum is open from 10:00 a.m.–3:00 p.m. on Good Friday, Memorial Day, Labor Day, and New Year's Eve.

Closed: Easter, July 4, Thanksgiving, Christmas Eve, Christmas, New Year's Day.

Minimum time required to see exhibit: 2 hours

Entrance Fees:

Adults $3.50
Seniors $2.50
Children (3–15) $2.00
Children under 3 free

Address:

Peabody Museum of Natural History
Yale University, 170 Whitney Avenue,
P.O. Box 6666, New Haven, CT 06511-8161
Telephone: (203)432-5050

Directions:

From I-91, take exit 3 and head west on Trumbull Street. Turn right (north) on Whitney Avenue. The museum is on the Yale University campus at the corner of Whitney Avenue and Sachem Street.

Map to Peabody Museum

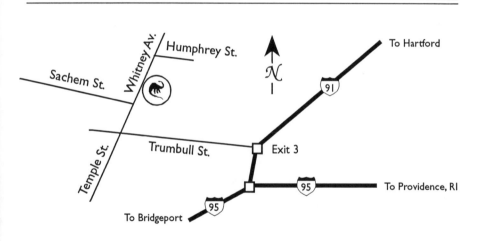

8.15 Dinosaur State Park
Rocky Hill, CT

Near the beginning of the Jurassic Period, this area consisted of mud flats along an ancient lake. Flesh-eating dinosaurs such as *Dilophosaurus* walked along the edges of the lake, leaving their footprints in the mud. The dinosaur tracks lay hidden for 185 million years until 1966, when the construction of a new state building exposed 1,500 tracks. A year later, 500 more tracks were discovered. A geodesic dome was built over the later find to preserve and display the tracks.

Dinosaur State Park offers you the chance to make your own cast of a real dinosaur footprint. Park rangers will show you how, and you can take the cast home with you. Bring at least 10 pounds of plaster-of-Paris, a quarter-cup of cooking oil, a five-gallon plastic bucket (for mixing your plaster), some rags, and a putty knife. Be sure to wear clothes you can get dirty!

Exhibit Features:
- Over 500 dinosaur footprints.
- Full-size models of *Dilophosaurus, Coelophysis, Stegomosuchus*.
- Nature trails.

Hours:
Tuesday–Sunday 9:00 a.m.–4:30 p.m.
You may cast footprints from May 1 to October 31, 9:00 a.m. to 3:30 p.m.
Closed: Mondays; Thanksgiving, Christmas, New Year's Day.
Minimum time required to see exhibit: 45 minutes

Entrance Fees:
Adults $2.00
Children (6–17) $1.00

Address:
Dinosaur State Park
West Street, Rocky Hill, CT 06067-3506
Telephone: (203)529-8423

Directions:
Rocky Hill is a few miles south of Hartford, Connecticut. Located on West Street, the park is one mile east of exit 23 off I-91.

Map to Dinosaur State Park

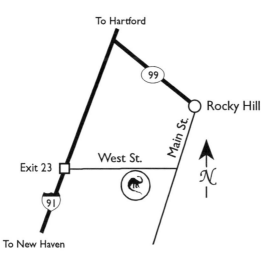

8.16 Springfield Science Museum
Springfield, MA

This hands-on museum is great for kids. Touching is encouraged and the emphasis is on learning. This is one place where you can walk right up to *Tyrannosaurus rex* and not worry about being eaten.

Articulated Skeletons:

- *Stegosaurus.*

Exhibit Features:

- Life-size models of *Tyrannosaurus rex* and *Coelophysis.*
- Dinosaur tracks.
- Slide show.

Hours:

Thursday–Sunday Noon–4:00 p.m.

Closed: Monday–Wednesday; July 4, Thanksgiving, Christmas Eve, Christmas, New Year's Day.

Minimum time required to see exhibit: 1 hour

Entrance Fees:

(free on Fridays)
Adults $4.00
Children (6–18) $1.00

Address:

Springfield Science Museum
236 State Street, Springfield, MA 01103
Telephone: (413)733-1194

Directions:

From I-91, take exit 7 (Columbus Ave/Springfield Center). Turn left at
the second light onto State Street. Turn right at Dwight and then loop
around to your left to Chestnut. Go north (left) on Chestnut. The museum is in the Quadrangle at the corner of State and Chestnut streets in
downtown Springfield.

Map to Springfield Science Museum

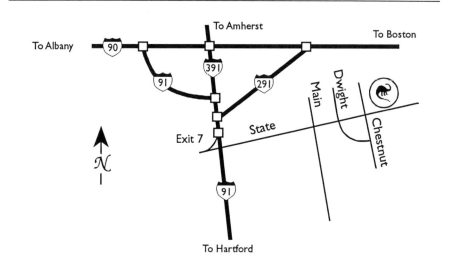

8.17 Nash Dinosaur Land
near South Hadley, MA

In 1933, Carlton Nash found dinosaur footprints in South Hadley, Massachusetts. The owners of the land were not interested in the footprints and were
planning to use the land to quarry building stone. Nash bought the property
and turned it into a museum and roadside attraction.

Exhibit Features:

- Dinosaur bones and footprints.

Hours:

Memorial Day to Labor Day:
Daily 8:30 a.m.–5:00 p.m.
Saturday–Sunday 10:00 a.m.–5:00 p.m.
April through Memorial Day and Labor Day through first snow:
Open weekends and by appointment.
Closed: December 23 to mid-March.
Minimum time required to see exhibit: 20 minutes

Entrance Fees:

Adults $3.00
Children $1.50

Address:

Nash Dinosaur Land
Route 116, South Hadley, MA 01075
Telephone: (413)467-9566

Directions:

Nash Dinosaur Land is about three miles north of South Hadley, just north
of Springfield on Highway 116.

Map to Pratt Museum and Nash Dinosaurland

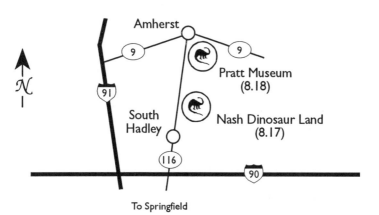

8.18 Pratt Museum of Natural History Amherst, MA

The museum has an extensive collection of dinosaur tracks. The first people to find them thought they were the tracks of giant birds. That may have been close to the truth: Some of today's theories hold that birds are descendants of dinosaurs. Thus, birds are dinosaurs (a paleontologist's perspective) or dinosaurs are birds (an ornithologist's perspective).

Articulated Skeletons:
- *Coelophysis, Edaphosaurus, Kritosaurus,* ichthyosaur, *Platecarpus, Eryops,* mastodon, mammoth, Irish elk, sabertoothed cat, dire wolf, cave bear.

Exhibit Features:
- Dinosaur tracks from the Connecticut River valley (open only by appointment).
- Evolution of horses.
- *Triceratops* skull and cast of *Tyrannosaurus* skull.
- *Compsognathus* cast.
- *Archaeopteryx, Diplodocus* limbs, *Gorgasaurus.*
- Dinosaur egg fragments.
- Eggs from *Hypsilophodon.*

Hours:
Weekdays 9:00 a.m.–3:30 p.m.
Saturday 9:00 a.m.–4:00 p.m.
Sunday Noon–5:00 p.m.
Summer hours:
Saturday 10:00 a.m.–4:00 p.m.
Sunday Noon–5:00 p.m.
Minimum time required to see exhibit: 1 hour

Entrance Fees: free (donations accepted)

Address:
The Pratt Museum of Natural History
Amherst College, Amherst, MA 01002
Telephone: (413)542-2165

Directions:

Amherst is about 25 miles north of Springfield and 7 miles northeast of Northhampton. The Pratt Museum is on the southeast outskirts of Amherst, on the Amherst College campus.

8.19 Museum of Comparative Zoology Cambridge, MA

The museum was founded by Louis Agassiz in 1859.

Articulated Skeletons:

- *Tenontosaurus tilletti.*
- *Herrarasaurus.*
- *Diononychus.*
- Partial skeleton of *Allosaurus.*
- *Heterodontosaurus, Plateosaurus, Staurikosaurus.*
- *Rhamphorhynchus* and *Pteranodon.*
- *Kronosaurus, Dimetrodon* (a mammal-like reptile), mammoth.

Exhibit Features:

- *Triceratops* skull and a 7-foot turtle shell.
- *Massospondylus* skull.
- Remains of the coelacanth *Latimeria.*
- One of the finest collections of Triassic reptiles in the world.

Hours:

Monday–Saturday 9:00 a.m.–4:30 p.m.
Sunday 1:00 p.m.–4:30 p.m.
Closed: July 4, Thanksgiving, Christmas, New Year's Day.
Minimum time required to see exhibit: 1 hour

Entrance Fees:

(Saturday 9:00 a.m.–11:00 a.m. admission is free)
Adults $4.00
Seniors $3.00
Students (with ID) $3.00
Children (3–13) $1.00

Address:

Harvard University Museums of Natural History
Museum of Comparative Zoology
26 Oxford Street, Cambridge, MA 02138
Telephone: (617)495-3045

Directions:

Cambridge is a suburb of Boston. The Museum of Comparative Zoology
is on the Harvard University Campus in Cambridge.

Map to Museum of Comparative Zoology

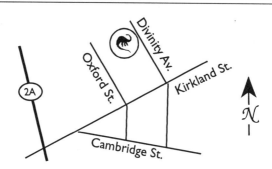

8.20 Maine State Museum
Augusta, ME

The museum has an exhibit of Ice Age mammals including mammoth and
mastodon remains.

Hours:

Monday–Friday 9:00 a.m.–5:00 p.m.
Saturday 10:00 a.m.–4:00 p.m.
Sunday 1:00 p.m.–4:00 p.m.
Closed: Easter, Thanksgiving, Christmas, New Year's Day.
Minimum time required to see exhibit: 15 minutes

Entrance Fees:

Families $6.00
Adults $2.00
Seniors $1.00
Children (6–18) $1.00

Address:

Maine State Museum
Station 83, State House Complex, Augusta, ME 04333
Telephone: (207)287-2301

Directions:

Augusta is in south-central Maine. Take I-95 to the Augusta/Winthrop exit. Follow Western Avenue to Memorial Circle and turn right onto State Street. Turn right again onto Union Street; the museum will be on your left.

8.21 Nova Scotia Museum
Halifax, NS

Around the beginning of the "Age of Dinosaurs" (about 225 million years ago), Nova Scotia was wedged between North America and Africa, near the equator. Fossils of the smallest dinosaurs ever discovered were found in the cliffs along the Bay of Fundy. These fossils are important because they tell us how dinosaurs came to dominate the earth.

Erosion by the rise and fall of tides continues to reveal new fossils. The Bay of Fundy boasts the world's highest tides (40 to 50 feet twice a day). Inexperienced fossil hunters searching these cliffs could easily be drowned by the rapidly rising tides.

Exhibit Features:

- Dinosaur models.
- Local fossils from the Triassic, Jurassic, and Carboniferous.

Hours:

Tuesday–Sunday 9:00 a.m.–5:00 p.m.
June 1 to October 15:
Daily 9:00 a.m.–5:00 p.m.
Closed: Mondays; Good Friday, December 24–26, New Year's Day.
Minimum time required to see exhibit: 45 minutes

Entrance Fees:

(June 1 to October 15 only)
Families $5.50
Adults $2.25
Children (5–17) $.50

Address:

Nova Scotia Museum
1747 Summer Street, Halifax, NS, Canada B3H 3A6
Telephone: (902)424-7353

Directions:

Follow Highway 3 towards the Atlantic Ocean as you come into town. The road will bend to the right and the museum will be to your right.

Nearby:

Minas Basin, Joggins Fossil Cliffs, and the area around Parrsboro offer opportunities to walk along the beach and see fossils *in situ*.

8.22 Parc de Miguasha
Nouvelle, PQ

Shallow lakes and lagoons dominated the Parc de Miguasha landscape during the Devonian Period, 370 million years ago. The waters were filled with strange fish without jaws, armored fish, and a curious fish whose flippers resembled limbs. Vertebrates had not yet ventured onto land. These were the ancestors of the first fish to walk on land and become amphibians. These fish are your ancestors.

Discovered in 1842, the beautiful fossils were highly prized for their exceptional clarity of detail. Quebec created the Parc de Miguasha in 1985 to protect and display the fossils. The park invites visitors into the laboratory to share the excitement of discovery firsthand.

Exhibit Features:

- One of evolution's most exciting stories, the conquest of the land by the fish that became amphibians.
- A history of life on earth including dinosaurs and the origin of humans.
- A guided tour of the fossil cliffs and the paleontology laboratory.
- A collection of remarkably preserved Devonian fossils.

Hours:

June 1 to August 29:
Daily 9:00 a.m.–6:00 p.m.
August 30 to October 2:
Daily 9:00 a.m.–5:00 p.m.
Minimum time required to see exhibit: 90 minutes

Entrance Fees: free

Address:

Parc de Miguasha

Ministere du Loisir, de la Chasse et de la Peche

270, Route Miguasha Ouest, C.P. 183, Nouvelle, PQ Canada G0C 2E0

Telephone: (418)794-2475

Directions:

Nouvelle is about 400 kilometers (250 miles) northeast of Quebec City, on the Baie des Chaleurs. The park is located off Highway 132 just outside of Nouvelle.

Map to Parc de Miguasha

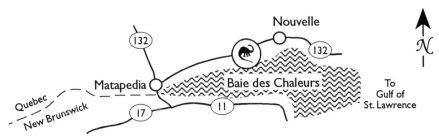

8.23 Redpath Museum
Montreal, PQ

Founded in 1882, the Redpath is one of the oldest museums in Canada. The museum's paleontology collection is primarily for teaching and research.

Articulated Skeletons:
- *Deinonychus, Hylonomus* (the most ancient reptile).

Exhibit Features:
- A collection of fossils housed in a very magnificent building.

Hours:
Monday–Friday 9:00 a.m.–5:00 p.m.
Closed: Saturdays, Sundays; all public holidays
Summer hours (June 15 to August 31):
Monday–Thursday 9:00 a.m.–5:00 p.m.
Saturday–Sunday 10:00 a.m.–5:00 p.m.
Closed: Friday–Sunday; all public holidays.
Minimum time required to see exhibit: 30 minutes

Entrance Fees: free

Address:
Redpath Museum
McGill University, 859 Sherbrooke Street West
Montreal, PQ Canada H3A 2K6
Telephone: (514)398-4086

Directions:
The museum is at the McGill University in downtown Montreal. From Route 10 take exit 64 northeast to McTavish. The museum is located off Sherbrooke Street (138).

8.24 Canadian Museum of Nature
Ottawa, ON

The Canadian Museum of Nature houses an excellent display entitled "Life Through the Ages." The display takes you from the origin of life to the present. Canada is well known for its wealth of Cretaceous dinosaur fossils and the exhibit emphasizes Cretaceous dinosaurs.

Articulated Skeletons:

- *Daspletosaurus, Styracosaurus, Anchiceratops, Triceratops, Brachylophosaurus, Edmontosaurus, Dromiceiomimus, Leptoceratops, Panoplosaurus.*

Exhibit Features:

- You can feel casts of dinosaur skin.
- Films on the origin of life and the extinction of the dinosaurs.
- Displays of plants from the Mesozoic.

Hours:

Daily 10:00 a.m.–5:00 p.m.
Summer hours (May 1 to Labor Day):
Sunday, Monday, & Thursday 9:30 a.m.–8:00 p.m.
Tuesday, Wednesday, Friday, & Saturday 9:30 a.m.–5:00 p.m.
Closed: Christmas.
Minimum time required to see exhibit: 3 hours

Entrance Fees:

Families $12.00
Adults $4.00
Students $3.00
Seniors and Children (6–16) $2.00

Address:

Canadian Museum of Nature
P.O. Box 3443, Station D, Ottawa, ON Canada K1P 6P4
Telephone: (613)990-2200 or (613)996-3102

Directions:

From Highway 417 (The Queensway), exit onto Metcalfe heading north. The museum is on the corner of Metcalfe and McLeod.

Map to Canadian Museum of Nature

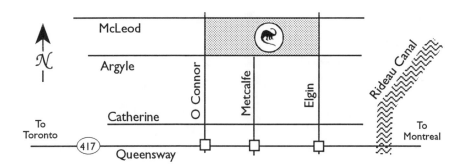

8.25 Royal Ontario Museum
Toronto, ON

This is one of the world's premier dinosaur displays. Magnificent paintings and dioramas provide intriguing settings for the fossil displays. Several hadrosaurs are displayed as wall mounts in simulated badlands. The fossil displays breathe life into the ancient bones.

Articulated Skeletons:
- *Prosaurolophus, Hadrosaurus, Anatosaurus, Albertosaurus, Parasaurolophus, Chasmosaurus, Corythosaurus, Lambeosaurus, Ornithomimus, Stegosaurus,* two *Allosaurus, Camptosaurus.*
- Plus the Mesozoic sea reptiles *Dolichorhynchops, Platecarpus,* and *Tylosaurus* set in an underwater display.
- Sabertoothed cats, mastodons, mammoths, and giant beavers.

Exhibit Features:
- Video terminals discuss dinosaurs.
- Many partial dinosaur skeletons and elements.
- Ornithopod trackway and a large fossil invertebrate gallery.
- Eerie music sets the mood for a fascinating diorama of a pair of *Allosaurus* attacking a *Stegosaurus.*

Hours:
Tuesday and Thursday 10:00 a.m.–8:00 p.m.
Wednesday, Friday–Sunday 10:00 a.m.–6:00 p.m.
Closed: Mondays; Christmas, New Year's Day.
Summer hours (Victoria Day to Labor Day):
Tuesday and Thursday 10:00 a.m.–8:00 p.m.
Monday, Wednesday, Friday–Sunday 10:00 a.m.–8:30 p.m.
Minimum time required to see exhibit: 6 hours

Entrance Fees:
Families $15.00
Adults $7.00
Seniors and students $4.00
Children (5–14) $3.50

Address:
Royal Ontario Museum
100 Queen's Park, Toronto, ON, Canada M5S 2C6
Telephone: (416)586-5551

Directions:
From Highway 2, exit to Avenue Road north. Located in downtown Toronto, the Royal Ontario Museum is at the southwest corner of Bloor Street and Avenue Road at the museum subway stop.

Map to Royal Ontario Museum

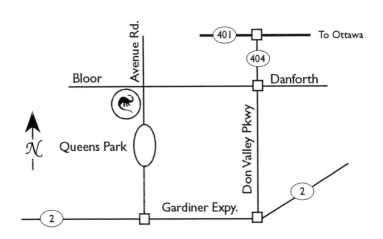

Safari Notes

Use these four pages to keep track of your own findings from your dinosaur safaris!

Safari Notes

Safari Notes

Safari Notes

Index to Selected Site Features

Looking for a particular dinosaur or other prehistoric animal? This list includes some of the features highlighted in *The Dinosaur Safari Guide*.

Alphabetical Index to Sites

References

In addition to the hundreds of informative phamplets available at the sites, these sources were used for *The Dinosaur Safari Guide*. Those listed in boldface are excellent sources for further reading about prehistoric life including dinosaurs.

Alexander, R. McNeill. *Dynamics of Dinosaurs and Other Extinct Giants*. New York: Columbia University Press, 1989.

Averett, Walter R., editor. *Paleontology and Geology of the Dinosaur Triangle: Guidebook for 1987 Field Trip*. Grand Junction, CO: Museum of Western Colorado, 1987.

Bakker, Robert T. *The Dinosaur Heresies: New Theories Unlocking the Mystery of the Dinosaurs and Their Extinction*. New York: William Morrow & Co., 1986.

Bakker, Robert T. "The Return of the Dancing Dinosaur," in *Dinosaurs Past and Present*, edited by Sylvia J. Czerkas and Everett C. Olson, vol. 1. Los Angeles: Natural History Museum of Los Angeles County, 1987.

Bakker, Robert T. "Cretaceous Park." *Earth*, Sept. 1993: pgs. 24–43.

Benton, Michael J. "Late Triassic Extinctions and the Origin of Dinosaurs." *Science*, vol. 260, 1993: pg. 769.

Carpenter, Kenneth, and Philip J. Currie, editors. *Dinosaur Systematics: Approaches and Perspectives*. New York: Cambridge University Press, 1990.

Carroll, Robert L. *Vertebrate Paleontology and Evolution*. New York: W.H. Freeman and Co., 1987.

Cohen, Daniel and Susan. *Where to Find Dinosaurs Today*. New York: Cobblehill Books, 1992.

Colbert, Edwin H. *Dinosaurs: An Illustrated History*. Maplewood, NJ: Hammond Inc., 1983.

Dawkins, Richard. *The Selfish Gene*. New York: Oxford University Press, 1989.

Dawkins, Richard. *The Blind Watchmaker: Why the Evidence of Evolution Reveals a Universe without Design*. New York: W.W. Norton & Co., 1987.

Diagram Group Staff. *The Dinosaur Data Book*. New York: Avon Books, 1990.

Gillette, David D., and Martin G. Lockley, editors. *Dinosaur Tracks and Traces*. New York: Cambridge University Press, 1989.

Gould, Stephen Jay. *Wonderful Life: The Burgess Shale and the Nature of History*. New York: W.W. Norton and Co., 1989.

Gould, Stephen Jay, general editor. *The Book of Life: An Illustrated History of the Evolution of Life on Earth.* New York: W. W. Norton & Co., 1993.

Hawking, Stephen W. *A Brief History of Time: From the Big Bang to Black Holes.* Toronto: Bantam Books, 1988.

Horgan, John. "In the Beginning," *Scientific American*, Feb. 1991: pgs. 116–125.

Horner, John R., and James Gorman. *Digging Dinosaurs.* New York: Workman Publishing Co., Inc., 1988.

Lessem, Don. *Kings of Creation: How a New Breed of Scientists is Revolutionizing our Understanding of Dinosaurs.* New York: Simon & Schuster, 1992.

Lessem, Don, and Donald F. Glut. *The Dinosaur Society's Dinosaur Encyclopedia.* New York: Random House, Inc., 1993.

Mason, Stephen F. *Chemical Evolution: Origin of the Elements, Molecules and Living Systems.* New York: Clarendon Press, 1991.

McGowan, Christopher. *Dinosaurs, Spitfires and Sea Dragons.* Cambridge, MA: Harvard University Press, 1991.

Mitchell, James R. *Gem Trails of Utah.* Baldwin Park, CA: Gem Guides Book Company, 1987.

Morell, Virginia. "Dino DNA: The Hunt and the Hype." *Science*, vol. 261, 1993: pg. 160.

Morell, Virginia. "How Lethal was the K-T Impact." *Science*, vol. 261, 1993: pg. 1518.

Norman, David, editor. *The Illustrated Encyclopedia of Dinosaurs.* Avenal, NJ: Outlet Book Co., 1985.

Paul, Gregory S. *Predatory Dinosaurs of the World: A Complete Illustrated Guide.* New York: Simon & Schuster Inc., 1989.

Sereno, Paul C. "Basal Archosaurs: Phylogenetic Relationships and Functional Implications." *Journal of Vertebrate Paleontology*, vol. 11, Dec. 31, 1991.

Stokes, William Lee. *Dinosaur Tour Book.* Salt Lake City, UT: Starstone Publishing Co., 1988.

Vickers-Rich, Patricia, and Thomas Hewitt Rich. "Australia's Polar Dinosaurs." *Scientific American*, Jul. 1993: pgs. 50–55.

Weishampel, David B., Peter Dodson, and Halszka Osmolska, editors. *The Dinosauria.* Berkeley, CA: University of California Press.

Wilford, John Noble. *The Riddle of the Dinosaur.* New York: Alfred A. Knopf, 1985.

Will, Richard and Margery Read. *Dinosaur Digs: A Guide to Museums, Sites and Opportunities to Learn about Dinosaurs in U.S. and Canada.* Castine, ME: Country Roads Press, 1992.

About the Author

Vincenzo Costa is a senior research engineer at Lockheed and has a Masters of Science in mechanical engineering from the University of California at Santa Barbara. An avid motorcycle road racer, he claimed the 1985 AFM National Formula One Mortorcycle Championship and in 1988 patented a new shock absorber design for racing cars and motorcycles. In addition, Vincenzo is developing an advanced robotic appendage to be used for animated dinosaur models. His engineering research has taken him on frequent trips to Utah, where he developed a life-long love of dinosaurs. The amazing quarries and museums of the Dinosaur Triangle of Utah and Colorado inspired Vincenzo to travel to all of the dinosaur exhibits in North America. His journey to our prehistoric past forms the backbone of this book.

Searching for a Better Way

Searching for a Better Way

by
Monroe Hawley

ISBN 0-89137-525-2

TABLE OF CONTENTS

CHAPTER 1

There Has to Be
a Better Way

A few years ago a congregation of undenominational Christians began a campus ministry at a state university. Its program included setting up a number of Bible study groups. They were so successful in influencing those with no or minimal commitment to the Christian faith that opposition developed from some who felt threatened.

At the beginning of one school year the following notice was printed in the student paper: "Warning! Evangelist loose. A word of warning to all freshmen. In the next few days a student will knock on your door and invite you to a religious Bible study. These discussions have only one purpose. They are designed to attract you to their religious worship services and eventually to become a Christian by being baptized into their church. . . . Before you accept any invitation to a Bible study, contact your pastor or priest and if the problem becomes too big for you to handle, consult the university counseling center located at Little Hall."

Two months later the paper published a letter to the editor dealing with the same topic. The writer strenuously voiced his disapproval of those involved in the campus study groups. His basic objection was that they believed they were right. He, on the other hand, felt that since there is no set standard in religion, everyone ought to do his own thing. Acknowledging that he was from a liberal Protestant background, he stated that his church did not feel that its beliefs were any more valid than those of other people.

A Response

A few days later the following response from an associate professor appeared in the paper: "Their beliefs are okay, for them, if they don't become self-righteous and start believing that their way is the only way,' says Scott B. Martin in a recent letter. . . .

"Martin was speaking from the perspective of an active member of a liberal Protestant church which does not feel that its beliefs are the only valid ones.

"I speak with the same credentials. My three-generation heritage has led me to an active role in such a church, including positions at the state and national level. My two daughters grew up in such a church, leading what all would term a 'good life.'

"They fitted well into society, worked hard, supported good causes and, in general, followed in their father's footsteps. They were sufficiently biblically illiterate, passively religious and worldly so that they could pass on a university campus as a member of any faith or no faith at all. . . ."

The professor went on to explain that this was before his daughters had become involved in the Bible study program. He continued:

"In recent months they have been exposed to what I term First Century Christianity. By biblical standards, the genuine article, rather than a 20th century adaptation or scholarly-defined interpretation of it. As a result they have become devout, disciplined, assertive, and . . . most apparent to me . . . radiant. To my chagrin, they look back on their past life—my life—as empty. In their new life, they have been transformed; in their old life, they had been, frankly, conformed.

"It has been easier for me to be a 24-hour, no-nonsense, fully dedicated 'true believer' of my favorite candidate than it has for me to demonstrate the same outward commitment to Jesus Christ. What has constrained me? Tolerance. In politics, one way; in religion, everybody charts his or her own course.

"Now that I think about it, that isn't very scriptural. I would have never thought about it if it hadn't been for the witness of my loving daughters. . . ."

The professor then stated that the Bible study groups made the letter writer and himself uncomfortable just as Jesus did in his day. He explained:

"The problem then was that good people focused their attention on their own discomfort. In the process they missed power, beauty, righteousness, commitment, and triumph. A few who felt they had nothing to lose found all of this and more.

"The 'good news' of the gospel is that the same choice is available today. But it speaks of sacrifice, too, and perhaps our concept of 'religious tolerance' stands in our way more than the traditional sins of greed, selfishness, etc. I can say this, if it were in my power to restore my daughters to the conventional, tolerant individuals they were before their religious awakening, I wouldn't choose that for a minute.

"As I reexamine the scriptures, I find Jesus empathetic and forgiving, but not tolerant. Rather than Mr. Martin's prescription. . ., I say, Right on!"

A Form of Religion

The professor's description of his own religious experience calls to mind the statement of the Apostle Paul: "For men will be lovers of self, lovers of money, proud, arrogant, abusive, disobedient to parents, ungrateful, unholy, . . . *holding the form of religion but denying the power of it*" (2 Timothy 3:2, 5). The professor held to the externals of Christianity, but lacked a commitment to its principles and the truth upon which it is based. Accordingly, his religion gave no joy, no strength to meet problems, and no genuine satisfaction.

In most Western nations the number of people claiming a religious profession has drastically declined. In America, on the other hand, the majority still espouse some kind of faith, and most of these call themselves Christians. At the same time moral values have been eroding and the philosophy that in ethics anything goes is now generally accepted. To stand for moral purity is to find oneself in the minority. This combination of moral laxity with formal religion can lead only to the conclusion that many of those making religious professions have frankly abandoned the spiritual precepts of Jesus, if, in fact, they have ever followed them.

It is not surprising, therefore, that some find their religion inadequate in meeting their emotional and spiritual needs. It cannot help them in making ethical decisions. It does not sustain them in human suffering. It is not a source of joy in this life nor does it provide faith when one is confronted by death. It is a form of religion, but with no power. As the professor said of the Jews of

9

Jesus' time, many religious people have "missed power, beauty, righteousness, commitment, and triumph."

"Now, That's Religion!"

This religious poverty is illustrated in an incident related to me by a friend. She was working in a factory where profanity was common. Because she was a Christian this bothered her. As kindly as she could she expressed her disapproval. A fellow worker observed her behavior and commented, "You're very religious, aren't you?" Connie responded, "No, I'm very Christian." Diane, her fellow worker, couldn't see the difference between being a Christian and being religious. Connie continued, "There are a lot of religious people in this world, but very few Christians." This comment surprised Diane who then inquired, "What do you mean?" Connie explained, "Christians live what they hear on Sunday. A lot of religious people go to church on Sunday and pay their debt on Sunday and they figure they're done for the week. But the next day you find them cursing and swearing. And then they inquire, 'Why didn't it work? I went to church and paid my dues.' "

About this time the boss walked by, cursing and swearing. A machine had given him trouble. He exploded, "I went to Mass Sunday and paid my missionary dues, and now what's wrong? Everything is going wrong. I don't think it paid at all to go." The two women witnessed the scene. Connie turned to Diane and quietly observed, "Now, *that's* religion!"

The Priority of Truth

Why do so many feel this spiritual vacuum in their lives? The answers vary according to the experiences of the person. The professor's letter to the editor pinpoints part of the problem as a lack of commitment to spiritual truth. It is easier to stand for nothing at all than to hold to a principle. How often has it been said, "It doesn't make any difference what you believe so long as you are sincere. We are all going to the same place, but just traveling different roads to get there." Now, sincerity is important, but the philosophy revealed by this statement is that truth does not exist, or if it does, it is unimportant.

However, if anything stands out in the teaching of Jesus it is his commitment to truth. Because of truth he taught moral precepts that would cause others to persecute him. Because of truth he refused to water down his teaching when many of his disciples left him and his popularity declined. And because of truth he surrendered his life on a cross outside Jerusalem! One cannot be a true disciple of Jesus without sharing in this commitment. Indeed, it was Jesus who prayed to the Father, "Sanctify them in the truth; thy word is truth" (John 17:17).

Some insist that tolerance forbids us to disagree about matters of the Christian faith. But this is a false tolerance which would have been condemned by Jesus. True tolerance requires that we listen respectfully to the views of other people. False tolerance insists that religious beliefs are unimportant, and insinuates that the one who dares to argue for his convictions is bigoted.

However, the religion which stands for nothing is worth nothing. The true Christian faith is rooted in God's truth, and the disciple of Christ must be willing to adhere to it regardless of the consequences. For many early Christians this meant dying as martyrs for that truth. Would we do the same? Perhaps no one knows for sure until confronted with the choice, but of this we may be certain—no man will die for that for which he will not first live. So, before your religion can be truly meaningful to you it must be firmly grounded on God's eternal truth. As the wise man observed, "Buy truth, and do not sell it" (Proverbs 23:23).

However, the truthseeker may find it hard to discover that truth which reveals the true religion of Jesus. When he questions others about his spiritual needs he is given many answers. He soon decides that religious teachers can't agree among themselves. He is totally confused and may become so discouraged that he concludes that further search for truth is futile.

The Denominational System

The two major alternatives usually considered by those who believe in Jesus are Protestantism and Catholicism. The Protestant Reformation resulted from a sixteenth century rejection of Catholic authoritarianism by those who were a part of the Catholic system. Luther, Zwingli, and Calvin—denying that spiritual authority is vested in the church—called for a return to the Bible as the ultimate source of knowledge of God's will. Each reformer agreed that Catholicism needed to be changed, but unfortunately they did not all seek changes in the same areas. This lack of agreement resulted in different religious bodies being established.

11

Some stressed the biblical doctrine of justification by faith, some the scriptural aspects of New Testament baptism, others the apostolic concept of congregational church government, and still others the essentiality of the holy life. The resulting division and confusion is evident everywhere today. How can these differences be reconciled with the teachings of Jesus? The denominational system has thus become a major impediment to one seeking the way of the Lord.

I must emphasize that the great leaders of the Protestant Reformation made many positive contributions. Unfortunately some of them have been lost in contemporary mainline Protestantism. Many denominations no longer stress biblical authority and some even deny the inspiration of the Bible. Humanism has been substituted for the ethical teachings of Jesus. The church is molded by society, not society by the church. One can be a church member in good standing even when his life contradicts the plain teachings of Jesus. That is why the professor commented that in their previous spiritual condition his daughters "were sufficiently biblically illiterate, passively religious and worldly so that they could pass on a university campus as a member of any faith or no faith at all."

Furthermore, many people conceive of their denominations merely as social clubs, promoters of civil causes, or fund raisers to support the denominational machinery. They don't believe their church cares about them. This conception may be reinforced by personal experiences. Often I have been told of churches that published the annual donations of their members—in descending order. No doubt this proceedure was designed to produce larger contributions from the less generous givers, and you may be sure that the point was made. A lady once told me, "When I got sick no one from the church visited me, but they sent me a bill telling how much I owed them!" It is not surprising that those who take time to read the Bible see little resemblance between this picture and that of first century Christianity. They feel a spiritual hunger which they know is not being satisfied. The cause of much of the problem is found in the denominational system which evolved from the Protestant Reformation. By its very nature it is divisive and deeply sectarian. Quite naturally each body is interested in promoting and defending its own brand of Christianity. In recent years there has been a growing recognition of the negative factors in the system and the ecumenical movement has sought to promote religious unity. This is encouraging, but the problem will not be solved so long as denominationalism continues to exist.

Of course, it is unfair to characterize everyone in the same way. There are denominations that continue to stress the fundamentals of the Christian faith, and which believe that one must be transformed by Christ rather than being conformed to the world. Even within liberal Protestant bodies there are individuals who have had the courage to cry out against the bland version of Christianity to which they have been exposed. Among Protestants the growing influence of evangelicalism, which stresses the inspiration of the scriptures and the authority of the written word, has been most encouraging. We should not become despondent as did Elijah who cried out to God after fleeing from the wicked Jezebel, "I, even I only, am left; and they seek my life, to take it away" (1 Kings 19:14). The Lord informed him that he was not alone for there were still seven thousand in Israel who had not bowed the knee to Baal. We must remember, therefore, that in the midst of what appears to be a turning away from God there are still many who are vitally interested in a return to original Christianity.

Those with Catholic roots have had different experiences from those raised in Protestantism. Unlike many Protestants they have not been taught that what one believes is unimportant. On the other hand, they have been indoctrinated with the view that their church is the one true church because it is in the spiritual lineage of apostolic Christianity. A line of succession is traced back to the first century. This is considered evidence that the present day Catholic Church is the true church, though it vastly differs from the body described in the New Testament. Moreover, it is taught that authority is not found in the written word alone, but is invested in the church which speaks through its popes, church councils, and traditions as well as through the Bible. Since the church is the guardian of truth, it has the God-given right to insist that its members accept its pronouncements.

Authoritarianism

The result is an authoritarian system in which Catholics are expected to accept the teachings of the church, no questions asked. Unlike many Protestants who believe they can let the scriptures respond to their questions, Catholics must listen to the voice of the church to find their answers. If the pope makes an "ex cathedra" declaration (when he infallibly teaches the faithful regarding faith and morals), all must regard this as truth, even though some may privately question the legitimacy of the position.

13

On the other hand, we live in an age in which people are taught to think for themselves. The system of public education is geared to that end. In the sciences the student solves problems on the basis of information learned and personal reasoning. The physician applies his knowledge to the condition of his patients and makes life and death decisions. The electors in a democratic society try to make enlightened choices in selecting those to serve in public. Yet in religion the Catholic is taught not to think for himself and to unquestioningly follow the official declarations of the church.

In recent years a number of changes have been made in the Catholic Church. These include saying the Mass in the language of the people rather than in Latin, and the removal of restrictions against eating meat on Friday. Since these are laws of the church, they are considered susceptible to change. On the other hand, some restrictions, such as those pertaining to birth control, have not been modified because it is believed that they are unalterable laws of God. The changes have caused consternation among those who are deeply traditional, and confusion among others who would prefer an even greater liberalization. Some inquire, "If they can change some of the laws, why can't they change others as well?"

The result has been disenchantment among those who believe they should be able to think for themselves, and those who feel that the changing doctrine reveals that the church is not so infallible as they had been led to believe. One lady bitterly related her disillusionment to me. She said that all of her life she had been taught that eating meat on Friday was a mortal sin (not a venial sin, she stressed.) As a child she once succumbed to temptation and secretly ate some meat on Friday. And then she said, "I have been living with that all of these years, and now they tell me that it's all right to eat meat on Friday!" As a result she became an atheist.

The authoritarian approach does not satisfy those who are unwilling to delegate their thinking and decision making to others. Many feel a spiritual void that is not being met by theological declarations from church divines. The spiritual longings of those in this condition were expressed to me a few years ago by a young friend. She wrote: "A Sunday service at my church is very dull to me. No one puts any feeling into the words. They talk of revival, but it is not filled with the spirit. I know my church turns a lot of people off."

14

A Better Way?

Denominationalism, authoritarianism, lack of conviction—these are the things which many find in the various brands of Christianity to which they have been exposed. Is there any wonder that millions are spiritually dissatisfied? Did not Jesus promise, "Blessed are those who hunger and thirst for righteousness, for they shall be satisfied" (Matthew 5:6)? **There has to be a better way! Thank God, there is!**

CHAPTER 2

The Undenominational Church

Have you ever wondered how many churches there were in the first century? Of which denomination were the early Christians members? It may surprise you to learn that there was then but one church and that the earliest Christians were undenominational. Would it not be wonderful if we could turn back the clock and recapture that condition today? Perhaps we can by examining the biblical concept of undenominational Christianity.

Before considering how the early disciples of Jesus could be just Christians, we need to take a good look at present day denominationalism. What is a denomination? Broadly speaking, to denominate is to name. Thus, a ten dollar bill is called a ten dollar denomination. In the religious sense:

"A denomination is a group of professed Christians with an existence which is not identical to the entire body of Christ. At best it is but part of the church, having separated itself by its actions from other disciples of Christ. At worst it may be totally outside the limits of the Christian faith, and hence, it may be argued, is not a denomination at all since it is not even Christian. However, *denomination* is here used in the popular sense to apply to all groups that call Jesus Lord."[1]

Denominational Characteristics

There are at least five characteristics of denominationalism, although a denomination may not display them all. To the extent that any of these marks is present, the body is denominational.

First, a religious group is denominational if it is governed by *a legislative or executive organization which is foreign to God's word*. Most denominations have some kind of human structure to authorize teachings and regulate practices. Catholics and some

17

Protestants have a hierarchical government in which doctrines and policies originate at the top. In contrast the presbyterian form of government places the decision making process in the hands of congregational representatives who collectively reach decisions in a presbytery. Some denominations are quite democratic. However, in each instance there is some kind of machinery which reduces the independence of the local church. A congregation which is unwilling to concur in the decisions passed down from above is excluded from denominational fellowship.

Next, a group is denominational if it accepts *an authoritative creed* as its official position in doctrinal matters. The creed may be a collection of historic pronouncements of the church, or perhaps a single manual of discipline or confession of faith which is regarded as binding. The Protestant Reformation began on the presumption that the scriptures are authoritative in divine-human relationships. Soon, however, different interpretations resulted in the adoption of conflicting confessions of faith as official commentaries on the meaning of the Bible. These creeds, in turn, became a barrier to badly-needed unity.

We should observe that it is not wrong to commit our understanding of the scriptures to writing. What you now read is itself a reflection of the author's thinking. Should this book, however, be accepted as the official position of any group of people it would become a creed in the denominational sense. It would assume a position of importance beside the Bible, and would become an obstacle to unity with those refusing to subscribe to its conclusions. The specific objection to creeds is not that they express a point of view, but that they become an authoritative expression of that position.

It is true that some are ignorant of the disciples of their denominations. They may not even feel obligated to accept them as authoritative. However, since the bodies of which they are members do acknowledge the creeds, public teaching reflects the accepted point of view. To the extent one is loyal to his denomination he is influenced by its creed, though he may be personally unfamiliar with it.

Third, a religious body is denominational if it adopts *a basic doctrine which contradicts the word of God.* The Montanists were a denominational group of the second century. The founder of the sect was Montanus, who, among other things, was accepted by his followers as the "Paraclete" (or Counselor) promised by Jesus to his apostles (John 14:26). Since Jesus explained that the Paraclete is the Holy Spirit, this was blasphemy. Since other Christians would not accept this and related views, the Montanists soon became a distinct denomination growing out of their false doctrine.

Of course, no religious body would acknowledge that its teachings are erroneous. Many people are where they are because they believe that the doctrine of their denomination is essentially correct. However, there obviously comes a time when a group ceases to represent the true Christian faith. John labeled the Gnostics of his day antichrists because they denied that Jesus is the Christ (1 John 2:22). There is a danger, however, of choosing a set of arbitrary issues which are too inclusive or too exclusive and on this basis declaring that all who do not give "the right answers" are thereby denominational. No two thinking persons see eye to eye on every biblical interpretation. There must be some latitude for different understandings while at the same time recognizing that sectarianism results from thought systems which do not meet Christ's approval.

Next, denominationalism is evident when a group wears *a distinctive name* which "denominates" it and separates it from others following Jesus. These names are usually without biblical authority. They may be derived from the name of the founder, the type of church government adopted, or even a major church doctrine. This symptom is easily recognized. However, it is also possible to use biblical terms in an unbiblical way. The adoption of a biblical phrase as the official denominational name does not make it less sectarian. It is not only important that Christians "speak as the oracles of God," but they must also be sure that their words reflect a non-sectarian viewpoint.

Finally, a religious body becomes denominational when its members display *a sectarian spirit*. Sectarian thinking is nothing new. It was a problem among the Corinthian Christians who gave their loyalty to great leaders of the church (1 Corinthians 1:10-13). They possessed the party spirit and didn't even realize that this was wrong. It is easy to detect sectarian attitudes among others, but more difficult to see it among ourselves. Even the one who professes strict loyalty to Jesus and to the authority of the written word may unconsciously think in sectarian terms. The problem arises from viewing spiritual matters from one's personal perspective rather than from God's.

Faults of Denominationalism

The faults of denominationalism are easy to detect. To begin with, *it devides the followers of Jesus.* Just before his crucifixion Jesus petitioned the Father, "I do not pray for these only (his apostles), but also for those who believe in me through their word, that they may all be one; even as thou, Father, art in me, and I in thee, that they also may be in us, so that the world may believe that thou hast sent me" (John 17:20, 21). Obviously this prayer is not being fulfilled in our generation and the existence of the denominational system is a major reason. Surely none of us believes that religious division is right.

In his prayer Jesus indicated that the unity of his disciples would promote faith on the part of others. This points to a second fallacy of denominationalism—*it discourages seekers of truth.* The average person is poorly versed in the scriptures. He does not know how to use the Bible to determine the will of God. The many answers to his spiritual problems which are given by different denominations may cause him to turn away in despair. But if all disciples of Jesus were truly one in Christ, what a wonderful testimony that would be to the world!

Furthermore, *denominationalism perverts the gospel of Christ.* This charge may seem to be overly broad; but consider this. The creeds of Christendom are often contradictory. Where they disagree, there must also be error. Truth does not contradict itself. It logically follows that those creeds containing untruths pervert the gospel and perpetuate error. Since these confessions of faith are essential ingredients of the system they cannot be separated from the denominations for which they speak.

Many recognize the bankruptcy of denominationalism and have sought solutions to the problem. The ecumenical movement, which promotes religious unity by advocating denominational mergers, provides one answer. This is a step in the right direction, but it fails to get at the root of the problem. When denominations merge there are usually dissidents who refuse to accept the union because they feel that truth has been compromised. In the end there is not a reduction in the number of denominations, but rather a realigning of allegiances.

The Undenominational Alternative

Is there a better way? I think there is. It is found in *undenominational Christianity*. This is different from interdenominationalism which promotes cooperation among those of differing faiths without disturbing their basic beliefs. Interdenominationalism lessens sectarian rivalry, but leaves the basic problem unsolved.

In contrast, undenominational Christianity requires the abolition of every denomination. All followers of Jesus would be just Christians, without prefix or suffix to that distinguished name. This proposal raises several important questions. Since we live in a divided world, how can an individual be a Christian only? Is it even possible? Viewed in a larger sense, will the denominations willingly sacrifice their identities in the interest of Christian unity?

Before answering we need to consider the implications of undenominational Christianity. The best place to start is the New Testament. The first century church which it describes was truly undenominational. By examining its features we can also determine what it now takes for people to be just Christians.

In the days of the apostles there was but one body. Paul stressed this when he wrote, "There is one body and one Spirit, just as you were called to the one hope that belongs to your call" (Ephesians 4:4). It was clear that he spoke of the church when he also declared of Jesus, "He is the head of *the body, the church*" (Colossians 1:18).

That body was united. Paul exhorted the Ephesians "to maintain the unity of the Spirit in the bond of peace" (Ephesians 4:3). True, first century congregations did have their problems. We have already alluded to sectarianism at Corinth. There was a dispute over circumcision which threatened the unity of the early disciples. A conference to discuss the difficulty was held in Jerusalem (Acts 15). But in spite of these factors unity still prevailed in the early church. Just as sin in the Corinthian church did not prevent Paul from addressing those Christians as "saints" (1 Corinthians 1:2), so the occasional disharmony among Jesus' followers did not destroy their basic unity.

21

Who were the people who composed this body? A study of the word *church* will help answer the question. In our language the term may mean a building, a congregation, or a society of religious people. We must realize, however, that we are concerned about how the word was used in the New Testament, not in current English usage. The New Testament books were written in Greek and then translated into the various tongues in which they may now be read. Our interest centers about the Greek *ekklesia* from which church comes.

Ekklesia never meant a building or place of worship. It always referred to people. In the classical sense it meant "the called out." It designated a body of people "called out" of their homes to a public assembly similar to a New England town meeting. There is some question as to whether the "called out" idea inheres in the New Testament use of the word as applied to the disciples of Jesus. Nevertheless, Peter does speak of the Christian's "call and election" (2 Peter 1:10), and he further declares, "But you are a chosen race, a royal priesthood, a holy nation, God's own people, that you may declare the wonderful deeds of him who called you out of darkness into his marvelous light. Once you were no people but now you are God's people; once you had not received mercy but now you have received mercy" (1 Peter 2:9, 10). God's people, then, are those who have been called from the world by the good news of Jesus to become part of the family of God.

There are three primary uses of *ekklesia* in the New Testament. Often it denotes a local group of Christians. Thus Paul addresses a letter "to the church of the Thessalonians in God the Father and the Lord Jesus Christ" (1 Thessalonians 1:1). In this sense *ekklesia* is best rendered "congregation."

Occasionally the word identifies the actual gathering of a group of Christians as when Paul writes, "When you assemble as a church, I hear that there are divisions among you" (1 Corinthians 11:18). (See also 1 Corinthians 14:19, 28, 35). In these passages the best translation would be "assembly."

A third important use of *ekklesia* is the universal signification which designates all Christians on earth. Jesus used it this way when he declared, "On this rock I will build my church" (Matthew 16:18). It is the universal body of which Paul speaks when he says "that through the church the manifold wisdom of God might now be made known to the principalities and powers in the heavenly places" (Ephesians 3:10). It is this sense which is so vital to our under-

standing if we are to grasp the concept we are considering—
undenominational Christianity.

The historic document of early Christianity is the *Acts of the Apostles.* In its beginning it records the establishment of Christ's church on the first Pentecost after the resurrection and ascension of Jesus. In the four Gospels which chronicle events before this time the church is always spoken of in the future tense. After that day the book of Acts always speaks of it as an existing body. Following the baptism of 3,000 on Pentecost we are told, "And the Lord added to the church daily such as should be saved" (Acts 2:47—King James Version). The Revised Standard Version renders the verse, "And the Lord added to their number day by day those who were being saved." Most versions omit *church* from this verse because of doubtful Greek manuscript support for its inclusion. However, it is evident from the language that the people who became Christians were added to something. Few would deny that it was the church which Luke, the writer, had in mind.

The passage also states that those who were added were the saved. Biblically speaking then, the church is the saved. When one is redeemed from his sins the Lord simultaneously adds him to his universal church. The identity between the saved and the church is expressed in this statement:

"The church Christ built includes all the saved; and it includes no one else. There is not one saved who is not in it. There is not one in it who is not saved. The guarantee of this is that the same one does both the saving and the adding to the church. The church is the saved."[2]

The undenominational church, therefore, is God's body of saved people. It is he who determines those who compose it on the ground of his knowledge of the redeemed. "The Lord knows those who are his" (2 Timothy 2:19). Men do not have the right on the basis of their creeds to try to define the boundaries of the kingdom of God. When we in human judgment seek to do so we are certain to include some whom the Lord will not claim while excluding others who rightly belong in the divine family.

The undenominational ideal is beautifully expressed in an editorial in *Christianity Today:*

"It is important to remember that the New Testament equates the Church with all the people of God. . . . From the Bible (or for that matter from ordinary common sense) it ought to be clear that the Church is people—not a bureaucracy, not clergy, not denominational leaders. It is the community of the redeemed. It is the family of God."[3]

The editorial gets to the heart of the problem which many have in grasping this concept:

"There is a great readiness to confuse the Church with institutional denominationalism. But the two are not the same. The New Testament knows nothing of institutional denominationalism. It indeed provides for the order of the visible church. It knows the people of God, the body of Christ, the bride of Christ, the household of God. It speaks of believers, of the elect, of those 'in Christ,' and much more. It sees the Church as a band of redeemed and committed men and women in whom the Spirit of God dwells."[4]

For us, therefore, to understand the meaning of undenominational Christianity, we must first remove our denominational misconceptions. Then we must go to the Bible to discover that the church is made up of those whom God through Christ has saved from their sins.

This body of saved people was a family with all that this term implies. Paul wrote the Ephesians, "So then you are no longer strangers and sojourners, but you are fellow citizens with the saints and *members of the household of God,* built upon the foundation of the apostles and prophets, Christ Jesus himself being the cornerstone" (Ephesians 2:19, 20). In the right kind of human family there is love. That love prompts brothers and sisters to be so concerned about their mutual welfare that they will share as need requires. The same was true in God's spiritual family. The love was so great in the early Jerusalem church that many sold their possessions and shared them with others to satisfy their physical needs (Acts 2:44, 45). While we do not find similar actions elsewhere in the New Testament, there is abundant evidence of Christians sharing in other ways because of the love which bound them together. It is sad that this family perspective is largely lacking in today's organized religion.

The early Christians knew that their lives separated them from a world of evil. Peter wrote, "But you are . . . God's own people, that you may declare the wonderful deeds of him who called you out of darkness into his marvelous light" (1 Peter 2:9). In discussing their relationships with sinful people Paul warned, "Therefore do not associate with them, for once you were darkness, but now you are light in the Lord; walk as children of light" (Ephesians 5:7, 8). Of course, they did not disassociate with those in the world so completely that they could not influence them for good, but intimate relationships were forbidden because "bad company ruins good morals" (1 Corinthians 15:33). The pure living of the disciples separated them from those who had not been "called out" of sin. Unfortunately today it is often impossible to distinguish those who wear the name of Christ from those who do not by the conduct of their lives.

The undenominational church was congregational. Each local unit made its own decisions without seeking authorization from some kind of hierarchy. Congregations, when fully organized, were shepherded by its elders or overseers. Of course, the inspired apostles gave the church the body of teaching which guided it in its infancy, but after their death they were not replaced. We may wonder how the church could function without some kind of denominational structure. It may seem that religious anarchy would result.

However, at least three things bound them together. In Jesus they recognized a common head of the church. "He (God) has put all things under his feet and has made him head over all things for the church, which is his body" (Ephesians 1:22, 23). This common allegiance promoted their unity. They also believed and taught the same things, and thus shared a common doctrine. Finally, their mutual love was so strong that congregations willingly cooperated with one another in the work of the Lord.

How were they identified? Individually they were simply *disciples*. A disciple is a follower or learner, and they followed Jesus. Other terms used to designate them were *saints* (Romans 1:7), *brethren* (Colossians 1:2), *priests* (1 Peter 2:5, 9), and *heirs* (Romans 8:17). However, it was by the term *Christian* that Jesus' followers came to be known to the world. We are first introduced to the word in Acts 11:26. "And in Antioch the disciples were for the first time called Christians." The word was accepted by the disciples as a fitting term for followers of Jesus. They were "Christ-ians," disciples of Christ.

Viewed collectively the New Testament applies a variety of descriptive expressions to the apostolic church. It was *the kingdom*

(Hebrews 12:28), *the household of faith* (Galatians 6:10), *the house-hold of God* (1 Timothy 3:15), *the body of Christ* (1 Corinthians 12:27), and *the way* (Acts 19:9, 23). The latter term is used six times in Acts to describe the fellowship of the saints. Each phrase tells us something about the nature of the divine body.

The most common designation of this spiritual family was *the church.* Sometimes the word was modified to show possession. "Or do you despise the *church of God* and humiliate those who have nothing?" (1 Corinthians 11:22). Congregationally we are told that "All the *churches of Christ* greet you" (Romans 16:16). The composition of the body by Christians was shown in Hebrews 12:23 which speaks of *"the assembly (church) of the first-born* who are enrolled in heaven." However, none of these terms is a proper name. In fact, there is no proper name applied to the universal church in the New Testament.

Christians Only Today?

The biblical picture we have drawn of the undenominational church is quite different from institutional denominationalism. Earlier we inquired if one can be just a Christian today in view of his religious surroundings. Our examination of the early church has revealed nothing about undenominational Christianity which we cannot duplicate in our time. It *is* possible to be just a Christian, and it is also possible for a congregation made up of Christians to be truly undenominational. Whether the religious community will accept this alternative to the present sectarianism is another matter. Certainly it will not until it is first presented for its consideration.

However, we face a problem which the early disciples did not encounter. Denominationalism was then unknown and the mere fact that one was a Christian was enough to insure his identification. Today, however, for a group to be undenominational it must first remove itself from the system. Does its act of separation also cause it to become sectarian because it has become distinct? G. C. Brewer states the dilemma facing undenominational Christians and proposes an answer:

"But if we group undenominational Christians, separate them into a party and distinguish them from other Christians, have we not made them a denomination? Yes, indeed, and in that sense we are denominational and we must admit it. But it is not our fault. We are forced to it. We are forced to be denominational by reason of the fact that we are undenominational. I can illustrate that this way: Let us suppose that we have on this desk a great heap of cards. Some of the cards are stamped with figures, 2, 4, 6, 8, etc., and there is a great number of them that are unstamped—have no figures on them. I am set to the task of separating these cards and classifying them. I place the 'twos' in one stack, the 'fours' in another stack, the 'sixes' in still another stack and so on until I have stacked all the different numbers in separate stacks; and then I have a stack of cards that we would call nondescript—unstamped cards. They are a stack of cards just as much as the others are. But let us give to the cards human intelligence and place in them the purpose that we have as Christians and we will witness a great debate. A card from the stack of 'fours' arises and says, 'Here you fanatical and inconsistent fellows, you claim to be unstamped and unstacked and yet you are bunched, stacked and classified as much as any of us.' Then a card from the nondescript bunch arises in his righteous indignation and vehemently denies. He says, 'We are not classified. We are not a stack of cards. We are just cards.' But they are a stack of cards, as you can see. They are forced to be in a stack to themselves because the others are separated into stacks and left them alone. They are classified by reason of the fact that they are unclassified. It is not their purpose to be a separate and distinct division of cards. They think that all cards ought to be just cards and all be stacked together in one big stack, but these other cards are all stamped with different figures and are therefore distinguished from one another and from those unstamped. The stamp differentiates them and that forces the unstamped cards to be *classed* as unclassified or else be stamped and go into different stacks, and they know that they can never all be one stack as long as they are separated into different classes.

"You can all see the application. It is in this sense that we are denominational. We are forced to be a separate body of people because we are undenominational; because we will not have put upon us the party names, marks and brands of the different denominations. We want the fellowship of all of God's people and we will affiliate with anybody in anything the Bible sanctions, but we can not have the fellowship of our denominational brethren without going into their peculiar and several denominations. We are therefore left in the predicament of being a separate people by virtue of the fact that we are undenominational. . . . If we are denominational then it is because our purposes and work as a body of Christians—undenominational Christians, simply Christians, Christians only—make it necessary for us to labor apart from the

27

denominations or else become members of some one or different denominations and thus perpetuate divisions."[5]

The matter can be illustrated in another way. Let us suppose that a farmer owns forty acres of land, one quarter of a mile square. On each side his land is joined by that of another farmer. Each of his four neighbors decides to build a fence around his property. In the process of fencing themselves in they also fence the first farmer out. He is completely surrounded by fences which he did not build and which he cannot legally tear down. If his land is separated from his neighbors it is their fault, not his.

Likewise, those who stand for undenominational Christianity have no control over the spiritual fences built by others. If they are separated from them on this account it is not of their doing. However, they can plead for the removal of the fences and to the degree that they are successful in persuading others to subscribe to undenominational Christianity they have contributed to the unity of the religious world and the exaltation of the name of Christ.

Whether the undenominational plea is accepted by others, it is still valid and is the correct response to the confusion of our day. The real problem facing one who advances this ideal is that he must go against the grain. But so did Jesus. His entire ministry was in opposition to an entrenched system. While one cannot be Jesus, he can be his disciple and as such have the courage to stand up for truth.

In the history of ancient Israel, God's people continually turned to idolatry, in spite of numerous efforts at reformation led by the prophets and some of the kings. Their problem was that they were completely surrounded by idolatrous people and were constantly influenced by them in their thinking and practices.

We face the same difficulty respecting denominationalism. Because the system is everywhere around us, it is difficult to think or act in undenominational terms. Yet Paul warns, "Don't let the world around you squeeze you into its own mould" (Romans 12:2—Phillips Translation). True followers of Jesus must resist all efforts to make them conform to anything which compromises the will of God. If this means standing in opposition to a divisive system, let us have that courage.

FOOTNOTES

[1]Monroe E. Hawley, *Redigging the Wells* (Abilene, Texas: Quality Publications, 1976), p. 22.

[2]Cecil May, Jr., "Undenominational Christianity," *Firm Foundation,* June 10, 1969.

[3]Editorial, "Isolated from the Church?", *Christianity Today,* September 16, 1966, p. 31. Used by permission.

[4]*Ibid.,* p. 31.

[5]G. C. Brewer, *Murfreesboro Addresses* (Cincinnati: F. L. Rowe, 1917), pp. 161, 162.

CHAPTER 3

Jesus, My Lord

Sunday! Fearing for their lives, ten disciples of a martyred teacher anxiously hide in a house in Jerusalem. Just three days earlier their leader was crucified by the Roman governor at the urging of angry Jewish leaders. They have seen him die and their hope of a kingdom over which he will reign is now gone. Only Judas, the betrayer, and Thomas the Twin are absent from the tightly knit group that walked with the Master for three and a half years. Suddenly, he stands before them. "Peace be with you," he greets them. He extends his hands revealing the nail prints of his death, and shows them the side into which a soldier has thrust a spear. Truly, he has risen from the dead.

Suddenly, he is gone. Thomas returns, unaware of what has happened. The ten excitedly relate what they have seen, only to be met by skepticism. "Unless I see in his hands the print of the nails, and place my finger in the mark of the nails, and place my hand in his side, I will not believe" (John 20:25), Thomas declares.

A week passes. It is again the first day of the week. The setting is the same, except that Thomas is now present with the ten. The disciples' course of action is yet undecided. Once more Jesus suddenly appears. "Peace be with you," he again greets them. Then fixing his eyes on the doubter, he says, "Put your finger here, and see my hands; and put out your hand, and place it in my side; do not be faithless, but believing." What an impact! Thomas cries out, "My Lord and my God!" (John 20:26-28).

Meaning of "Lord"

In calling Jesus his God Thomas acknowledged his deity. In addressing him as "my Lord" he expressed that deep personal relationship which ought to govern the lives of all disciples of

Jesus. "Lord" is used 747 times in the New Testament, often being applied specifically to Jesus. The dictionary defines the word as "one having power and authority over others."

In the Middle Ages the term had particular significance in the feudal system which dominated Europe for five hundred years. After the death of Charlemagne in 814, his Carolingian Empire began to disintegrate. His heirs then decreed that every freeman must have a lord, that no man should leave his lord without good cause, and that every freeman should follow his lord to war. Theoretically even the most important noble had a lord to whom he owed allegiance, perhaps ultimately to the king himself. Thus the lord assumed a vital role in the development of feudalism.

"Lord" had special significance to the ancient Israelites. They believed that the written name of God in the Old Testament, usually rendered "Jehovah" or "Yahweh" in English, was too sacred to be spoken. In reading the scriptures aloud they would pronounce this word, *Adonai* or *Lord*. New Testament writers followed the same practice when quoting the Hebrew Old Testament by translating Jehovah as "Lord."

Over and over in the New Testament Jesus is called the Lord Jesus or the Lord Jesus Christ, or perhaps, Jesus Christ our Lord. To his early followers "Lord" was of great significance. In a very personal way the disciples sought to make Jesus the Lord of their lives. They knew that in return he was the guarantor of their protection and redemption. Today if we are to recapture the spirit of early Christianity, we too must be willing to elevate him to that position.

My Authority

To make Jesus my Lord I must acknowledge his *authority* in spiritual matters. In his Great Commission to his apostles Jesus directed, "All authority in heaven and on earth has been given to me. Go therefore and make disciples of all nations, baptizing them in the name of the Father and of the Son and of the Holy Spirit, teaching them to observe all that I have commanded you; and lo, I am with you always, to the close of the age" (Matthew 28:18-20). Notice that Jesus claimed all authority over his followers, that authority coming from God. His instructions to his apostles were based on this premise. Earlier, when Jesus was on the Mount of Transfiguration with three of his disciples, the Father declared, "This is my beloved Son, with whom I am well pleased; listen to him" (Matthew 17:5). Because Jesus is my Lord, I must be guided by his authority in all teachings which apply to me. If Jesus teaches me to live by the Golden Rule, and he does, I am obligated to do so, not just because I think it is a good idea and is the best way to handle my human relationships, but because he is my Lord and I have submitted myself to his authority. I have no right to alter that command to suit my personal whims.

The writings of the New Testament have been given by the inspiration of God's Holy Spirit under the authority of Jesus. Since Jesus is now in heaven and the inspired men of apostolic times have died, our sole source of the revealed authority of Jesus is to be found in that part of the sacred scriptures which we call the New Testament. One of the fundamental principles of the Protestant Reformation was the recognition of the absolute supremacy of the Bible in faith and conduct. This sharply contrasted with Catholicism which contended that authority is vested in the church. Ultimately authority has its source in Christ, but the issue is whether Christ has revealed his will through the written word or through the church. "Jesus Christ is the same yesterday and today and for ever" (Hebrews 13:8). But the witness of the church as demonstrated in Catholicism is constantly changing. What is regarded as truth today may not be tomorrow. If we must depend on the church—anybody's church—for authority, we can never hope to recover the Christianity which Jesus and his apostles gave to the world.

My Leader

As my Lord, Jesus is also my *leader*. Just before he was betrayed he took a basin and washed his disciples' feet. When he had finished he said, "Do you know what I have done to you? You call me Teacher and Lord; and you are right, for so I am. If I then, your Lord and teacher, have washed your feet, you also ought to wash one another's feet. For I have given you an example, that you also should do as I have done to you" (John 13:12-15). Observe that Jesus declared that because he was their Lord they should follow his example of service. His lordship not only implied his authority over them, but also required that they copy his pattern. Do I wish to know how to live an upright life in the midst of my daily frustrations? I have only to look to Jesus of whom it is said, "For to this you have been called because Christ also suffered for you, leaving you an example, that you should follow in his steps" (1 Peter 2:21).

My Master

My Lord is also the *master* of my life. Jesus warned his disciples, "Neither be called masters, for you have one master, the Christ" (Matthew 23:10). T accept him as my master implies that I will do what he asks of me without questioning. Jesus once inquired, "Why do you call me 'Lord, Lord,' and not do what I tell you?" (Luke 6:46). Of some professed followers he declared, "Not every one who says to me, 'Lord, Lord,' shall enter the kingdom of heaven, but he who does the will of my Father who is in heaven. On that day many will say to me, 'Lord, Lord, did we not prophesy in your name, and cast out demons in your name, and do many mighty works in your name?' And then will I declare to them, 'I never knew you; depart from me, you evildoers' " (Matthew 7:21-23). It is not enough for me to simply call Jesus, "Lord." To make him the Lord of my life I must be willing to do what he asks and go where he asks me to go.

> "I'll go where you want me to go, dear Lord,
> Over mountain, or plain, or sea;
> I'll say what you want me to say, dear Lord,
> I'll be what you want me to be."
>
> Mary Brown

My Ruler

The lordship of Jesus means that he is my *ruler*. In feudal times the chief lord was the king. Paul describes Jesus as "the blessed and only Sovereign, the King of kings and Lord of lords" (1 Timothy 6:15). God's people constitute a kingdom. Jesus identified the kingdom of God on earth as his church when he said to Peter, "I will build my church. . . . I will give you the keys of the kingdom of heaven" (Matthew 16:18, 19). The church is not a democracy, but a monarchy with Jesus Christ, the Lord of our lives, as its absolute king and ruler. This means that I must always be willing to accept his will, even when it contradicts my personal wishes. Once some Christians sought to dissuade Paul from going to Jerusalem, fearing that he would be imprisoned. Their fears were justified, but when it became apparent that it was God's will that Paul go to Jerusalem they said, "The will of the Lord be done" (Acts 21:14). Sometimes it is hard to accept the will of the Lord, especially when it seems that his wishes conflict with our plans, or perhaps when we are faced with difficulties we cannot understand. Still, he is our Lord and King, and to our Sovereign we must yield.

Denying the Lordship of Jesus

I have stressed the lordship of Jesus because of its vast implications as we seek to recover true Christianity in our modern age. We live in a day of *humanism* in which man proceeds on the assumption that he, unaided by the divine, can discover the answers to the secrets and problems of life. Although man was created in the image of God, man has reversed the roles and has sought to shape God in human form. In religion this humanism assumed the form of twentieth century *liberalism* which was in turn the outgrowth of the German *rationalism* of the last century. Essentially liberalism denies the reality of anything which cannot be scientifically demonstrated. Thus the supernatural is rejected. Many liberals deny that Jesus is the son of God, affirming only his human greatness. To them the Bible is not the word of God, although it contains elements of truth. The miracles recorded in the scriptures could not have occurred. The creation of Adam, the great flood, and the feeding of the five thousand by Jesus are myths or distortions.

But, we need to inquire, if those events recorded in the Bible did not actually occur, how can we accept with any certainty the teachings of Jesus as correct? The doctrine of Christ is so interwoven with the historical events of the Bible that it is virtually impossible to distinguish these happenings from the message. If the occurrences of the Bible are inaccurate at best and myths at worst, how can we separate the historical Jesus from the truths he proclaimed? The validity of Jesus' teaching rests squarely on his claim to be the son of God and his place in history as one who has been correctly represented in the gospels. If Jesus was not what he claimed to be, he is the greatest fraud in the history of the world and his teachings must be rejected as the boasting of a charlatan.

Some, realizing the bankruptcy of religious liberalism as a valid expression of true Christianity, have propounded a neo-orthodox existentialism. In essence this theology asserts that in the area of reason the Bible makes mistakes, but that it can nevertheless provide a valid religious experience in the area of human feeling. Practically speaking, it declares that facts are unimportant and that our relationship with God is determined on the basis of our inner feelings. This may take the form of some kind of subjective conversion experience which is quite unrelated to the specific message of Jesus Christ. It may assume the charismatic approach of one who wants to "get high on Jesus" without having any real knowledge of what Jesus demands of his disciples. This kind of religious subjectivism falls far short of revealing genuine Christianity because, like religious liberalism, it seeks solutions from within man himself rather than in the lordship of Jesus.

If we accept Jesus as Lord and acknowledge the validity of his claims, we will then regard his teachings as coming from God. True Christianity is a revealed religion in which man seeks divine solutions to human problems instead of searching for the answers purely from a human perspective. Humanism, in whatever form it appears, gives no absolutes. It teaches that what is right today may be wrong tomorrow because truth is always variable. The so-called new morality or situation ethics which denies that an action can be always right or wrong is an extension of that philosophy. But the Christian who is committed to the lordship of Jesus believes that because God knows what is right and has given us absolute truth, we can always know that certain things are right or wrong. True, we may have difficulty in knowing how to apply the principles and sometimes we will make mistakes because of our human frailties. But the solutions to the problems are there, revealed to us in the word of God.

To accept the lordship of Jesus, therefore, is to acknowledge the absolute supremacy of his authority as revealed to us in the written word, and having acknowledged it, to let Jesus govern our lives, trusting him completely as one who truly knows what is best. We can recover genuine Christianity only if we have a prior commitment to the lordship of Jesus. For as Peter informed those Jews who had earlier demanded the life of Jesus, truly Jesus is "both Lord and Christ" (Acts 2:36).

CHAPTER 4

The Restoration Principle

Imagine finding a description of treasure telling where you can locate 90 tons of gold and silver buried in 64 places! It is inscribed on a badly oxidized copper scroll which must be meticulously cut in strips before the message can be deciphered. Add to this the likelihood that the treasure has never been found. You have all the elements of an intriguing mystery that would send a confirmed treasure hunter around the world in quest of the prize.

The treasure "map" exists. The only problem is that in the 19 centuries that have elapsed since it was made, the places mentioned have been so obscured that it is unlikely that the gold and silver will ever be found. The copper roll was discovered in 1952. It was in a cave overlooking the Dead Sea among the famed Dead Sea Scrolls which have cast so much light on the Old Testament scriptures and the times of Jesus. Interestingly, the copper manuscript seems unrelated to those other writings. It is thought that it **may reveal** where the Jews hid the treasure of Herod's Temple when **the fall of** Jerusalem to the Romans was imminent near the close of the first century. The mystery will probably never be solved and our curiosities must be content to speculate about the missing pieces.

Treasure in the Temple

About 700 years before that temple treasure was hidden, another treasure was found in Solomon's Temple. The king of Judah at the time was Josiah, one of the best kings ever to rule over God's chosen people. He ascended the throne of David when he was only a boy. His rule followed the wicked reigns of his father, Amon, and his grandfather, Manasseh. Beyond doubt Manasseh was the worst king in the history of Judah. For most of his fifty-five years on the throne he turned the people from Jehovah to the depravity of Canaanitish worship. He venerated Baal and Asherah and even burned his own sons as an offering to the god Molech.

It was little wonder that the worship of Jehovah was totally corrupted when Josiah began his reign. When he was old enough to evaluate the situation he instituted a series of reforms designed to bring the people back to God. One of his acts was to authorize the repair of the temple. One day while this work was being done, Hilkiah, the high priest, found an unidentified document. It was probably in a corner, covered with dust. What could it be? The blueprints of the temple, perhaps? Investigation revealed something far more precious. Here indeed was a treasure. It was not, to be sure, a hidden hoard of gold and silver. This was a spiritual treasure revealing the solution to the ills of the nation. It was the book of God's law. So complete had been the apostasy of Judah during the 57 years that Manasseh and Amon turned the people's hearts from God that even their great spiritual guidebook, the Law of Moses, had been lost!

Hilkiah at once realized the importance of this discovery. He sent the book to Josiah to whom the secretary read the words of God. The king was so distraught at what he heard that he tore his clothes. He ordered his officials to consult the Lord through a prophet to determine the penalty for Judah's continued violation of the law. For, you see, it was only when the lost book was read that Josiah fully realized how completely his people had departed from God. He immediately instituted a great reform. It was much more than a reform; it was an effort to truly restore the worship of Jehovah to Israel. From the corners of the small kingdom the leaders of the people were summoned and in the presence of all the law was read. Then, using the book of the law as his pattern, Josiah set out to make the service of Judah conform to what was written. He knew that only by returning to the original, the true treasure, could the purity of Judaism be recovered.

In a sense we today confront the same problem faced by good King Josiah. True, we do not live amidst pagan idolatry. It may be plausibly reasoned that what passes for Christianity should not be compared to the excesses that Manasseh introduced among his people. Yet it would be difficult to deny that the face of Christianity today differs sharply from that described in the New Testament. Not only do the outward forms contrast, but the inner spirit which prompted the first Christians to lay down their lives for the Lord when called upon to do so is seldom seen. As with Josiah, if we are to recover the early Christian faith, we must seek to restore the original.

Is Restoration Desirable?

The concept of *restoration,* sometimes called *restitution,* is not new. There are many examples of restoration efforts in the history of Christianity. Before further exploring the ideal, however, we ought to consider whether restoration is really desirable in today's society.

Some people feel that the divided state of the religious world is not necessarily bad because it provides an opportunity for each one to find his own niche. It is reasoned that there is so much variety that anybody can discover some brand of the Christian faith to suit his needs. The most important thing is finding people and ideas with which one can feel comfortable. This approach makes truth secondary to one's personal desires. But Christianity is by nature based on the primacy of truth, and that can never rightly be relegated to an inferior position. Moreover, the true church of Jesus Christ is sufficiently broad to include those of every race, culture, and social status, even as the early Christians were drawn from every walk of life. Different congregations may have different personalities reflecting the diverse backgrounds of those who compose them. However, the truth taught by all ought to be the same.

Others believe that Christianity should be continually modified to reflect the ever-changing needs of our day. Our scientific knowledge greatly surpasses that of the first century. Life is far more complicated in the nuclear age. The teachings of Jesus were largely directed to an agrarian society and illiterate people. They must be altered to fit the demands of our century. In response it must be acknowledged that our circumstances vary greatly from biblical times. There is a whole host of devices that the devil has dreamed up to lead human beings astray. We confront many ethical questions that have been recently introduced by current scientific technology. For some of them the answers are not found in so many words in the New Testament. It is easy to understand how some feel that Christianity should be updated rather than restored.

Before evaluating this approach we must first seek the answer to another question: *What is Christianity?* If the Christian faith is of human origin, it is hard to defend the ideal of returning to the original. No human philosophy was ever perfect. Therefore, since Christianity was imperfect in its conception, it must continually be altered to meet changing conditions.

On the other hand, Christianity claims to be of divine origin. Paul stated, "For I would have you know, brethren, that the gospel which was preached by me is not man's gospel. For I did not receive it from man, nor was I taught it, but it came through a revelation from Jesus Christ" (Galatians 1:11, 12). The book you are reading is based on the presupposition that the Christian faith is from God. We shall, therefore, proceed on the supposition that Christianity is divinely conceived, and that we are dealing with God-given principles which, being perfect, never need updating. God is all-knowing, and those maxims which come from him can never be improved. Certainly the application of divine truth varies from time to time and culture to culture, but the principles themselves remain unchanged. They are valid in every age, but must be individually applied by Christians to the immediate circumstances. Unlike the Law of Moses, Jesus does not give us a lawbook of specifics that directs one to a given page and paragraph for every detailed condition. Rather we have a guidebook of broad principles adaptable to living situations. Of course, there are specifics relating both to the church and to ethics. These must be observed. However, in some areas human judgment is involved. Two Christians will disagree on how the scriptures should be applied. It is vital that we seek answers from the revealed word, even when we disagree, rather than allowing personal desires to control our actions.

Is there, then, truly a need to restore apostolic Christianity? If it is of divine origin, it cannot be improved. When man departs from divine truths, they must be restored. Thus, Christianity by its very nature as a religion of divine origin validates the restoration principle.

The desirability of restoration can be illustrated in this way. Cannot all Christians agree that the golden rule (Matthew 7:12) is (1) not being widely followed, and (2) its use needs to be restored? While this is in the ethical realm, it at least establishes the desirability of restoring some elements of the religion of Jesus.

Is Restoration Biblical?

Is the idea of restoration really biblical? The restoration concept is based on the supposition that some vital truth has been lost. So long as a people is truly following the will of God there is no need for restoration. Also, in order to restore something there must first be some kind of pattern to follow. We must first search for the pattern, and when we find it, try to discover whether there are biblical examples of men returning to the divine model.

In the Old Testament there are numerous instances of patterns being given to the people of God. The Law of Moses was itself a pattern. Even the specifics of the building of the tabernacle and its furnishings were spelled out. "And see that you make them after the pattern for them, which is being shown you on the mountain" (Exodus 25:40). Jesus alluded to the scrupulous way in which the scribes and Pharisees carried out the Mosaic pattern. He said, "Woe to you, scribes and Pharisees, hypocrites! for you tithe mint and dill and cummin, and have neglected the weightier matters of the law, justice and mercy and faith; these you ought to have done, without neglecting the others" (Matthew 23:23). These Jews were so meticulous in their pattern keeping that they even gave 10 percent of their spices. Jesus' condemnation, it should be noted, was not that they carried out the tithing pattern, but that they failed to observe the spiritual aspect of God's law.

In the New Testament the importance of the scriptures as a divine guideline is stressed by Paul. "All scripture is inspired by God and profitable for teaching, for reproof, for correction, and for training in righteousness, that the man of God may be complete, equipped for every good work" (2 Timothy 3:16, 17). There are also warnings against any alteration of God's revealed message. Consider a few. "I am astonished that you are so quickly deserting him who called you in the grace of Christ and turning to a different gospel—not that there is another gospel, but there are some who trouble you and want to pervert the gospel of Christ. But even if we, or an angel from heaven, should preach to you a gospel contrary to that which we preached to you, let him be accursed. As we have said before, so now I say again, if any one is preaching to you a gospel contrary to that which you received, let him be accursed" (Galatians 1:6-9). "Any one who goes ahead and does not abide in the doctrine of Christ does not have God; he who abides in the doctrine has both the Father and the Son" (2 John 9). "I warn every one who hears the words of the prophecy of this book: if any one adds to them, God will add to him the plagues described in this book, and if any one takes away from the words of the book of his prophecy, God will take away his share of the tree of life and in the holy city, which are described in this book" (Revelation 22:18, 19).

Since the New Testament was then in the process of being written, these passages are not cited as teaching that it is wrong to change the New Testament as an entity. The point is that the will of God, whatever it is and however revealed, cannot be changed by us without divine approval. "For who has known the mind of the Lord, or who has been his counselor?" (Romans 11:34). God has given us a pattern to follow. Today our sole source of knowledge of its nature is found in the Bible.

An example of the pattern idea is found in Paul's first letter to Timothy. In chapter one he discusses doctrinal matters, in chapter two worship, and in chapter three church organization. Then he admonishes Timothy, "I hope to come to you soon, but I am writing these instructions to you so that, if I am delayed, you may know how one ought to behave in the household of God, which is the church of the living God, the pillar and bulwark of the truth" (1 Timothy 3:14, 15). In effect Paul is declaring that his divinely revealed writings constitute a pattern for the family of God.

Having discovered divine patterns in both testaments, it remains for us to determine if there are also biblical examples of the restoration principle. In the Old Testament the time span from the writing of the books of Moses to Malachi, the last of the prophets, was several centuries. In that period Israel often departed from God. When this happened there were always efforts to bring the nation back. The restoration of Josiah, already mentioned, was one of these (2 Kings 22:3-23:25). Hezekiah, the great-grandfather of Josiah, also instituted one of the greatest restoration efforts during his reign (2 Kings 18:1-6). One of the primary functions of the prophets was to cause God's wandering people to return to the old paths laid out by Moses. Jeremiah cried out to Judah, "Thus says the Lord: 'Stand by the roads, and look, and ask for the ancient paths, where the good way is; and walk in it, and find rest for your souls' " (Jeremiah 6:16). Ezekiel, prophet of the exile, went even further and spelled out details of an anticipated restoration when the Jews should return to their homeland (Ezekiel 40-48).

In the New Testament Jesus introduced the restoration concept in discussing divorce. When his disciples inquired about the Jewish practice of putting away wives "for any cause," Jesus called them back to the pre-Mosaic ethic as authority for his teaching (Matthew 19:3-9). In denouncing the scribes and Pharisees he showed the need to restore the spirit of the Law of Moses, while not denying that the letter of the law in which the spirit was expressed was essential (Matthew 23). He was calling them back to the true meaning of the system under which they lived. These people were Jews, subject before God to the Law of Moses. We, on the other hand, are subject to the teachings of Jesus and the apostles whom he commissioned.

An examination of the Acts of the Apostles and the epistles does not reveal a call to return to pure Christianity because what is presented in these books is the model itself. But clearly, the restoration principle is set forth in the New Testament as well as in the Old.

Presuppositions

Every system of thought has underlying presuppositions. This means that there are always certain fundamental ideas upon which the philosophy rests. The presuppositions are assumed rather than proved. This may be because they are incapable of proof, or perhaps all believers in the ideology accept them unquestioningly. The Moslem proceeds on the premise that Mohammed was the prophet of God. The atheist denies that the Bible is God's word because he first of all rejects the idea of a supreme being. The Christian, on the other hand, assumes that there is a God and may spend little or no time trying to establish that this is true.

Acceptance of the restoration principle hinges on several presuppositions. Not everyone will acknowledge their validity. Failure to grant the presuppositions will lead to rejection of the restoration approach to Christianity. The scope of this book is not broad enough to discuss these presuppositions in detail, but we should at least be aware of them.

First, Christians are bound by the authority of Jesus in their faith and practice. In the previous chapter we studied the lordship of Jesus and observed that because he is our Lord he is also our leader, master, ruler, and authority. On this basis Jesus informed his apostles in the Great Commission, "All authority in heaven and on earth has been given to me," (Matthew 28:18). Until recently few have questioned the authority of Jesus in spiritual matters.

Second, the New Testament as we know it is the sole expression of the authority of Jesus in our day. Here we encounter more disagreement. In the early days of the church the authority of the apostles (who taught by the sanction of Christ) was expressed both orally and in writing. At first their teaching was totally oral since the twenty-seven New Testament books remained to be written. In time inspired men put these teachings on paper and these came to constitute a permanent record of what the Holy Spirit desired that we know. Should Peter or Paul appear on the scene today we would be bound to accept their inspired oral utterances as having as much authority as their writings. But Peter and Paul are not with us in the flesh. We do, however, have their writings along with those of other inspired men of God, and these constitute God's message for us.

This presupposition necessarily excludes several things. It denies that there have been latter-day prophets like Joseph Smith or Mary Baker Eddy to whom God has privately revealed his will. It denies that authority reposes in the church giving it the right to change fundamental teachings at will or to reveal some new principle as vital truth. And it denies that God subjectively reveals additional truths in a personal way to each individual.

Third, the New Testament reveals a pattern of Christianity and of the church to be restored. Some concede that the ethical facets of faith should be restored, but they also deny that the picture of the early church described in the New Testament is clear enough to make its restoration possible. The position taken here is that we should seek to restore Christianity in its totality rather than limiting restoration to morals.

What Should Be Restored

If one believes that the Christian religion is from God, the real question is not whether the restoration principle is valid, but what elements of primitive Christianity should be restored. Some point to flaws in early local churches and inquire if we propose to restore these defects. The Corinthian congregation was plagued with divisiveness and immorality. Even the great Jerusalem church had its Ananias and Sapphira, and soon had to cope with disunity. There were no perfect congregations in apostolic days. While the universal church was perfectly constituted by our Lord, it has always been composed of human beings with all their frailties. The divine part of the church is perfect; the human part is not. The divine construction is described by Paul: "You are fellow citizens with the saints and members of the household of God, built upon the foundation of the apostles and prophets, Christ Jesus himself being the cornerstone, in whom the whole structure is joined together and grows into a holy temple of the Lord" (Ephesians 2:19-21). It was the human element that prevented early congregations of Christ from attaining the ideal. There is, however, an ideal church which emerges from the scriptures. If we are told that some of the early Christians quarreled among themselves, we also learn that Jesus desires only love and peace and harmony in the spiritual body. If some abused the Lord's supper, and they did, the scriptures also clearly point out how the sacred meal should be eaten (1 Corinthians 11:17-32). It is the ideal from the New Testament which we are to seek in our restoration effort.

In restoring the apostolic pattern we must consider the relationship between the principles of Jesus and the culture from which the Christian faith emerged. Christianity appeared on the world scene at a particular time and place in history. Had it been the will of God, Jesus could have been born in our day and in our land. Since it was not his will, "*When the time had fully come,* God sent forth his Son, born of woman, born under the law, to redeem those who were under the law, so that we might receive adoption as sons" (Galatians 4:4, 5).

Jesus was born a Jew. Though he often condemned the ways and attitudes of his people, he lived according to Jewish custom. He was raised in a Roman world, in a culture greatly influenced by Greek thought. The external aspects of primitive Christianity reflect Jewish, Greek, and Roman influence. Similarly, contemporary Christianity necessarily mirrors the customs and habits of those who embrace it, whether they be American, European, African, or Asiatic.

In our restoration quest we must seek to filter out the cultural aspects of early Christianity from those elements which are the essence of the revealed faith. The Christian faith was set in the culture and mores of the first century. That the early Christians may have dressed in long robes is unrelated to how we should be attired. In biblical times the kiss was the customary form of greeting; in most Western nations today it is the handshake. Kissing as a greeting then was a part of the culture, not vital Christianity. When Peter wrote that the disciples should "greet one another with the kiss of love" (1 Peter 5:14), he was not ordering that kissing be made a church ordinance, but that our greetings should be in the spirit of love. Kissing was a custom; greeting in the proper spirit is the principle that applies to us.

We must also avoid the mistake of trying to restore incidental things. We are given several specific facts about Paul's visit to the church in Troas (Acts 20:5-12). (1) The disciples assembled on the first day of the week. (2) They met in a third story room. (3) There were many lights in this place. (4) The purpose of the assembly was to partake of the Lord's supper. The location of the assembly and the lights were obvious incidentals. We would misapply the restoration principle to require men to worship God only on the third floor with the lights on! Yet the context of the passage also indicates that the breaking of bread (the Lord's supper) was carried out by intent and served as the focus of their worship. This was not an incidental. Neither was the day of worship since this chapter, coupled with other evidence in the New Testament, shows that the first day assembly was by design and represented the practice of Christians of that period.

Since the New Testament is not a big lawbook spelling out specifics in creedal form, the search for pure Christianity is not simple. The New Testament is a collection of biographies, history, and personal writings given by the inspiration of the Holy Spirit from which must be distilled those truths which ought to govern the people of God in every age. We will next consider how others have sought to achieve this goal through the centuries.

CHAPTER 5

Surveying the Past

It was in the year 1054 that three legates of Pope Leo IX came to Constantinople to try to heal a major breach within Catholicism. For several centuries a great schism had been developing between Greek and Latin churches. In fact, a complete rupture nearly came in the eighth and ninth centuries during the iconoclastic controversy. This had to do with whether images should be worshipped and even resulted in the Roman Pope and the Patriarch of Constantinople excommunicating one another. However, the difficulties were temporarily assuaged and for another two hundred years East and West tenuously held together.

The crack between the two parts of the Catholic Church continued to widen. New issues were injected into the fray. Should unleavened bread be used in communion? Should clerical celibacy be enforced? Should milk, butter, and cheese be used during the week of Quadragesima? Should the "Hallelujah" be omitted from the liturgy during Lent? To further his own ambitions, Michael Cerularius, Patriarch of Constantinople, provoked a confrontation with the Pope. The latter, in turn, sent his emissaries to Constantinople to seek a solution to the controversy. However, their attitudes were so insolent that Cerularius refused to make any concessions or even to negotiate. Finally, in retaliation on July 16th the papal representatives, on behalf of the Roman Pope, laid on the altar of the Church of St. Sophia a bull of excommunication of the Patriarch "and his followers, guilty of the above mentioned errors and insolences . . . along with all heretics, together with the devil and his angels."[1]

The Patriarch immediately convened a counsel of his own which excommunicated the papal legates and their sympathizers. The final break had come. The Catholic Church was now irreparably divided into two parts represented today by Roman Catholicism and Eastern Orthodoxy.

How did all of this come about? How could the prayer of Jesus for unity be so subverted that men would divide over such things as whether milk, butter, and cheese should be eaten during Lent? How, for that matter, did the religious world get in the condition in which it finds itself today?

To find the answers we need to briefly sketch the history of the Christian faith to the present. Even before the close of the apostolic age disruptive forces were at work in the church. Jewish and Gentile conflict erupted in the circumcision controversy. The disagreement was largely settled at the Jerusalem conference involving the apostles (Acts 15). Later, Gnosticism, an alien philosophy built around the idea of salvation by mystical knowledge, so influenced the thinking of some that John had to denounce the ideology (1 John 2:18, 19; 4:1-3). In spite of these factors, it appears that when John, the last of the apostles, died around the year 100 the Christian faith was largely unchanged and general unity prevailed.

Christianity Spreads

The next two centuries saw tremendous numerical growth. The gospel covered the Roman Empire and extended far beyond its limits. The Christians' zeal was fanned by persecution and martyrdom as thousands died for their faith in periodic Roman persecutions. When the Emperor Diocletian began the final imperial effort to exterminate the Christian faith at the beginning of the fourth century, perhaps as much as one-tenth of the populace was Christian. But the terrible persecution was not to succeed. Just a few years later in 313 a new emperor, Constantine, issued the Edict of Milan which recognized Christianity as lawful. In 392 pagan worship was made illegal. Christianity was now the state religion. It was popular to be a Christian and thousands embraced the faith. The battle had been won!

But had it? Christianity had been spread by people of conviction. When persecutions ceased, so did much of the dedication. With paganism forcibly stamped out the world embraced the church. The bride of Christ was compromised as many people without doctrinal or moral convictions nominally subscribed to the tenets of the Christian faith. History has repeatedly demonstrated that Christianity can never remain pure so long as it is in alliance with the world as represented by the state.

Internal Controversies

Although the church outwardly prospered during the second and third centuries, there were serious internal doctrinal difficulties. A group of Jewish Christians called Ebionites, mixing elements of Judaism with Christianity, gradually separated themselves from the mainstream. Gnosticism became so widely diffused among the congregations that for several centuries it threatened to stifle Christianity. Its lasting influence in the church became apparent in more elaborate liturgical worship, asceticism, veneration of the saints, and worship of the virgin Mary, the counterpart of Sophia of Gnosticism.

In the mid-second century Montanus, a former heathen priest, appeared in Phrygia to promote a purported band of Christianity which became known as Montanism. In some ways his followers were orthodox. They even emphasized some aspects of the faith neglected by others. They were dedicated to the point of ascetisism, but they also laid undue stress on prophecy. They looked for a new Jerusalem in the village of Pepuza in Phrygia, accepted Montanus as the instrument through which the Holy Spirit promised by Jesus spoke, and went into ecstatic visions and wild frenzies. Naturally they provoked great opposition.

Besides Gnosticism, the third century saw other pagan influences on Christianity. Neo-Platonism, Manichaeism, and Mithraism affected the thinking of the church. Other controversies dealt with the natue of God and the relationship of the Father, Son, and Holy Spirit. The most serious was the Arian heresy which denied the Trinity.

Beginning of Creeds

These controversial teachings prompted changes in the church. Some felt that the church was obliged to set up standards which would be acknowledged by anyone claiming to be a Christian. From this there came the first creed which, by the fourth century, was recited by candidates for baptism. Its earliest known form is *The Old Roman Symbol* which was later revised as *The Apostles' Creed,* although it was not authored by the apostles. The ancient Greek rendition is as follows:

"I believe in God Almighty; and in Christ Jesus, his only Son, our Lord, who was born from the Holy Spirit and the virgin Mary, who under Pontius Pilate was crucified and buried and on the third day rose again from the dead, ascended into heaven, and sits at the right hand of the Father, whence he is coming to judge the living and the dead; and in the Holy Spirit, the holy Church, forgiveness of sins, the resurrection of the flesh, life eternal."[2]

This confession, with which most Christians could agree today, posed a problem in that it became the precursor of other human creeds which were regarded as religiously binding. The Nicene Creed soon followed, and whenever there was a major dispute, a church council would convene to issue another creed stating the official position of the church. The collective decisions of men, rather than of God, became authoritative.

Organizational Changes

The threat of doctrinal error was also a factor in another change beginning in the second century. This related to church organization. In apostolic times each independent congregation was shepherded by a group of men called elders or overseers (bishops). They were assisted by servants known as deacons. Early in the second century this began to change, partly by way of containing false teachers who were spreading their insidious doctrines. Soon a distinction was made in the congregation between the plurality of elders and a single overseer or bishop. The bishop came to be regarded as an authority figure rather than a shepherd of the flock. Early in the second century Ignatius of Antioch set forth these ideas and in seven letters which have been preserved, he seemed almost obsessed with the authority of the bishop. Typical is a comment addressed to the Trallians:

"For when ye are obedient to the bishop as to Jesus Christ, it is evident to me that ye are living not after men but after Jesus Christ, who died for us, that believing on His death ye might escape death. It is therefore necessary, even as your wont is that ye should do nothing without the bishop; but be ye obedient also to the presbytery, as to the Apostles of Jesus Christ our hope. . . .

"In like manner let all men respect the deacons as Jesus Christ, even as they should respect the bishop as being a type of the Father and the presbyters as the council of God and as the college of Apostles. Apart from these there is not even the name of a church."[3]

It is easy to see how such an authoritarian bishop could effectively combat heresy. By maintaining dictatorial control he could exclude all false teachers. This method was augmented by the development of the doctrine of apostolic succession which held that only those tracing a line of authority back to the apostles could pronounce on the authenticity of apostolic tradition.

The New Testament concept of congregational participation is that of a brotherhood in which each Christian has distinct functions to discharge. Quite obviously Ignatius saw it otherwise. His writings clearly mirror a developing clergy-laity relationship in which all functions are controlled by the clergy.

The church rapidly developed an organization paralleling the Roman government. The bishops of the major cities extended their authority to adjoining communities and it was not long before each province had but a single bishop. While all bishops were theoretically equal, practically speaking those in the larger cities exerted the greatest influence. they were called metropolitan bishops or patriarchs, and much later, archbishops. Much of this development came in the fourth and fifth centuries. By the time of the Council of Nicea the dignity of the metropolitan was recognized, and his consent was required in choosing an ordinary bishop. That conference recognized the bishops of Rome, Alexandria, and Antioch as superior metropolitans of equal stature. Later councils added the bishops of Constantinople and Jerusalem to that exalted position. Although the Roman bishop was held in deference by virtue of his location in the capital of the empire, the authority of the Pope was by no means yet established.

The threat of heresy posed the question of how orthodoxy should be determined. The bishops did not always agree. Accordingly the Emperor Constantine convoked the first universal church council in Nicea in 325, although some geographic areas were not represented. Other councils at Constantinople and Chalcedon followed. Compromises were reached and creeds hammered out. Bishops, councils, creeds—the church was well on its way to becoming an ecclesiastical hierarchy replacing the simple structure of the early church.

Doctrinal Innovations

Doctrinal changes accompanied the structural modifications. Many of these were so gradual that they were largely unrecognized.

Others provoked strong controversy. It is hard to pinpoint the inception of some of these teachings and practices. Our chief interest is in observing that many changes did occur over the course of the centuries.

Baptism is a case in point. The original form of baptism was immersion. In fact, the Greek word from which baptize comes means to immerse. The first documented case of sprinkling or pouring as a substitute related to Novatian, who in the mid-third century had water poured on him in his sick bed. This came to be called clinical baptism which was administered only in the case of extreme illness. Later Novatian's right to serve as a bishop was challenged because of his baptism. It was many years before affusion was generally substituted for immersion.

The first unambiguous reference to infant baptism appears early in the third century in the writings of Tertullian who opposed the practice. The doctrine of original sin, the rationale for infant baptism, came a few years later. Origen became the chief proponent of this theory which holds that we are born with the guilt of Adam's sin and that the one who dies without baptism, even if an infant, is lost because of that guilt.

Mandatory celibacy for the clergy is mentioned in the Catholic *Question Box* as having first been enforced in Spain about the year 300.[4] The practice was never universally adopted, especially among the eastern churches.

Praying for the dead seems to have originated in the fourth century. Some references in the church fathers are susceptible to more than one interpretation and documentation is difficult. Belief in purgatory accompanied this practice, for, if prayer for the dead is of value, there must be a place where the objects of those prayers are found.

Doctrinal changes relating to the Lord's supper were gradual. They included the teaching of transubstantiation (the bread and wine are changed into the literal flesh and blood of Christ) and the Mass (the sacrifice of Christ is reenacted in an unbloody way.)

As multitudes of pagan converts sought substitutes for their old habits, the veneration of saints became widespread. Martyrs were canonized. The practice of praying *for* the saints was altered to pray *to* them. Thinking that the relics of martyrs possessed miraculous powers, Christians eagerly sought them in order to receive God's blessings. The adoration of Mary, the mother of Jesus, exceeded the veneration of the saints and in time amounted to worship. It was thought that she remained a perpetual virgin after the birth of Jesus, and that she was the "mother of God." Eventually believers began to pray to God through Mary as a mediator.

Gradually a sacramental theology evolved. It was taught that in addition to baptism God requires certain human actions through which he bestows special blessings. At an early date the Lord's supper was thought of this way. Centuries later the number of sacraments was officially fixed at seven by the addition of confirmation, extreme unction, penance, marriage, and ordination.

Other doctrinal changes were introduced. Special festivals and holy days were adopted. As a clerical system emerged, the clergy began wearing priestly garments. After the Council of Nicea the confessional was incorporated into church life.

These theological concepts and practices developed over a long period of time. Some were not officially sanctioned by Catholicism for a thousand years. Typically the germ of an idea in the second or third centuries would be enlarged and refined by the scholars of the Middle Ages until it grew into a full-fledged theology.

What was this church when persecution ceased at the beginning of the fourth century? Was it still the church of which we read in the Bible, or had it already evolved into the Catholic Church of later centuries? *Catholic* simply means *universal*. Ignatius applied it to the body of Christ early in the second century. Its use was widespread by the end of the century. At first the word was used generically to designate the universal body of believers. In time it distinguished the main body of Christians from the heretics. Eventually "Catholic" was adopted as a proper name, and after the schism between East and West is signified the Greek Catholic or the Roman Catholic Church as the case might be.

Organizationally the church, prior to the council of Nicea, rapidly developed an ecclesiastical system, but as yet there was no papacy. Doctrinal changes were numerous, but in some ways the church of this period was closer to apostolic Christianity than to medieval Catholicism. The church was in a transition. The Romans had a deity named Janus whose two faces pointed in opposite directions. Similarly, as one historian suggests, the church had one face pointed back toward apostolic Christianity and the other toward Catholicism.[5]

The Papacy

The rise of the papacy completed the transformation of early Christianity into Catholicism. The Council of Nicea had designated the bishop of Rome as one of three superior metropolitans. In time the Roman bishop and the Patriarch of Constantinople became the chief rivals for supremacy. Practically, the power of the Roman bishopric was enhanced by its location, and when the empire fell it was the only available authority to fill the political vacuum. Theoretically, the claim of the Roman church stemmed from the belief that Peter and Paul had established it and that Peter was supposedly its first bishop. Leo the Great, bishop from 440-461, spelled out the papal concept, claiming authority for the Roman pontiff through Peter. To claim power and to have others acknowledge it, however, were two different things. In 451 the Council of Chalcedon voted the Patriarch of Constantinople the chief bishop of the entire church, much to the displeasure of Leo.

The date of papal domination is hard to fix. It can probably be said that by about 600 the Roman Pope was generally acknowledged as head of the church except among those eastern churches where the influence of the Patriarch of Constantinople loomed large. The conflict between Rome and Constantinople described at the beginning of this chapter resulted from the power struggle between these two ecclesiastical forces.

The Middle Ages

With the fall of Rome in 476 the Roman Empire technically ended, although it had been disintegrating for a hundred years. The next thousand years were the Middle Ages with the earlier part of that period called the Dark Ages. Roman civilization came to an end and with it much of the accumulated knowledge of the centuries was lost. The comforts which were so much a part of Roman life disappeared. Life was hard and some fled to monasteries to escape. Within a few hundred years political Europe was dominated by the feudal system.

The Dark Ages was a time of great spiritual decline. Knowledge of the Bible was hidden in the recesses of the monasteries. Even the clergy was ignorant of the scriptures. In the ninth and tenth centuries the papacy became the pawn of Italian nobles. The faction that controlled Rome chose the Pope. It was a period of religious anarchy. The degradation of the day is illustrated in the person of Pope Formosus (891-896). After his death his remains were exhumed by the order of his enemy and successor, Stephen III. Dressed in his pontifical vestments he was given a mock trial. He was condemned, stripped of his robes, the three fingers with which he gave the papal blessing were chopped off, and his body was consigned to the Tiber River.

Moral standards greatly declined. Many of the popes had illegitimate children. Their actions reflected the general condition of the clergy. Simony, the practice of buying and selling church offices, became the rule. Unfortunately the light of true Christianity had been so diminished that few knew the difference.

Catholicism Divides

In the midst of these turbulent times the division of 1054 occurred within Catholicism. Rome's domination had never been absolute. From the earliest days some churches outside the Roman Empire had maintained an independent existence. The churches of the East aligned, with the Patriarch of Constantinople, suffered greatly with the continuing advance of Mohammedanism. Ultimately, Constantinople itself fell in 1453 to the forces of the Moslem Ottoman Empire. The sphere of influence of Orthodox Christianity was largely reduced to Russia and the Balkan area of Eastern Europe.

Portents of Reform

Throughout the Middle Ages there were numerous dissidents who challenged Catholicism. To combat heresy the Fourth Lateran Council of the Roman Catholic Church instituted the Inquisition in 1215. This provided that those accused of false teaching would be ferreted out and tried by the church. If found guilty they would be turned over to the state for punishment or death, often by burning. Since the source of much disquiet among the populace was the reading of the Bible by the educated, the Council of Toulouse in 1229 prohibited the laity to possess the scriptures. This rather local prohibition was soon extended to other places.

History reveals that truth cannot be permanently surpressed by force. The revival of learning during the Renaissance prompted a renewed study of the ancient writings, including the Bible. Few translations into the language of the people had yet been made. The Latin Vulgate version of Jerome was the official Bible of Catholicism. In 1384 John Wyclif translated the scriptures into English. He also expressed his dissenting theological views in numerous writings. The Lollards, his disciples, spread his views across England. Soon other translations into different tongues were made. The Englishman, John Tyndale, was burned at the stake in 1536 for daring to produce his version of the Bible. With the development of printing by John Gutenberg in the 1450's, it became possible to greatly multiply copies of the scriptures. Had it not been for the great proliferation of the word of God made possible by the printing press the Protestant Reformation would have progressed more slowly. In spite of the prohibitions of Catholicism, the Bible was read.

Wyclif's writings influenced a Bohemian priest, John Huss, who lead a reformatory effort in what is now Czechoslovakia. This was the time of the Great Schism in which two rival popes presided over the Catholic Church for forty years. The Council of Pisa in 1409 deposed both popes and elected a third. Unfortunately, neither of the others would step down so now Catholicism had three infallible popes anathematizing one another! To settle the problem the Council of Constance was convened in 1414. Into this seething caldron of controversy John Huss was summoned to account for his teachings. The emperor promised him safe conduct to Constance. The promise was not honored and Huss was arrested, tried, and burned at the stake. His martyrdom hardened the determination of the Bohemians to promote more aggressively the principles for which he died. The Council of Constance deposed all three popes and healed the schism, but it also paved the way for the Reformation by trying to stamp out principles by force. In another 100 years Protestantism would change the face of Europe.

The Protestant Reformation

The Reformation was inevitable. Its direction was determined by the forces and personalities that shaped it, but had they been different there still would have been a reformation. Truth can be forcibly suppressed only so long. The longer it is held down, the more violent its eruption.

The term *Protestant* originated with a formal protest by 19 German states against a governmental edict in 1529 restricting reformatory efforts in Germany. It came to be applied to all reformers who protested against the abuses of Catholicism and who eventually separated from the Roman Catholic Church.

The Protestant Reformation had four main fountainheads—distinct, and yet interrelated. All begun in Europe with 17 years. The movements were the Lutheran, Reformed, Anabaptist, and Angelican. For the most part they arose from within Catholicism as reformatory efforts and culminated in complete separation from the Catholic Church. Responding to these efforts was a Counter Reformation within Catholicism which aimed at correcting the most flagrant perversions. The leading spirit of the Counter Reformation was Eramus, a contemporary of Martin Luther. While sympathetic to many of the aims of the Protestant Reformation, Eramus thought separation from the Catholic body was a mistake.

Lutheranism

The Reformation dates from October 31, 1517, when Martin Luther, German monk and professor at the University of Wittenberg, issued his famous Ninety-five Theses in which he proposed debate on some of the abuses of Catholicism. The immediate object of his attack was the sale of indulgences to raise money to build St. Peter's Cathedral in Rome. He stressed the importance of the scriptures as sole spiritual authority. His continued study caused him to reject the idea of salvation by works and to accept Paul's teaching of justification by faith. His writings ignited a fuse that shook the religious and political world. For his supposedly heretical ideas he was ordered to recant his teachings. When he refused he was excommunicated by the church. Ordinarily he would have been burned at the stake, but Frederick the Wise, Elector of Saxony where Luther lived, protected him. His teachings became the dominant religious force in Northern Germany and the Scandinavian countries. In most of these places Lutheranism was made the state religion.

The Reformed Movement

Contemporary with Luther was Ulrich Zwingli, another Catholic priest who led a Swiss reformation from his home city of Zurich. The two men had much in common, but differed in emphasis. Luther was vitally concerned about the biblical conception of salvation; Zwingli's greatest interest was in conforming to the will of God. Their greatest difference related to the Lord's supper. Luther held to the Catholic position of the real presence of Christ in the elements; Zwingli viewed the Lord's supper as a memorial. Their failure to reconcile their views prevented a union of the two forces.

Their approaches to the scriptures also resulted in different treatment of other matters. Luther retained images, altars, ornaments of the churches, and organs because he did not find them condemned in the Bible. Zwingli rejected these same things because he did not find them authorized. D'Aubigne focuses on their contrasting attitudes in this way:

"Luther was desirous of retaining in the Church all that was not expressly contradicted by Scripture,—while Zwingle was intent on abolishing all that could not be proved by Scripture. The German Reformer wished to remain united to the Church of all preceding ages, and sought only to purify it from everything. that was repugnant to the word of God. The Reformer of Zurich passed back over every intervening age till he reached the times of the apostles; and, subjecting the Church to an entire transformation, laboured to restore it to its primitive condition."[6]

Thus Luther was essentially a reformer, while the guiding principle of Zwingli was restoration. Unfortunately, Zwingli never completed his labors as he was killed in 1531 in a Swiss war between Catholics and Protestants. A few years later his work was absorbed and modified by John Calvin who moved to Geneva in 1536. Like Zwingli, he sought to purge the church of everything not expressly allowed in the scriptures. But he also developed a distinctive theology of election and predestination which became the cornerstone of the Reformed Movement. In Geneva he established a city-state which he dictatorially controlled. Copying the tactics used against the Reformation, he banished or executed dissenters. His teachings leavened the thinking of Protestant Europe and became the dominant force in the Reformed Church of the Netherlands and the Presbyterian Church of Scotland in the late sixteenth century.

The Anabaptists

The Anabaptists were a diverse group appearing throughout Europe in the time of Zwingli and Luther. They had no single great leader and their churches were largely independent. They were nicknamed *Anabaptists* for their practice of "rebaptizing" those previously baptized as infants. While differing among themselves, they held several things in common. They universally rejected infant baptism. They believed in complete separation of church and state, and in this differed from other elements of the Reformation. Many were pacifists. Some tended toward mysticism and a dependence on an "inner light" of the Spirit. Even more than Zwingli, they sought a restoration of primitive Christianity.

The Anabaptists were terribly persecuted by both Catholics and Protestants. Persecution stemmed largely from two things—their rejection of infant baptism and a debacle at Munster, Germany, in which some fanatical revolutionaries took over the city and proclaimed a kingdom. Before the tragic episode ended in 1535 many people had died. Although this action was disavowed by the Anabaptists, hundreds of innocent believers were unmercifully executed. Dispersed and disspirited, their existence was threatened until Menno Simons, a former priest who was wise and peace-loving, assumed direction of the movement. His followers were called Mennonites.

The Anabaptists were numerous in the Netherlands, Moravia, and parts of Germany. The most lasting Anabaptist influence resulted from the emergence of the Baptists in the seventeenth century. Although they rejected some Anabaptist positions, they agreed in their oppostion to infant baptism. They also believed that biblical baptism is performed by immersion. The Baptist movement dates from 1608 when John Smyth of England led a group of followers to Amsterdam and founded a congregation on Baptist principles.

The Anglicans

The English Reformation differed from the others in that it was motivated by political rather than religious factors. King Henry VIII wished to marry Anne Boleyn, a lady of the court. He asked the Pope to annul his marriage to Catharine. The Pope refused to grant the divorce. Henry, who earlier by the Pope had been awarded the title of "Defender of the Faith" for his opposition of Luther, was greatly angered. He had his new archbishop, Thomas Cranmer, secretly marry him to Anne Boleyn. Soon afterwards Cranmer declared Henry's marriage to Catharine null and void. The Pope excommunicated Henry in 1534. The king immediately responded by having the English parliament declare Henry to be "the only supreme head on earth of the Church of England."

By a single stroke Henry severed English Catholicism from the papacy. Henceforth it was to be the Church of England. The American counterpart which separated during the Revolution is the Episcopal Church. Some changes were made. Monasteries were abolished. Worship was conducted in English. The clergy was allowed to marry. The Bible was given to the people in their language. But the English Reformation was quite limited when compared to the other three efforts. Most Anglicans still think of themselves as English Catholics rather than Protestants.

The Rise of Denominations

Most contemporary non-Catholic bodies trace their origin to one or more of the movements we have examined. For example, in the early seventeenth century a group of Independents within the Church of England stressed the importance of congregational church government. From this, Congregationalism began. The first settlers in Massachusetts were of this faith. In 1957 the Congregational Church merged with the Evangelical and Reformed Church to found the United Church of Christ denomination.

Also originating in England in the eighteenth century were the Methodists. They began as a distinct society within the Church of England under the guidance of John Wesley. They sought an evangelical revival. Wesley died as a member of the Church of England, but after his death the Methodists formed a separate denomination.

Several denominations have American origins. The Holiness Movement of the last part of the nineteenth century gave birth to several, the largest being the Church of the Nazarene. The Pentecostal Movement at the start of the twentieth century spawned many religious bodies, the largest being the Assemblies of God.

This story could be greatly expanded, but this is enough to tell how the religious world got where it is. There is another part yet to be related. That will be told next.

---

[1]James W. Thompson and Edgar Nathaniel Johnson, *An Introduction to Medieval Europe, 300-1500* (New York: W. W. Norton and Co., 1937), p. 136.

[2]Everett Ferguson, *Early Christians Speak* (Austin, Texas: Sweet Publishing Co., 1971), pp. 25, 26. Used by permission.

[3]Ignatius, "Epistle to the Trallians," J. B. Lightfoot, *The Apostolic Fathers* (Grand Rapids, Michigan: Baker Book House, 1970), p. 73.

[4]Bertrand Louis Conway, *The Question Box* (New York: Paulist Press, 1929), p. 313.

[5]Lars P. Qualben, *A History of the Christian Church* (New York: Thomas Nelson and Sons, 1942), p. 71.

[6]J. H. Merle D'Aubigne, *History of the Great Reformation of the Sixteenth Century in Germany, Switzerland, Etc.* (New York: Robert Carter, 1843), vol. III, pp. 258, 259.

CHAPTER 6

The Search for Truth

It was in the autumn of 1891 that Fred C. Conybeare went from England to Armenia in search of an ancient version of the Book of Enoch. Instead he discovered a copy of an unknown document called *The Key of Truth.*[1] Originally written no later than 850, this manual of church life pictures a group of simple Christians in the midst of a world that had long since forsaken apostolic Christianity.

The people of *The Key of Truth* were Paulicians or Thonraks, and arose about the fifth century. For several centuries they and their spiritual relatives—the Bulgarians and the Gogomils—played a role in the political and religious history of Asia Minor, Armenia, and southeastern Europe. *The Key of Truth* reveals a people seeking to duplicate the apostolic faith. They considered themselves to be "members of the universal and apostolic church." They taught that baptism by immersion was to be preceeded by faith and repentance. They rejected the baptism of the "unbelieving, the reasonless, and the unrepentant." Elders, called "the elect," were carefully chosen and were impressed with the possibility that their service might require suffering and imprisonment. (Thousands of these people were martyred by their enemies.) When children were born the elders went to their homes with the congregation and stressed parental responsibility in training the young in godliness and faith. Believing that only Christ can be our mediator, they rejected images, relics, and the confessional.

The Paulicians observed the Lord's supper, apparently accepting the doctrine of the real presence. They stressed the teaching of the scriptures and emphasized Bible reading. If we can judge by *The Key of Truth,* this was a movement seeking to reproduce original Christianity in an age in which the light of the scriptures had almost gone out. How well the Paulicians succeeded in this we do not know. They are, however, typical of the many efforts through the centuries to find in the Bible the true religion of Jesus.

63

Unfortunately, not all struggles designed to recover lost truth have been successful. Controversy, and even division, have often followed in the wake of the introduction of new ideas. Many times this has been because human beings resist change or anything which threatens the security represented by the status quo. Too often we fear learning new truth because acceptance of it might require a change in our lives.

Religious movements generally fall into four categories—*heretics, dissenters, reformers,* and *restorers.* Some Groups overlap these classifications. For example, movements that were heretical in some respects often aimed at reformation in others. We will consider each of these groups with major attention on restoration efforts.

The Heresies

The Greek word from which *heresy* is translated has different shades of meaning in the New Testament. Sometimes it implies a sect. Because they viewed Christianity as a deviation from true Judaism, Jews of the first century considered it to be a sect or heresy (Acts 24:5, 14; 28:22). It was a false teaching to be vigorously opposed.

The ecclesiastical definition of heresy involves "the open espousal of fundamental error." A heretic is considered to be one who is so wrapped up in the promotion of his error that he will push it regardless of cost. It is not just error, but the militancy associated with it that has come to be considered heresy. The heretic has an obsession which impels him to promote his peculiar views at the expense of equally vital matters.

Defined in this way, heretical movements can be thought of as moving *away* from pure Christianity. Gnosticism and Montanism in the post-apostolic period fall into this category. So does Arianism, the fourth century teaching which denied the full deity of Jesus Christ.

Many heresies revolve around the supposed revelations received by their leading figures. These revelations claim divine knowledge not previously given in the scriptures. Contemporary examples are Mormonism and Christian Science, whose founders each claimed direct revelations from God.

Heretical movements often teach some biblical truths. In some areas they may be closer to genuine Christianity than established religions. There is a danger of condemning *all* of the tenets of a body because some of them are erroneous. Many present day cults appeal to the social outcasts of society who find in them a sense of community, a feeling of being loved and cared for, which they do not find in conventional denominations. The cults may succeed because they stress an aspect of the Christian faith neglected by others. Unfortunately they also present a package deal in which error must be accepted along with the positive aspects of the faith.

The Dissenters

Not all controversies center on doctrine. Although the eleventh century Catholic division had doctrinal overtones, it was largely political in nature. Similarly, the separation of the English church from Rome during the reign of Henry VIII was motivated by Henry's desire to marry Anne Boleyn and to increase his own authority. Some doctrinal changes resulted, but they were the effect, not the cause of the separation.

In the American Civil War, Methodists, Baptists, Presbyterians, and Episcopalians all divided along North-South lines either during the war or before it. Attitudes toward slavery were involved, but it can hardly be denied that sectional political feelings were the major factors in these separations. Such divisions are usually neither toward nor away from apostolic Christianity. The intent in these struggles is not to promote new doctrine (as with heresies) nor to return to a more pure form of Christianity.

The Reformers

Probably most religious divisions come about from reformatory efforts. Reform often begins within a body and results in the reformers being driven out by those who are unwilling to accept the changes proposed. This was true of Martin Luther and his followers.

An early type of reformation was monasticism in which dedicated people secluded themselves in cloisters to devote themselves more fully to the service of God. Their action was prompted by disilluisionment with the secular and empty form of Christianity to which they had been exposed. In the monasteries they devoted themselves to religious work (such as copying the scriptures), prayer, and Bible reading. Such reforms were more concerned with improving one's personal relationship with God than in changing the practices of the church.

The fourteenth century saw several reformatory efforts. Pointing to the New Testament as the standard of truth, Marsilius of Padua and John of Jandun wrote a book in which they denied that the pope has any more authority than any other bishop. A few years later the English reformer, John Wyclif, struck out against the concentration of wealth among the clergy. He denied the infallibility of the pope and even called him the Antichrist. He regarded the Bible as the sole source of truth. John Huss, one of his disciples, lead a reformation in Bohemia in which, among other things, he called for the abolition of indulgences.

One of the greatest of all reformers was Martin Luther. With the Bible as his guidebook, Luther called for changes in many areas of Catholicism. We should note, however, that Luther was interested in changing the established church in those areas in which he felt it needed to be purified rather than in restoring New Testament Christianity as such.

Dozens of other examples of reformation could be given. One common characteristic is found in all. Each sought to reform some corrupted element of Christianity. The monks sought a return to the consecrated life. Wyclif called for removal of the papal office. Luther emphasized justification by faith. John Wesley, founder of Methodism, stressed one's personal relationship to Christ. The Congregationalists called for a return to the apostolic form of church government. The Baptists taught the importance of immersion as biblical baptism.

While these reformations were usually valid in the areas in which they sought change, they dealt with different things. The result is the current religious division. If one group seeks a return to biblical baptism, another to correct church organization, and a third to the proper role of the Lord's supper, these people are not going to agree because they start at different places. While a vast improvement over a corrupted Christianity, reformation as a system fails because it is partial. It has the wrong objective. It seeks to correct an existing institution in one respect while neglecting vital needs in other areas.

The Restorers

A more comprehensive approach to gaining the total truth of the Christian faith is found in restoration. Unlike reformation, which seeks to remodel an existing structure, it strives to return to the original "blueprints" as a spiritual guide.

The history of Christianity is replete with efforts to restore the pure religion of Jesus and his apostles.[2] Many of these stories have never been fairly told because the records of these people have been lost in antiquity, and we know them only through the writings of their enemies. Some movements were blemished by heretical teachings. Often these restorers were severely persecuted. Many were martyred. Almost always they were motivated by a desire to let the Bible guide them as they struggled to recapture the essence of pure Christianity.

The centuries following the apostolic period reveal few restoration efforts. This was partly because men, not yet having drifted far from Christ's original teachings, saw little need to return to the original pattern. As the dissimilarity between early Christianity and medieval Catholicism became more pronounced, the number of these movements increased.

The Paulicians have already been mentioned. They originated in Syria as early as the fifth century and spread into Armenia. In succeeding persecutions they were widely scattered. Later we read of the Bogomils and Bulgarians in the Balkans who were their spiritual descendants. They considered themselves to be just Christians and adhered to the authority of the New Testament.

The Waldenses emerged in the twelfth century. They were led by Peter Waldo, a wealthy French merchant who gave his goods to the poor and began preaching the gospel. Called the "Poor Men of Lyon," the Waldenses went beyond Waldo's intent of preaching penance and a life of poverty. They stressed the pure life and made the Bible their rule of faith. Whatever they could not find in it they rejected, and hence renounced many practices and teachings of Catholicism such as clerical usurpation and purgatory. Some can still be found today in the Alps of Northwest Italy.

The sixteenth century Protestant Reformation saw numerous efforts to return to New Testament Christianity. Reference has been made to the differing views of Luther and Zwingli. Luther was a reformer while Zwingli was more in the tradition of a restorer. We must wonder if Zwingli would have carried his approach to its logical conclusion had he not died before his reformation was completed. The true restorers of this era, however, were the Anabaptists. They were not homogeneous and the actions of the fanactical fringe has obscured the true restoration elements among them. They believed that the original church fell when it was wedded to the state during the reign of Constantine in the fourth century. They urged complete separation of church and state. Fundamentally they accepted the scriptures, especially the New Testament, as the only standard for the individual and the community. A letter from Conrad Grebel, an Anabaptist leader, shows their attitude toward the Bible:

"Therefore we beg and admonish thee as a brother . . . that thou wilt take earnest heed to preach the divine word without fear, to set up and guard only divine institutions, to esteem as good and right only what may be found in pure and clear scripture, to reject, hate and curse all devices, words, customs, and opinions of men, including thine own . . . whatever we are not taught by clear passages of examples must be regarded as forbidden. . ."[3]

This total acceptance of the scriptures as authority is the restoration principle in action. Using this approach the Anabaptists rejected infant baptism because they did not find it in the early church, and regarded the Lord's supper simply as a memorial in the way it was originally viewed. They sought to organize congregations after the primitive pattern and recaptured the missionary zeal of the first Christians.

In England, restoration sentiments expressed themselves in numerous movements. In 1689 the noted English philosopher John Locke wrote:

"But since men are so solicitous about the true church, I would only ask them here, by the way, if it be not more agreeable to the Church of Christ to make the conditions of her communion consist in such things, and such things only, as the Holy Spirit has in the Holy Scriptures declared, in express words, to be necessary to salvation?"[4]

Here is a clarion call to return to God's word as the means of recovering the ancient faith. In the next two centuries others made similar pleas. The eighteenth century saw the planting of a number of independent churches in the British Isles through the influence of John Glas and Robert Sandeman. They stressed the importance of duplicating the New Testament pattern in restoring the simplicity of worship and the autonomy of the local church. This group remained small because of its legalistic approach to the scriptures and the lack of an evangelistic spirit.

A few years later the Haldane brothers, James and Robert, launched a similar effort in Scotland. They believed that the New Testament contains all that is needed to govern the worship and conduct of Christian societies. Accordingly they organized congregations patterned after the New Testament in structure, worship, and conduct of life. When they renounced infant baptism and adopted immersion, a division among their churches followed since not all would accept their conclusions.

The accounts of restoration efforts could be multiplied to include the Plymouth Brethren, the Evangelical Christians of Russia, and others. These are sufficient to demonstrate that for centuries restoration has been a recurring theme among truthseekers. We will examine one other movement in greater detail because of its fuller development of the restoration principle.

The American Restoration Movement

Often called the *Reformation of the Nineteenth Century,* the *Restoration Movement* was a coalescence of many efforts in the United States starting about 1800. Independent of it, but related, was a similar work in Great Britain.

The first effort, sometimes called the *Christian Connection,* was itself a fusion of three distinct attempts to return to the teachings of the early church. In 1793 James O'Kelly of Virginia led a revolt against the authoritarian domination of Francis Asbury in the Methodist Church. His associates called themselves *Republican Methodists,* but they soon abandoned this title in favor of the name Christian to the exclusion of all sectarian names. They regarded Christ as the only head of the church and adopted the Bible as their only guidebook.

Elias Smith and Dr. Abner Jones, two Baptist preachers, launched a similar effort in New England in 1801. The established churches rejected all sectarian names and adopted the New Testament as their only religious authority.

In Kentucky a third movement was crystalizing. Five Presbytern preachers, disenchanted with the narrowness of Calvinism, withdrew in 1803 from their synod to establish the Springfield Presbytery. However, they soon became convinced that this was a mistake as they had no biblical authority for beginning another denomination. They dissolved the presbytery by issuing *The Last Will and Testament of the Springfield Presbytery* on June 28, 1804. The most important leader of these churches was Barton W. Stone. The three groups soon established mutual contact, and though there was no organic union, they came to be viewed as a single effort.

The second major branch of the Restoration Movement was led by a father and son, Thomas and Alexander Campbell, who immigrated to Pennsylvania from Scotland. Thomas, who came first, was a Presbyterian clergyman. In that day the Presbyterians were badly splintered. This distressed him, and when he offered the Lord's supper to other Presbyterians than those in his own sect and declared that there is no divine authority for creeds and confessions of faith, he was suspended from the synod. Gathering a group sympathetic to his views of Christian union, he organized "The Christian Association of Washington." At its direction he wrote its *Declaration and Address* which was published in 1809. This set forth the principles by which Campbell felt Christian union might be achieved. About this time Alexander arrived from Scotland, and it was not long before he became a leading spirit of a new movement stressing that Christian unity could be achieved by the "restoration of the ancient order" of Christianity.

Both major movements spread rapidly in the West as hundreds of churches were planted. They soon discovered that their basic positions were the same. Both believed in Christian unity. Both taught that the scriptures alone constitute spiritual authority. Their emphasis differed somewhat, but this was not a major obstacle to unity. With no denominational machinery to facilitate their union, their forces were blended together as one, beginning in 1831. Not all congregations were willing to join hands, but most in the West did. The union provided a great impetus to their work and soon the plea of non-sectarian Christianity was heard throughout the western part of the country.

Space will not allow telling the story of other tributaries of this movement in such states as Indiana, Kentucky, and Georgia. But the efforts of religious leaders from diverse backgrounds calling for unity on the basis of the scriptures was highly successful as multitudes embraced the plea to abandon sectarianism in favor of being Christians only. Today thousands of congregations throughout the world are the spiritual heirs of those who strove to find their way out of sectarianism in the early nineteenth century. Neither they nor those involved in any similar search have recovered all the truth. Nor have we. Restoration is a never-ending struggle to discover the essence of the religion of Jesus.

Discovering the Principles

Our major concern is not the historical development of the Restoration Movement, but the principles that guided these searchers for truth. Some early documents chart the course which was followed. One was *The Last Will and Testament of the Springfield Presbytery,* already referred to. Part is given here to help us breathe the spirit of that day:

"The Presbytery of Springfield, sitting at Cane-ridge, in the county of Bourbon, being, through a gracious Providence, in more than ordinary bodily health, growing in strength and size daily; and in perfect soundness and composure of mind; but knowing that it is appointed for all delegated bodies once to die; and considering that the life of every such body is very uncertain, do make, and ordain this our last Will and Testament, in manner and form following, viz:

"*Imprimis.* We *will,* that this body die, be dissolved, and sink into union with the Body of Christ at large; for there is but one Body, and one Spirit, even as we are called in one hope of our calling.

"*Item.* We *will,* that our name of distinction, with its *Reverend* title, be forgotten, that there be but one Lord over God's heritage, and his name One.

"*Item.* We *will,* that our power of making laws for the government of the church, and executing them by delegated authority, forever cease; that the people may have free course to the Bible, and adopt *the law of the Spirit of life in Christ Jesus.* . . .

"*Item.* We *will,* that the people henceforth take the Bible as the only sure guide to heaven; and as many as are offended with other books, which stand in competition with it, may cast them into the fire if they choose; for it is better to enter into life having one book, than having many to be cast into hell. . . .

"*Item.* Finally, we *will,* that all our *sister bodies* read their Bibles carefully, that they may see their fate there determined, and prepare for death before it is too late."[5]

This document clearly rejects sectarianism. The unity of the one divine church is affirmed, and a call to union in that body issued. Truly, if all followers of Jesus would unite upon this platform we would in fact have undenominational Christianity.

The *Declaration and Address* written by Thomas Campbell decries religious division and calls for Christian unity. The first three of its thirteen propositions are here reproduced:

"Prop. 1. That the Church of Christ·upon earth is essentially, intentionally, and constitutionally one; consisting of all those in every place that profess their faith in Christ and obedience to him in all things according to the Scriptures, and that manifest the same by their tempers and conduct, and of none else; as none else can be truly and properly called Christians.

"2. That although the Church of Christ upon earth must necessarily exist in particular and distinct societies, locally separate from one another, yet there ought to be no schisms, no uncharitable divisions among them. They ought to receive each other as Christ Jesus hath also received them, to the glory of God. And for this purpose they ought all to walk by the same rule, to mind and speak the same thing; and to be perfectly joined together in the same mind, and in the same judgment.

"3. That in order to do this, nothing ought to be inculcated upon Christians as articles of faith; nor required of them as terms of communion, but what is expressly taught and enjoined upon them in the word of God. Nor ought anything to be admitted, as of Divine obligation, in their Church constitution and managements, but what is expressly enjoined by the authority of our Lord Jesus Christ and his apostles upon the New Testament Church; either in express terms or by approved precedent. . . ."[6]

These three propositions summarized the basic principles of the Restoration Movement—*undenominational Christianity, Christian unity, and the sole authority of the scriptures as the means of attaining these objectives.*

72

Three mottoes often used in the movement should be noted. The first is Thomas Campbell's statement, *"Where the Scriptures speak, we speak; and where the Scriptures are silent, we are silent."* This calls upon us to respect the silence of the Bible, as well as its voice.

A second motto was also coined by Campbell. It was, "In faith unity; in opinions liberty; in all things charity." This distinguishes between essential doctrine and human opinion, laying stress upon the importance of love in all disagreements.

The third motto, of unknown origin, was, "While we claim to be Christians only, we do not claim to be the only Christians." These people called men to undenominational Christianity, but did not presume to stand in eternal judgment of those who disagreed.

The restoration principles can be clearly seen in the thinking of truthseekers of other generations. Restoration efforts have sometimes failed. Sometimes they have degenerated into sectarianism. Broadbent aptly describes what can happen:

"Sectarianism is limitation. Some truth taught in Scripture, some part of the Divine revelation, is apprehended, and the heart responds to it and accepts it. As it is dwelt upon, expounded, defended, its power and beauty increasingly influence those affected by it. Another side of truth, another view of revelation, also contained in Scripture, seems to weaken, even to contradict the truth that has been found to be so effectual, and in jealous fear for the doctrine accepted and taught the balancing truth is minimized, explained away, even denied. So on a portion of revelation, on a part of the Word, a sect is founded, good and useful because it preaches and practises Divine truth, but limited and unbalanced because it does not see all truth, nor frankly accept the whole of Scripture. Its members are not only deprived of the full use of all Scripture, but are cut off from the fellowship of many saints, who are less limited than they, or limited in another direction."[7]

As we seek to return to apostolic Christianity, the real danger is that we may only partially restore it. As Broadbent says, we may focus on one aspect while neglecting another. Some stress the externals and overlook the spirit; others emphasize purity of life and disregard the church. True restoration requires balance. In a writing of this length we cannot explore every facet of Christianity, but in the remaining chapters we will try to discover its basic elements.

FOOTNOTES

[1]Fred C. Conybeare, translator and editor, *The Key of Truth, a Manual of the Paulician Church of Armenia* (Oxford: Clarendon Press, 1898).

[2]Two books that trace restoration efforts in some detail are *The Pilgrim Church* (London: Pickering and Inglis, 1955) by E. H. Broadbent, and *The Restoration Principle* (St. Louis: The Bethany Press, 1960) by Alfred T. DeGroot. Both have their deficiences, but are of value for pursuing this topic in depth.

[3]Quoted by Pat E. Harrell, "The Anabaptist Doctrine of the Church," *Restoration Quarterly,* Vol. 3, No. 1, 1st quarter, 1959, p. 5.

[4]John Locke, *A Letter Concerning Toleration* (New York: The Liberal Arts Press, 1950), p. 22.

[5]Charles Alexander Young, *Historical Documents Advocating Christian Union* (Chicago: Christian Century, 1904), pp. 19-23.

[6]*Ibid.,* pp. 107-109.

[7]E. H. Broadbent, *Op. Cit.,* p. 197.

CHAPTER 7

Jesus Saves?

The gaudy colors of the bumper stickers proclaimed their messages: I CONFESS I BELIEVE IN JESUS; HEAVEN IS JUST OUT OF THIS WORLD; THE KING IS COMING; BE A CHRISTIAN; I'M STICKING AROUND TO TELL YOU ABOUT JESUS.

I don't know your reaction to those five slogans I saw on the car in front of the post office, but I had several. First, I suspected that the owner was an egotist. One or two bumper stickers for a non-egotist; five—never. Second, advertising Jesus in this way cheapens his name. Third, a bumper sticker does not a Christian make.

I suppose I have a conditioned reflex to this sort of thing, but it strikes me that the context of our message to a degree determines our effectiveness. Somehow an automobile bumer doesn't seem to me the best place to advertize Jesus. One of the more common bumper stickers is JESUS SAVES. I have often wondered how the non-believer reacts when he reads this short message on the car ahead of him as he waits at the stop light. Does it turn him off about religion? We live in an age of gimmicks and I have to believe that some of the methods used on television, on the printed page—yes, and on bumper stickers—adversely affect some people who react by thinking, "If that's your approach to Christianity, I don't want any of it."

JESUS SAVES? Yes, I do think these words have been cheapened by the way they have been used. Even so, the message which they convey is not cheap. JESUS DOES SAVE! If we remove this simple statement from the Christian faith, we have cut out the heart of the religion of Jesus. Did not Jesus himself declare, "The Son of man came to seek and to save the lost" (Luke 19:10)?

To say that Jesus saves is to imply that somebody is lost. It is the drowning man who needs the life preserver, not the person on dry ground. But in what sense can one be said to be spiritually lost? When Adam and Eve disobeyed God's commandment in the Garden of Eden, they were cast from the garden and separated from God. They were at that point—LOST! The story of Jesus is the account of how God provided the means by which mankind might be restored to the favor of the Heavenly Father.

The Penalty for Sin

Adam and Eve were lost because they sinned. John said that "sin is lawlessness" (1 John 3:4). The King James Version says, "Sin is the transgression of the law." Our English word, *sin,* translates from a Greek word which literally means "a missing of the mark." Just as the ancient archer would miss the target with his arrow, so we in failing to obey God's commands miss the spiritual target. When one violates the law of the land it is called crime; when he violates the law of God it is sin.

God is absolutely perfect and holy. It is inconceivable that he could ever sin. Because of this God cannot tolerate sin, and when we sin we separate ourselves from his presence by the act. The Bible says that "the wages of sin is death" (Romans 6:23). As physical death separates the soul from the body, so spiritual death separates man from God. The ultimate penalty for unforgiven sin is eternal punishment. Jesus said of the unrighteous, "And they will go away into eternal punishment" (Matthew 25:46). This punishment is called hell and is described in terrifying terms: "But as for the cowardly, the faithless, the polluted, as for murderers, fornicators, sorcerers, idolaters, and all liars, their lot shall be in the lake that burns with fire and sulphur, which is the second death" (Revelation 21:8).

Of course, we may feel that we do not fall into any of these categories. How many of us have ever murdered a person or worshipped an idol? But our relief is shortlived when we read Paul's declaration, "All have sinned and fall short of the glory of God" (Romans 3:23). Paul then goes to great length to prove that "none is righteous, no, not one" (Romans 3:9). He reasons that no one is so morally good or has done so many good deeds that he can claim the right to go to heaven on his own merits. From God's point of view it just isn't possible, though one may sometimes get the feeling that he isn't so bad because there are lots of people worse.

This is a dismal picture until we read the Bible a little more and discover that all isn't as hopeless as it sounds. Paul encouraged some early Christians, "But we would not have you ignorant, brethren, concerning those who are asleep, that you may not grieve as others do who have no hope" (1 Thessalonians 4:13). While many have died without hope in the afterlife, it doesn't have to be that way!

The Good News

The first Christians proclaimed a message to the world that they called the *gospel*. Gospel means *good news*. When one became a disciple of Jesus he shared with his neighbors the good news of how Jesus had transformed his life and given him hope. This gospel is the story of how God through his son Jesus has made the forgiveness of our sins possible so that we might be restored to divine favor. The Golden Text of the Bible beautifully sums up this idea: "For God so loved the world that he gave his only Son, that whoever believes in him should not perish but have eternal life. For God sent the Son into the world, not to condemn the world, but that the world might be saved through him" (John 3:16, 17).

There it is! Although all of us are separated from God by our sins—lost, if you please—God still loves us and wants us back in his favor. That love was so great that he sent his son, who assumed human form and lived on this earth for some thirty years before being murdered by his enemies.

God's Remedy for Sin

But how could one man, even a great one, make possible the salvation of *all* human beings? Before Christ came, the Law of Moses provided that the people of Israel should offer animal sacrifices for their sins. The blood of these animals was sprinkled upon the altar or mercy seat of the ark of the covenant for the transgressions of the Israelites. Of these sacrifices it is said, "Indeed, under the law almost everything is purified with blood, and without the shedding of blood there is no forgiveness of sins" (Hebrews 9:22). Why God required that blood be shed in order for sins to be forgiven we are not specifically told. Some indication of the purpose is seen in the statement, "For the life of the flesh is in the blood; and I have given it for you upon the altar to make atonement for your souls; for it is the blood that makes atonement, by reason of the life" (Leviticus 17:11). Whether or not we completely understand God's reason for requiring the shedding of blood in granting forgiveness, we do know that this is his divine plan.

However, the sacrifices of the old law were inadequate. What they lacked is explained in the Hebrew letter. "For since the law has but a shadow of the good things to come instead of the true form of these realities, it can never, by the same sacrifices which are continually offered year after year, make perfect those who draw near. Otherwise, would they not have ceased to be offered? If the worshipers had once been cleansed, they would no longer have any consciousness of sin. But in these sacrifices there is a reminder of sin year after year. For it is impossible that the blood of bulls and goats should take away sins" (Hebrews 10:1-4).

The problem with the animal sacrifices of the Law of Moses was that the animals were themselves imperfect. They were but a temporary expedient for God's people until a perfect sin offering for all mankind should be given for the sins of dying man.

The Perfect Sin Offering

Where could such a sacrifice be found? Was there no human being so perfect that he might die for his fellowmen? There was none, for every son and daughter of Adam has fallen far, far short of the holy perfection required by our Maker. There was but one answer. The Father had to send his Son to earth to assume human form. He had to endure the trials which each of us faces in order to demonstrate his sinless perfection. So, "The Word became flesh and dwelt among us, full of grace and truth; and we have beheld his glory, glory as of the only Son from the Father" (John 1:14). To a Jewish peasant woman named Mary, Jesus, the Son of God, was born in human form in the village of Bethlehem to share our trials and triumphs, our joys and sorrows. For a third of a century he faced every kind of temptation we encounter, but unlike the rest of us he never slipped, never spoke an evil word, never did an evil deed. He was "one who in every respect has been tempted as we are, yet without sin" (Hebrews 4:15). "He committed no sin; no guile was found on his lips. When he was reviled, he did not revile in return; when he suffered, he did not threaten; but he trusted to him who judges justly" (1 Peter 2:22, 23).

Because Jesus was exposed to every sort of human stress, he can identify with us and understand our needs. "For because he himself has suffered and been tempted, he is able to help those who are tempted" (Hebrews 2:18). Truly, Jesus is our friend!

Jesus began his teaching ministry when he was about thirty years old. Three and a half years later he had so incurred the wrath of the Jewish leaders by his teachings that they arrested him and delivered him to the Roman governor, demanding his life. Although Pontius Pilate acknowledged his innocence, he capitulated to the demands of Jesus' accusers, had him scourged, and delivered him to be crucified. In perhaps the most painful death ever devised by men, Jesus surrendered his life upon a Roman cross. He was buried in the tomb of a Jewish leader, Joseph of Arimathea, and three days later arose from the dead to appear again to his followers. Forty days after his resurrection he ascended to the Father, having accomplished his mission of seeking and saving the lost.

What is the significance of the death of Jesus? After all, others have died as martyrs to a cause, and certainly Jesus was not the only one ever crucified. Even as he died two thieves met the same fate. It is in the light of his resurrection that the death of Jesus assumes special importance. For if Jesus did in fact rise from the grave, there is also hope that his followers may do the same.

What Jesus Did for Us

The major significance of Jesus' death is that he died as the substitute for those who accept him. Sometimes this act of dying is called the *atonement* because in it he atoned for our sins. Paul put it this way: "While we were still weak, at the right time Christ died for the ungodly. Why, one will hardly die for a righteous man—though perhaps for a good man one will even dare to die. But God shows his love for us in that while we were yet sinners Christ died for us" (Romans 5:6-8). God loved me; he loved you so much that he sent his Son to pay the supreme sacrifice for each of us. He did not die just for the mass of humanity, but for each individual. It has been said that had there been but one sinner on earth, Jesus would have died for that person. Thus Christ's sacrifice becomes very personal for each one.

But how does the offering of Jesus accomplish this? When Jesus died he shed his blood. Remember that God requires that blood be shed before he will *forgive* our sins. As Jesus died "one of the soldiers pierced his side with a spear, and at once there came out blood and water" (John 19:34). Unlike previous animal sacrifices, he became a perfect sacrifice making it possible for Paul to write, "In him we have *redemption* through his blood, the *forgiveness* of our trespasses, according to the riches of his grace which he lavished upon us" (Ephesians 1:7, 8). God forgives us because Jesus died for us. Paul calls this *redemption.* To redeem is to buy back. For a given amount of money one may reclaim what he has previously pawned. If he cannot redeem it himself, another may buy it back for him. In the spiritual sense my life has been put in pawn by sin. Regardless of how good a life I may live, I cannot redeem it. I can't raise the redemption price. So Christ by his blood pays the price for me.

A similar word is *ransom.* We usually think of a ransom as being paid to free a kidnap victim. In biblical times it was the price paid to liberate a slave. If one could not ransom himself, another could do it for him. Before one accepts Christ he is a slave of sin. He does not have the personal means to procure his release. So Christ ransoms him with his blood shed at Calvary. Jesus said of his mission, "The Son of man came not to be served but to serve, and to give his life as a *ransom* for many" (Matthew 20:28).

The legal term *justification* approaches the idea from another direction. To justify is to pronounce one innocent. As applied to the death of Jesus it pictures man as a sinner before God's judgment bar, unable to pay his debt of sin. He must either be found guilty and condemned to die or another must pay his debt. So Jesus pays the debt with his blood, and man is acquitted, not because of his own goodness, but because the charges have been dropped in view of Christ's offering. Paul explains it, "Since, therefore, we are now *justified* by his blood, much more shall we be saved by him from the wrath of God" (Romans 5:9).

This redemption and justification results in our being restored to the favor of, or *reconciled* to, God. As sin has separated us from the Father, so Christ in his sacrifice has brought us together. "All this is from God, who through Christ *reconciled* us to himself and gave us the ministry of *reconciliation;* that is, in Christ God was *reconciling* the world to himself, not counting their trespasses against them, and entrusting to us the message of *reconciliation"* (2 Corinthians 5:18, 19). This reconciliation has been accomplished by the blood of Christ. "For in him all the fulness of God was pleased to dwell, and through him to *reconcile* to himself all things, whether on earth or in heaven, making peace by the blood of his cross'' (Colossians 1:19, 20).

The Reality of Grace

The giving of Jesus is the supreme expression of divine grace to man. *Grace* is unmerited favor. We cannot be saved by doing so many good works or perfectly keeping God's law. Therefore God has made it possible for us to be "justified by his *grace* as a gift" (Romans 3:24). Paul explains, "For by *grace* you have been saved through faith; and this is not your own doing, it is the gift of God—not because of works, lest any man should boast" (Ephesians 2:8, 9). Though God has attached conditions to the acceptance of his grace, they in no way diminish the fact that God's favor is totally unearned and undeserved.

Why did God choose this means of saving us from sin? Perhaps it was to provide a means of his being just and merciful at the same time. Absolute justice requires that wrongdoing be punished; on the basis of our own merit none of us could hope to escape condemnation. Were God to forget about punishing us for wrong he would cease to be just. This is totally against the character of the Almighty.

On the other hand, the Father's merciful nature cannot be denied. He loves us and doesn't want anyone to be lost. Peter informs us that the Lord is forbearing, "not wishing that any should perish, but that all should reach repentance" (2 Peter 3:9). In sending Jesus to die for us, God is both just and merciful. Justice is served when the penalty for sin is paid in the death of Jesus; mercy is extended in offering us free forgiveness leading to everlasting life when we really do not deserve it. Or as Paul put it, "For our sake he made him to be sin who knew no sin, so that in him we might become the righteousness of God" (2 Corinthians 5:21).

Truly, JESUS SAVES!

CHAPTER 8

The Meaning of Faith

A new theory of forgiveness was developed by theologians in the Middle Ages. In the doctrine of *indulgences* they taught that Jesus, in his death, did more for man than God requires to restore human beings to his favor. A single drop of Christ's blood, it was said, was enough to reconcile man to God. With the rest of his shed blood Jesus established a spiritual treasury for the purpose of removing the temporal punishment for the sins of Christians, a treasury so vast that even eternity would not exhaust it. To this treasury were added the superabundant merits of the saints—those surplus good works of a very few good people who had more than earned their salvation.

It was explained to the people that this treasury of good works was under the guardianship of the Pope who could apply these credits against those sins which they committed after baptism. An individual could draw on this "bank" to pay for his sins by doing penance for each specific sin he committed. But, it was reasoned, since this was too heavy a burden for the average person, the penance could be performed by the priest who should be paid by the parishioner since "the laborer is worthy of his hire." A fixed fee for each kind of sin was set. The remission of the whole or part of a temporal punishment resulting from this sin being forgiven was called an *indulgence*.

In the sixteenth century funds were being raised to pay for the building of St. Peter's Cathedral in Rome. A papal emissary named John Tetzel traversed northern Germany selling indulgences for this purpose. Tetzel was a good salesman and even taught that an indulgence could be bought for a sin one intended to commit in the future. He proclaimed, "The very moment that the money clinks against the bottom of the chest, the soul escapes from purgatory and flies free to heaven."[1]

Martin Luther, a monk who taught at the University of Wittenberg, reacted against this teaching. His study of the scriptures led him to believe that the theory of indulgences as taught by Tetzel was wrong. On October 31, 1517, he nailed to the door of the Wittenberg Cathedral ninety-five propositions for debate in conformity with academic custom. These were his famous "Ninety-five Theses," the publishing of which touched off the Protestant Reformation. In them he challenged the teachings and practices of Tetzel, particularly the indulgence theory. Eventually he was arraigned by the Roman Catholic Church and excommunicated.

Luther took issue with the accepted view that man is saved by works. His study of Romans convinced him that man is saved by *faith alone,* and that works proceed from that faith. From this concept much of the theology of the Reformation developed. The controversy over faith and works was not new. It had been argued extensively in the fourth and fifth centuries. The relationship is also developed by Paul and James in the New Testament. Likewise, it deserves our close examination.

Is Salvation By Faith Alone?

Was Luther correct in concluding that salvation is by faith alone? Salvation by faith without regard to works of merit is often taught in the New Testament. Paul wrote, "For we hold that a man is justified by faith apart from the works of law" (Romans 3:28). Again, "For by grace you have been saved through faith; and this is not your own doing, it is the gift of God—not because of works, lest any man should boast" (Ephesians 2:8, 9).

But was Luther right when to *faith* he added *alone,* as the means of our salvation? On the face of it we must respond negatively. If faith "alone" saves, that eliminates the blood of Christ and the grace of God. Of course, Luther did not deny the necessity of these elements in our salvation. He was thinking of the human response to divine grace. An easy answer to our question would be simply to quote James 2:24: "You see that a man is justified by works and *not by faith alone.*" When salvation is approached from James' perspective, we are not saved by faith alone.

However, there is more involved in the matter than is suggested in quoting a single verse. Critical to the issue is our definition of faith. *Belief* and *faith* are derived from the same Greek word. To believe is to have faith. In the New Testament, though, faith is used in more than one sense. Sometimes it denotes *historical faith*—the mental act of believing something to be true. For example, we all accept as unquestioned truth that George Washington was the first president of the United States though none of us ever saw him. Nor do we doubt that Julius Caesar and Napoleon were once great generals. In this sense those who accept Jesus must first acknowledge that he lived and that he is the Son of God. It is also in this sense that we are told of some of the Jewish leaders in the time of Jesus, "Nevertheless many even of the authorities *believed in him,* but for fear of the Pharisees they did not confess it, lest they should be put out of the synagogue: for they loved the praise of men more than the praise of God" (John 12:42, 43). While they believed in Jesus, their faith lacked something, which deterred them from standing up for him. James tells us that "even the demons believe—and shudder" (James 2:19). Surely no one will affirm that the devil and his angels will be saved just because they admit the existence of God!

Trusting Faith

However, there is another kind of faith mentioned in the Bible. It is faith that not only believes in something *about* Christ, but also has confidence *in* him. One might acknowledge that an incumbent holds public office, but refuse to vote for his re-election because in another sense he does not believe in him. This would indicate that he lacks that personal confidence which we call *trust*. It is *trusting faith* that is described in Hebrews 11 where we are informed, "By faith Abel offered to God a more acceptable sacrifice than Cain. . . . By faith Noah . . . constructed an ark for the saving of his household. . . . By faith Abraham, when he was tested, offered up Isaac. . ." These great heroes of faith not only believed something about God, but they also trusted his promises. When the Bible speaks of the faith that saves, it speaks of the faith that trusts. Of course, to believe in Jesus one must first acknowledge that he is the Christ, the son of. the living God, but he must also trust him and his promises and be willing to follow wherever he leads because of that trust. The faith that will not "trust and obey" will not save.

Some think that Paul and James contradict one another regarding faith and works. Even Martin Luther called the book of James "an epistle of straw" because he could not reconcile the writings of the two men. Both Paul and James quote the Old Testament statement about Abraham, "Abraham believed God, and it was reckoned to him as righteousness." (See Romans 4:3 and James 2:23.) However, they draw different conclusions from the text. Paul quotes the passage to show that we are not saved by works while James is denying that we are saved by faith *only*. A close examination reveals no contradiction. James is thinking of historical faith; Paul is considering trusting faith. James is declaring that mere mental acceptance of facts will not save one unless that faith is coupled with obedience; Paul is denying that we can earn our way to heaven. Both conclusions are valid. Taken in context the two writers agree.

But what does trusting faith really imply for the one who accepts Jesus as Lord? Paul explains that it involves obedience by twice speaking in Romans of "the obedience of faith." (See Romans 1:5; 16:26.) He shows that obedience is not something distinct from faith, but an integral part of it. If one really trusts Jesus he will obey him, even when he cannot completely understand what lies behind his Lord's commands.

Once Paul and Silas were imprisoned in Philippi. When their jailor asked them what he needed to do to be saved they responded, "Believe in the Lord Jesus, and you will be saved, you and your household" (Acts 16:31). They were not just telling him to accept the facts about Jesus, but were also instructing him to so trust Jesus that he would obey him. And this is what he did! The story relates his repentance (he washed their wounds after they had been beaten) and his baptism. We are then informed that "he rejoiced with all his household *that he had believed in God*" (Acts 16:34). His faith included his obedience.

To return to our earlier question, can we correctly state that we are saved by faith *alone*? Viewed historically with faith as just the mental act of accepting the facts about Jesus, the answer is "no." This is what James meant when he declared, "you see that a man is justified by works and not by faith alone" (James 2:24). When faith is perceived as trust, including the whole of obedience, then the answer is "yes." In this sense those acts of obedience which Jesus requires of us are not distinct from faith, but essential elements of it.

Accepting God's Offer

If it is true that saving faith is trust and trust includes obedience, what is involved in accepting the sacrifice of Christ by faith? There is no better answer than is found in the account of the conversion of the three thousand on the first Pentecost after Christ's ascension into heaven. The story is related in Acts 2. On that occasion Peter preached a powerful message in which he told his hearers that they were responsible for killing the Messiah. They were so touched at what they heard that they cried out, "Brethren, what shall we do?" (Acts 2:37). Their question revealed that historically speaking they did believe in Jesus. But that was not enough. Their faith that Jesus was their Lord and Christ had to be enlarged to obedient faith before it could remove their guilt. Peter replied, "*Repent, and be baptized* every one of you in the name of Jesus Christ for the forgiveness of your sins; and you shall receive the gift of the Holy Spirit. For the promise is to you and to your children and to all that are far off, every one whom the Lord our God calls to him" (Acts 2:38, 39).

So the faith needed by those in Peter's audience included repentance. *Repentance is a change of heart,* not merely sorrow, although "godly grief produces a repentance that leads to salvation. . ." (2 Corinthians 7:10). Fifty-two days before many of these people had demanded the death of Jesus. Peter even said they had crucified him. Now, in order to follow Jesus they had to change their ways and surrender completely to him. This change was repentance.

There was more. Peter also said they must be baptized to have their sins forgiven. The book of Acts is sometimes called the book of conversions because it tells how people became Christians in the first century. Nine times in this book we are informed that those who accepted Christ were baptized as part of the process. In fact, in those days no one was considered to be a disciple of Jesus until his faith had been expressed in repentance and baptism.

In many circles the matter is viewed differently today. Some teach that conversion to Christ is accomplished at the instant of faith—the precise moment at which one intellectually acknowledges Jesus as Lord. The idea has been popularized by well-known evangelists who encourage their listeners to commit themselves to Jesus by raising their hands or walking down the aisle. If one is watching on television he may make this commitment at home. When one thus "believes" he is regarded as "saved," without regard to any further response or obedience. Since obedience is not part of this faith, one might, under the impulse of the moment, accept Jesus in faith without any intention of altering his life through repentance. Moreover, if he is baptized at all it is simply viewed as a means of declaring his faith by which he has already been saved before baptism.

This approach clearly conflicts with the biblical picture of how people accepted Jesus in apostolic times. In Acts, one was never regarded as having been saved until he had been baptized. Even Saul of Tarsus (Paul) was not saved when he was struck down on the Damascus road, but when as a penitent believer he obeyed the command to "be baptized, and wash away your sins, calling on his name" (Acts 22:16). Ananias would not have told him to be baptized to wash away his sins if he had already been forgiven when he intellectually believed on the way to Damascus. Perhaps the basic difficulty with this teaching is that it fails to view saving faith in the biblical perspective—that obedience is a vital part of trusting faith. The relationship between saving faith and obedience can be illustrated in the diagram on the next page.

Thus when one confesses that he believes that Jesus is God's son, that confession is actually his faith speaking. When he turns his life around to direct it to Jesus, that act of repentance is faith turning. And when he is baptized into Christ his action is faith obeying. Confession, repentance and baptism are simply elements of the faith that saves.

The Role of Baptism

We have observed that Peter instructed his audience on Pentecost to be baptized "for the forgiveness of your sins." Some have difficulty in reconciling his teaching with the fact that our salvation is by grace and is totally unmerited on our part. It is reasoned that if we teach that baptism is for the remission of sins as Peter did, we become water salvationists, making baptism a work and trying to earn eternal life.

Several observations are in order: (1) it was the Holy Spirit who declared through Peter that baptism is for the forgiveness of sins, and we do not have the right to deny that teaching; (2) when

SAVING **FAITH**

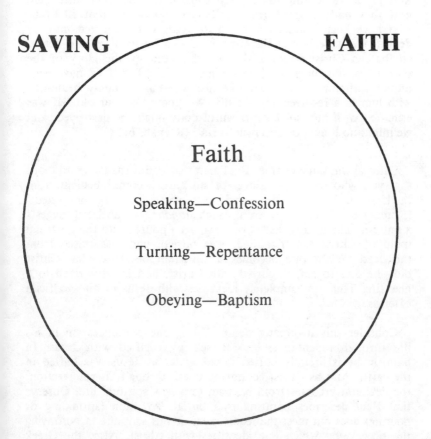

Faith

Speaking—Confession

Turning—Repentance

Obeying—Baptism

one is baptized he is passive, certainly doing no work; (3) baptism is not a work of merit, but rather an act of obedience, a required expression of our faith; (4) salvation is not in the water, but in the blood of Christ, the water being but the means by which we reach the blood.

The conversion process is beautifully portrayed by Paul in Romans 6. In writing the Roman Christians, Paul reminded them how they had accepted Jesus. "Do you not know that all of us who have been baptized into Christ Jesus were baptized into his death? We were buried therefore with him by baptism into death, so that as Christ was raised from the dead by the glory of the Father, we too might walk in newness of life. For if we have been united with him in a death like his, we shall certainly be united with him in a resurrection like his. We know that our old self was crucified with him so that the sinful body might be destroyed, and we might no longer be enslaved to sin" (Romans 6:3-6).

Later in the same chapter Paul affirmed, "But thanks be to God, that you who were once slaves of sin have become obedient from the heart to the standard of teaching to which you were committed" (Romans 6:17). The word from which *standard* is translated suggests a pattern. The idea is that "you have been poured into the doctrinal mold of Christ." Christ died, was buried, and was raised from the dead. When one becomes a Christian he does what Christ did—he dies to sin, is buried with Christ, and is resurrected to a new life. Thus he completely identifies with Jesus in his sacrificial offering.

Consider this in greater detail. When one renounces sin in his life through repentance, his old self is crucified with Jesus. In baptism he is literally buried in the water as Jesus was buried in the earth. And as Christ conquered death through his resurrection, the new convert rises from baptism to a new spiritual life. Observe that Paul describes baptism as a burial. Affusion (sprinkling or pouring) does not meet the requirement of this scripture in portraying the process by which one identifies with Christ. Also, the Greek word from which our English word baptize is translated literally means to immerse, submerge, dip, or overwhelm. Even Jesus, when he was baptized, "went up immediately *from* the water" (Matthew 3:16), showing that his baptism by John in the Jordan was by immersion.

Romans 6:3 also tells us that those who have been baptized into

Christ have been baptized into his death. In his death Jesus shed his blood to take away our sins. Paul declares that we reach his death by baptism. It is the final part of our faith that puts us in touch with the blood of Jesus. Baptism is said to be for the forgiveness of sins (Acts 2:38), to wash away sins (Acts 22:16), and to be necessary for salvation (Mark 16:16; 1 Peter 3:21) because it is the act of faith that puts us where the blood of Christ removes our sins.

One other observation regarding faith is in order. The faith that saves is personal. No one else can believe for you. Many stake their spiritual welfare on their baptism as babies. However, infants are incapable of believing in Jesus Christ. One catechism gets around the problem by asking and then answering a question: "Does God work faith even in infants also? Certainly; else all infants would be damned."[2] The idea is that somehow God imputes faith to a baby, even though the child is incapable of understanding the most elemental things. However, the catechism gives no proof of the assertion that infants can believe, nor is such found in God's word.

The Bible teaches neither infant nor adult baptism. It does teach believers baptism. Jesus said, "He who believes and is baptized will be saved; but he who does not believe will be condemned" (Mark 16:16). Infant baptism was introduced many years after Christ lived, and was defended on the basis that human beings born with the guilt of Adam's sin are lost unless they are baptized. This is the doctrine of original sin. However, the New Testament is totally silent about infant baptism. Small babies do not need to be baptized because they have never personally sinned. They are not lost until they do sin, and at that point they become old enough to believe in Jesus and be saved.

The faith one possesses when he becomes a child of God is but the beginning of a new life in Christ. It is that by which he will live as he begins his Christian journey. At times it will seem to be very feeble, and he will cry out as did the father of the demoniac boy whom Jesus healed, "I believe; help my unbelief!" (Mark 9:24). But by placing our hands in those of our Lord, that faith will daily increase and enable us to live the Christian life—triumphantly!

[1]J. H. Merele D'Aubigne, *History of The Great Reformation of the Sixteenth Century* (New York: Robert Carter, 1843), Vol. 1, p. 212.

[2]C. Gausewitz, editor, *Doctor Martin Luther's Small Catechism,* (Milwaukee: Northwest Publishing House, 1942), p. 143.

CHAPTER 9

A Day in Philippi

Come with me, if you will, to the city of Philippi, the leading city of Macedonia in northern Greece. It is the first day of the week in the year 58 A.D. in this Roman colony. Philippi, named for the father of Alexander the Great, enjoys a special status in the Empire. A group of Christians have assembled to worship God. They compose the first congregation planted by Paul the Apostle after his crossing into Europe to preach the good news of Jesus. These disciples are especially loved by their father in the gospel, Paul's "joy and crown" as he calls them (Philippians 4:1).

We cannot, of course, know exactly what occurred on this occasion. The sixteenth chapter of Acts relates the beginning of this beachhead in Greece. Paul's brief epistle to these people adds specific information about the congregation. Other apostolic writings supplement our knowledge of the early Christians. From these sources we can construct a reasonably accurate picture of what may have occurred that day.

A Christian Assembly

The assembly of the disciples of Jesus is possibly in the evening, Roman time, as this is a Roman city. Across the Aegean Sea the Christians in Troas met in the evening on the first day of the week (Acts 20:7, 8). At the beginning of the second century the Roman governor, Pliny, wrote the Emperor Trajan that the Christians assembled before dawn to worship. The unusual hours were probably determined by the fact that many of them were slaves, and they had to perform duties for their masters on what was just another work day for the Roman populace.

Luke's language in Acts 20:7 establishes that the first day of the week, rather than the Jewish sabbath, was the regular day of worship for the Christians. In relating Paul's visit to Troas he said,

"On the first day of the week, when we were gathered together to break bread, Paul talked with them." A description of their assembly follows. Moreover, Paul's request of the Corinthians that they make a special donation on the first day of the week for the needy in Judea (1 Corinthians 16:2) clearly implies that they regularly worshipped on that day. He wanted the donation to be ready when he came to visit, which would be true only if they gave at the time of their assembly. His direction that they should give on "the first day of every week" (1 Corinthians 16:2) establishes the regularity of their meeting.

The most likely place for their gathering is a rented hall. If their number is not too large they may meet in a home. In Troas they assembled in a third floor room (Acts 20:8). Although the Jewish community usually gathered in synagogues, Christians did not have their own church buildings until the close of the second century, if then. Theirs was a persecuted faith in which illegal houses of worship (and their assembly came to be regarded as illegal) could easily have been seized by the officials or destroyed by enemies. While such buildings are not wrong, and under ordinary circumstances today are expedient, the work and worship of God's people ought not to be tied to a physical structure. So great is the dependence of some on a building belonging to the church that they could not function as Christians should it be destroyed. True Christianity is rooted in Christ, not a material building.

The Christians Gather

Once we enter the Philippian assembly we observe a diversity of people. There is Lydia, a Jewish businesswoman who was Paul's first convert in the community. We notice that most of the people are Gentiles. There is the family of the jailor who was converted by Paul and Silas at the time of their imprisonment. Two Christian women, Euodia and Syntyche, are among the number. Although they were diligent workers with Paul in the early days of the congregation, they have recently had their personal differences with one another. Then there is Epaphroditus, a young gospel preacher trained by Paul. The audience is made up of slaves, masters, and freemen of which Roman society was basically composed. Shepherding the church are bishops or overseers, and much of its work is carried out by servants called deacons. This diverse assemblage is united as a single body with one mind, in spite of the varied cultural backgrounds and interests. For in Christ "there is neither Jew nor

Greek, there is neither slave nor free, there is neither male nor female; for you are all one in Christ Jesus" (Galatians 3:28).

On this occasion there is a love feast, commonly called the *agape*. This simple meal, referred to in Jude 12, was often eaten by early Christians as a means of expressing brotherly affection and mutual concern. According to Pliny the love feasts at the beginning of the second century were distinct from the worship. The food provided by the wealthy is shared by all. In Paul's time the Corinthian Christians seem to have confused the Lord's supper with the agape, and the consequent abuse brought a sharp reprimand from the apostle (1 Corinthians 11:20-22). While we can't be sure how often the early Christians ate together, we can be quite certain that when they did they viewed this fellowship as an expression of mutual love and concern as members of the same spiritual family.

The Meaning of Worship

Our understanding of the worship we are about to observe in Philippi will be enhanced if we first consider the Greek words rendered *worship* in our English versions of the New Testament. Three words are most frequently used. By combining their meanings we can gain a picture of the purpose and nature of true worship of God. *Proskuneo* means to do reverence by kissing the hand, or to prostrate oneself as a means of expressing homage. Hence, it involves the outward actions of worship. *Sebomai* reflects the attitude of worship—reverence and veneration. Thus we are to worship God in a spirit of awe. A third word, *latreuo,* signifies service rendered, and in this sense we may conclude that worship is not limited to the public assembly, but that all true service to God is worship. From these definitions it is apparent that worship involves both the form and the spirit. Jesus told the woman at Jacob's well, "God is spirit, and those who worship him must worship in spirit and truth" (John 4:24). The outward actions of worship are but the means of bringing the human spirit into the proper relationship with God. Unless the mind relates to the outward forms they are meaningless. It is possible to read the scriptures without following the thought or to sing praises to God with one's mind in another place. Such worship is as unacceptable to God as were the vain repetitions of the Pharisees which Jesus so strongly condemned.

Worship has been defined as "the conscious point of contact between the creature and the creator, a recognition of divine kinship." In it we express to the Father our praise, adoration, and thanks. In return we receive from him the blessings of faith, comfort, and forgiveness. It becomes our means of enjoying true communion with God. As we worship in spirit, our minds should be captivated by the divine presence. The world is shut out as the heart consciously reaches for the Father. The true worshipper is a participant, not just a spectator. The prayers that others direct to God in his presence become his prayers conveying his petitions to heaven. Worship is a personal experience in which one comes "to know the love of Christ which surpasses knowledge" and is "filled with all the fulness of God" (Ephesians 3:19). When we reach this state we can enjoy that intimate relationship with the Father which David felt when he wrote, "As a heart longs for flowing springs, so longs my soul for thee, O God. My soul thirsts for God, for the living God. When shall I come and behold the face of God?" (Psalm 42:1, 2).

The worship in Philippi strikes us by its utter simplicity. There is none of the elaborate ritual of the Jewish temple observances. Nor do we see the liturgy and formalism found today in so many communions. The function of the assembly is not to impress others or to create pleasing personal sensations, but to truly worship and edify. The acts of worship we observe are designed both to praise God and to mutually strengthen on another.

Their Singing

The Christians raise their voices in song. They have been enjoined, "Let the word of Christ dwell in you richly, teach and admonish one another in all wisdom, and sing psalms and hymns and spiritual songs with thankfulness in your hearts to God" (Colossians 3:16). They also have been told, "Make melody to the Lord with all your heart" (Ephesians 5:19). It may seem strange that their hymns are sung without musical accompaniment. It would be four or five hundred years before instruments of music would be introduced into Christian worship. You see, the emphasis in their singing is not on the beauty of the musical harmony, but on making music in the *heart*. To these people the words are the important thing, not the sensual effect of the melody on the ears. It appears that musical instruments were intentionally omitted from the worship of the church in the apostolic period. This view is reflected in the writings of the church fathers in the centuries immediately following. When they deal with the subject of musical instruments, they are preponderantly opposed to their use in Christian worship.[1]

As we listen to the Philippians sing we notice that their melodic form differs from that to which Western ears are accustomed. The singing is in unison in a minor key, and perhaps a chant, reflecting the typical singing of the Orient. The New Testament does not tell us what kind of melody or meter the early Christians used nor is this particularly important. Each culture uses its own musical forms, and even today the songs of Africa or the Far East will sound strange to those accustomed to the tonal patterns of the West. The important thing is not the key of the song nor the way it is sung by the lips, but rather the thoughts conveyed by the words of the psalms, hymns, and spiritual songs which draw the worshippers closer to God and to one another.

Their Prayers

We observe the importance they attach to prayer. Paul enjoined the Philippians, "Have no anxiety about anything, but in *everything* by prayer and supplication with thanksgiving let your requests be made known to God" (Philippians 4:6). Their prayers are not mere generalities, but are as specific as required by the circumstances. When Peter escaped from prison he found the disciples having a prayer meeting, probably on his behalf, in the home of the mother of John Mark (Acts 12:12-17). Paul exhorted that prayers be offered for kings and those in authority (1 Timothy 2:1, 2) and requested that Christians remember him in their prayers (1 Thessalonians 5:25). We can be sure that these Philippians pray for the sick and those in prison by name, and that they do not forget Paul, their spiritual father in the faith, who has recently been arrested in Jerusalem. There are no memorized prayers, no liturgy, but rather a spontaneity in which the heart addresses the Father in the name of Jesus.

Scripture Reading

Following the practice of the Jewish synagogue, the Philippian Christians devote much of the time in their worship to the reading of the sacred writings which they call the scriptures. Many of the people are uneducated and cannot read, but they can listen and the assembly period provides the ideal time to hear the Lord speak.

Paul stressed the importance of the scriptures when he declared that "all scripture is inspired by God and profitable for teaching, for reproof, for correction, and for training in righteousness, that the man of God may be complete, equipped for every good work" (2 Timothy 3:16, 17). From the Old Testament they read the fifty-third chapter of Isaiah which graphically foretells the coming of the Messiah. Paul's first letter to the church of the Thessalonians, a sister congregation in Macedonia, is also read. A copy of it has been made for the Philippian church. At this time only a few of the books which we call the New Testament have yet been penned. Paul's personal letter to the Philippians themselves is still some months from being written, but when it is received it will be a regular part of the public reading.

Edification and Exhortation

The scriptures are used as a basis for teaching and preaching. They are explained to the hearers by those appointed to the task of edifying. They can profit by the examples of the Old Testament heroes of faith. Those who know the story of the life and teachings of Jesus recite the account from memory. The first of the four gospels, Mark's memoirs of Jesus, will be written in a few years to provide an accurate record of the one on whom their faith rests.

If a preacher of God's word is present he is invited to speak as Paul was when he visited the Christians at Troas at the time of their weekly Sunday assembly (Acts 20:7). The public teaching also provides an opportunity for the disciples to exhort one another. Then, as today, it was the habit of some to neglect to meet with their brethren at the regular time. Therefore, when they gather they are urged "to stir up one another to love and good works" and to "encourage one another" (Hebrews 10:24, 25). To be a Christian in the first century means to be persecuted and to suffer the loss of one's possessions (Hebrews 10:32-34) and sometimes even to die for Jesus. Without mutual encouragement some would lose their faith in the face of the intimidations of Satan. They find their strength in one another, especially when they come together to worship.

The Lord's Supper

The focal point of the Philippian worship is the Lord's supper. This is a simple meal instituted by Jesus as a personal *memorial* on the night he was betrayed. Its elements were taken from the food he and his disciples were eating as they observed the Jewish Passover—unleavened bread and the juice of the vine or grape. Matthew describes the event in this way: "Now as they were eating, Jesus took bread, and blessed, and broke it, and gave it to the disciples and said, 'Take, eat; this is my body.' And he took a cup, and when he had given thanks he gave it to them, saying, 'Drink of it, all of you; for this is my blood of the covenant, which is poured out for many for the forgiveness of sins' " (Matthew 26:26-28). He exhorted them, "Do this in remembrance of me" (1 Corinthians 11:24). Following his instructions the early disciples met on the first day of the week to "break bread" (Acts 20:7), or eat the Lord's supper (1 Corinthians 11:20) in memory of the body and blood of their crucified and risen Savior. In it they also enjoyed a *communion* or *fellowship* with the Lord and with one another in the body and blood of Jesus (1 Corinthians 10:16). In turn it became an expression of their *unity* in Christ (1 Corinthians 10:16, 17). Moreover, it was a symbol of their *covenant* with Jesus who had informed them, "This cup is the new covenant in my blood" (1 Corinthians 11:25). It was also a mutual *proclamation* of their faith that one day Jesus would return. Had not he himself declared, "For as often as you eat this bread and drink the cup, you proclaim the Lord's death until he comes" (1 Corinthians 11:26)? A memorial, fellowship, unity, a covenant, a proclamation—all of these were bound up in the eating of this simple meal.

So it is that our visit finds the Christians meeting for the purpose of remembering their Lord in this way. This is not just a ritual which they discharge to obey a command, nor do they eat it to receive the forgiveness of sins. Forgiveness has already been granted them in the blood of Jesus. But because the elements do symbolize the death of Jesus, it is eaten with great solemnity. Paul had warned, "Whoever, therefore, eats the bread or drinks the cup of the Lord in an unworthy manner will be guilty of profaning the body and blood of the Lord. Let a man examine himself, and so eat of the bread and drink of the cup. For any one who eats and drinks without discerning the body eats and drinks judgment upon himself" (1 Corinthians 11:27-29).

The Lord's supper was intended only for the Christian. Only to him is it a memorial of the death of Jesus; only for the child of God is this communion a symbol of the divine covenant; only for him is it a proclamation of his faith in the return of the Son of God; only to the Christian is the bread a sign of the unity of the one body. For the non-Christian the sacred feast is meaningless and such a one should not partake of it until he has accepted Jesus as his Lord.

Their Giving

As we visit the Philippian assembly, shall we expect them to take up a contribution as is usually done today among most religious bodies? We do know that these Christians contributed to Paul's personal welfare when he preached the gospel in other places (Philippians 4:15, 16). This congregation was certainly also among those Macedonian churches which gave so liberally out of their deep poverty when Paul requested funds for the needy in Jerusalem and Judea (2 Corinthians 8:1-5). Paul instructed the Corinthians to give on the first day of every week, apparently at the time of their assembly (1 Corinthians 16:1, 2), and there is no reason to presume that it was done otherwise at Philippi. The money collected was put into a treasury, and although the contribution mentioned at Corinth was intended for a specific purpose, the Christians must have given on the Lord's day to meet the needs that arose, whether they related to benevolence or proclamation of the gospel.

Should such a contribution be considered worship? We have already observed that one of the Greek words translated "worship" carries the idea of service. A gift to Christ through the church is certainly service rendered and therefore worship. Paul speaks of the Philippians' gift to him as God's servant as "a fragrant offering, a sacrifice acceptable and pleasing to God" (Philippians 4:18). This certainly makes a monetary offering an act of worship. Of course, not all worship is carried out in the public assembly. Food given by a Christian to a needy family on Tuesday in the name of Jesus is quite as much worship as the offering of a ten dollar bill dropped in the collection plate when the saints assemble. A prayer offered or a hymn sung in praise to God in the privacy of one's home, if done in the proper spirit, is as truly worship as when prayers and hymns are directed to God collectively on the Lord's day.

Spiritual Gifts

We have yet to consider the exercise of spiritual gifts (1 Corinthians 12:1) at Philippi. Although nothing is said in Paul's letter to this church about these gifts, we should probably presume that they were present since they were at Corinth. Our knowledge of these miraculous spiritual abilities is largely limited to the discussion in chapters twelve, thirteen, and fourteen of 1 Corinthians. Paul there mentions nine distinct gifts—wisdom, knowledge, faith, healing, miracles, prophecy, ability to distinguish between spirits, tongues, and the interpretation of tongues (1 Corinthians 12:8-10). Although some of these talents, such as knowledge and faith, would not necessarily imply the miraculous, it is obvious in the context of the passage that a measure beyond normal human abilities is being considered. For example, Paul mentions a faith so great that it can remove mountains (1 Corinthians 13:2), which is obviously far beyond the ordinary measure of faith possessed by any of us.

Paul makes it clear that different Christians enjoyed different gifts. Probably no one possessed them all. Some had become puffed up because they could speak in tongues. Paul writes to correct their abuses of speaking when there was no interpreter, and of everyone trying to talk at the same time. An analysis of these gifts shows that they were given to reveal the truth of God, impart that truth to those who had not heard it, and confirm the truth once it was taught. The church was in its infancy, few of the New Testament books were yet written, and some kind of supernatural guidance was necessary for these young Christians. These spiritual gifts were God's answer to the problem.

There is special interest today in whether Christians should now expect to receive these gifts. Does the restoration of apostolic Christianity include miraculous healing and prophecy? Some are especially concerned about the gift of tongues which in the modern mind seems to eclipse all of the other gifts mentioned by Paul.

We should first observe that the tongues mentioned by Paul were real languages, not ecstatic speech which has no meaning in any known language. The only description of the nature of tongues in the New Testament is found in Acts 2:4-13. On the day of Pentecost the apostles spoke in these tongues and Jews from everywhere understood their words in their native dialects. The Egyptian understood the Egyptian language, the Arabian the Arabic.

In this way it was demonstrated to them that the message of the apostles was from God.

There is no justifiable reason to presume that the phenomenon of tongue speaking mentioned by Paul in his writings to the Corinthians was any different. The same Greek word is used in both accounts and certainly there is no mention of ecstatic speech in 1 Corinthians. Therefore, those who today profess to speak in ecstatic tongues that have no counterpart in known languages should realize that their practice does not correspond to that of the Corinthians.

The biblical evidence is that these gifts were transmitted by the laying on of hands of certain people who had the special talent of giving them to others. Paul gave gifts to the Ephesian Christians by laying his hands on them (Acts 19:6), and to Timothy in the same manner (2 Timothy 1:6). He wrote the Roman Christians, "For I long to see you, that I may impart to you some *spiritual gift* to strengthen you" (Romans 1:11). Perhaps the clearest case of how the gifts were transmitted is that of the Samaritans converted by the preaching of Philip the evangelist. Philip could not give these gifts to the new disciples of Jesus, but when the apostles Peter and John arrived in Samaria we read, "Then they laid their hands on them and they received the Holy Spirit. Now when Simon saw that the Spirit was given through the *laying on of the apostles' hands,* he offered them money, saying, 'Give me also this power, that any one on whom I lay my hands may receive the Holy Spirit" (Acts 8:17-19). What Simon the magician sought to buy was the ability to transmit miraculous gifts to others. His request was very wrong and he was sternly rebuked by Peter. This incident clearly shows that only certain people could give the gifts to others. Whether the apostles alone could transmit the gifts we are not told, but only the apostles are mentioned as possessing this talent. If they alone could give the gifts to others, we should expect them to cease after the end of the apostolic age. Historically this is what happened.

The basic question we must ask about spiritual gifts is whether they were intended to continue to the present. The answer is found in 1 Corinthians. After discussing the gifts in general in chapter twelve, Paul continued, "And I will show you a still more excellent way" (1 Corinthians 12:31). The better way, he explained in chapter 13, is love. It excels all spiritual gifts. Moreover, "Love never ends; *as for prophecies, they will pass away, as for tongues, they will cease; as for knowledge, it will pass away.* For our knowledge is imperfect and our prophecy imperfect, but when the perfect comes, the imperfect will pass away" (1 Corinthians 13:8-10).

Paul chose three of the nine spiritual gifts as typical of all—prophecy, tongues, and (miraculous) knowledge. He declared that spiritual gifts would end when their function had been completed. Our problem is determining if the ceasation of these gifts has yet occurred. The key phrase is, "When the perfect comes, the imperfect will pass away." What is meant by "the perfect"? Various explanations have been proposed. Some think the perfect is Christ. This explanation is deficient because in the original language there is not grammatical agreement between "Christ" and "perfect." Others think it is the second coming. But this would hardly make sense because it would have Paul saying, "When the coming comes."

The Greek word for *perfect* means "that which is brought to maturity; completeness; perfect in the sense of completeness or maturity." The sentence may be translated, "For we know in part, and we prophesy in part; but when the complete comes, the partial will be done away." One writer states, "From a grammatical standpoint, it appears that Paul is saying, 'We *know* in part, and we *prophesy* in part, but when the complete (*knowledge* and *prophecy*) comes, the partial (*knowledge* and *prophecy*) will be done away.'" [2] Thus, spiritual gifts (of which knowledge, prophecy, and tongues were typical) were partial and designed to last until God's complete revelation of his will had been made known. With the completion of the apostolic age and the revelation in written form of God's will for us in the books that make up the New Testament, this has been accomplished. The spiritual gifts have served their purpose and we should not now expect to receive them.

The order of worship of the churches of the first century undoubtedly varied. They probably didn't all meet at the same time on the Lord's day, sing the same songs, or do things in precisely the same way. But the basic picture of the worship of these early disciples emerges from the pages of the New Testament, and I hope that our visit to Philippi has helped us understand how they may have rendered homage to God so that we too may seek to observe the essential elements of that worship.

[1]A very fine historical examination of the attitudes of the church fathers toward musical instruments in worship is found in Everett Ferguson's *A Cappella Music in the Public Worship of the Church* (Abilene, Texas: Biblical Research Press, 1972), pp. 47-84.

[2]Hal Hougey, " 'When the Perfect Comes'—An Interpretation," *Koinonia*, January, 1973, p. 2.

CHAPTER 10

The Community of the Redeemed

Jesus and his disciples traveled north to the region of Caesarea Philippi. Here at the foot of snowcapped Mt. Hermon the Lord posed some of the most searching questions he ever asked of the twelve. "Who do men say that the Son of Man is?" he inquired. Several names were suggested including John the Baptist and Elijah. Jesus had asked his question to introduce another. "But who do *you* say that I am?" he pursued. Peter replied, "You are the Christ, the Son of the living God."

The response of Jesus to Peter's confession is of great significance. "Blessed are you, Simon Bar-Jona! For flesh and blood has not revealed this to you, but my Father who is in heaven. And I tell you, you are Peter, and on this rock I will build my church, and the powers of death shall not prevail against it. I will give you the keys of the kingdom of heaven, and whatever you bind on earth shall be bound in heaven, and whatever you loose on earth shall be loosed in heaven" (Matthew 16:17-19).

Most discussion of these verses focuses on the *rock* on which Jesus intended to build his church. Our interest here, however, relates to the *church* itself. Earlier we noted that our English word *church* is a translation of the Greek *ekklesia*. We also learned something of the derivation of *ekklesia*. Now we need to inquire what Jesus was talking about when he introduced this word, for this is the first time it is found in the New Testament.

"I will build my church." Some may suppose that Jesus was about to construct a cathedral or beautiful temple. This is not possible because *ekklesia* never meant a building. Others may think that Jesus was about to start a denomination. Neither can this be true since it was many years later that religious denominations began. Still others, viewing his statement from our modern

107

perspective, will envision a complex organization with a president, secretary, and chairman of the board. Although this last idea agrees closely with the contemporary use of *church,* a closer examination shows that Jesus had something quite different in mind. Our problem is that we tend to explain the Bible according to present day definitions rather than seeking the original meanings.

A clue to the thought of Jesus is that in this passage he equates the church and the kingdom. After stating that he would build his church, he then informed Peter that he would give him the keys of the kingdom of heaven, thus using church and kingdom interchangeably. Although *kingdom* suggests a government, Jesus always used the word spiritually to denote the people of God.

Moreover, *ekklesia* was not a new word to the disciples. The *Septuagint* translation of the Hebrew Old Testament (the Bible of the Greek speaking Jewish world) used it as the equivalent of an assembly. To the Jewish mind it designated the people of Israel. One authority comments:

"It is the Septuagint term for the community of Israel, whether assembled or no. In the gospels the word is confined to Matthew 16:18; 18:17, where it denotes Christ's new ekklesia, as distinguished from the old."[1]

When Stephen stood trial before the Jews, he described the people of Israel in their journey from Egypt to Canaan as "the church (congregation) in the wilderness" (Acts 7:38). Just as fleshly Israel in Old Testament times was God's church then, so the Christians, spiritual Israel, constitute God's church today. Paul even calls the followers of Jesus "the Israel of God" (Galatians 6:16).

A Spiritual Body

Viewed in this way it is apparent that we should think of Christ's church as an organism rather than an organization. Of course, it does have structure as we will notice, but it was created to be a living entity rather than an unfeeling corporation. Paul describes it as a spiritual body comparable to our physical organisms:

"For just as the body is one and has many members, and all the members of the body, though many, are one body, so it is with

108

Christ. For by one Spirit we were all baptized into one body—Jews or Greeks, slaves or free—and all were made to drink of one Spirit. For the body does not consist of one member but of many. If the foot should say, 'Because I am not a hand, I do not belong to the body,' that would not make it any less a part of the body. And if the ear should say, 'Because I am not an eye, I do not belong to the body,' that would not make it any less a part of the body. If the whole body were an eye, where would be the hearing? If the whole body were an ear, where would be the sense of smell? But as it is, God arranged the organs in the body, each one of them, as he chose. If all were a single organ, where would the body be? As it is, there are many parts, yet one body. The eye cannot say to the hand, 'I have no need of you,' nor again the head to the feet, 'I have no need of you.' On the contrary, the parts of the body which seem to be weaker are indispensable, and those parts of the body which we think less honorable we invest with the greater honor, and our unpresentable parts are treated with greater modesty, which our more presentable parts do not require. But God has so composed the body, giving the greater honor to the inferior part, that there may be no discord in the body, but that the members may have the same care for one another. If one member suffers, all suffer together; if one member is honored, all rejoice together. *Now you are the body of Christ and individually members of it"* (1 Corinthians 12:12-27).

Observe how the spiritual body compares to the physical:
1. The body is unified.
2. Each one became a part of it in the same way.
3. Each part has a function.
4. Each part is dependent on the other parts.
5. Each part is indispensable.
6. All parts suffer together.
7. All parts rejoice together.

The Family of God

These conclusions can also be applied to the human family. In it there is unity, each person became a part of it in the same way, each one has his own responsibilities, each individual depends upon the other members, each one is indispensable to the proper functioning of the family unit, and when one member suffers or rejoices, the others share that suffering or rejoicing.

The church is a spiritual family possessing many of the characteristics of the human family. It is composed of God's children (Romans 8:16), often called brothers and sisters in the New Testament. Their lives are closely interwoven in a spiritual unit in which the members have different roles. As such they love each other, are concerned for one another, and mutually bear one another's material and spiritual burdens.

As with human families, spiritual families (congregations) often fall short of the ideal. Nevertheless, they must always strive to carry out the family pattern which the Father has given.

When we view the church as a body or family, it alters our understanding of its organizational structure. We must cease thinking of it as an ecclesiasticism in which all planning is arranged at the top. We can no longer conceive of it in terms of a professional clergy paid by the laity to do all the work. Nor can we properly think of it as the clergy wielding heavy-handed authority and imposing its wishes on those not in the decision making process.

Instead we see a group of people working cooperatively for the benefit of all, each one fulfilling his proper role in the interest of the common good. Those who exercise authority do so at the will of the members because in any kind of body there must be leaders to direct activities and carry out the group's objectives.

God's Theocracy

In order to better understand the structure of the early church it is helpful to observe that the government of ancient Israel was a theocracy. The people recognized God as their king. The Law of Moses, given by God, regulated every facet of their lives—civil, political, and religious. For several hundred years after Israel entered the land of Canaan it was directed by judges who were more shepherds than rulers. Yet there was also the recognition that God was their king. In time the people tired of this arrangement and demanded of Samuel, their judge, that he give them a human king to replace the judges. When they made this request, God informed the prophet, "Hearken to the voice of the people in all that they say to you; for they have not rejected you, but they have rejected me from being king over them" (1 Samuel 8:7).

In a sense the church is also a theocracy. Christ is our king (1 Timothy 6:15), his word is our spiritual guide, and we acknowledge him as our sovereign. We are citizens of the kingdom he said he would establish (Ephesians 2:19). His monarchy is absolute. In his commision he told the apostles, "*All authority* in heaven and on earth has been given to me" (Matthew 28:18). We have no independent right to change any of his directives.

The Apostolic Office

The New Testament provides us with a picture of the structure of the early church. The lack of a detailed description is testimony to the simplicity of its organization. The first office of which we read is that of the apostles. During his personal ministry Jesus chose twelve men to lay the groundwork for his spiritual body. After training them for about three and a half years, he gave them authority to proclaim his message to the world. This they did after his death, resurrection, and ascension into heaven. To these original twelve may be added Matthias, who replaced the traitor Judas (Acts 1:26), and Paul, who received a special commission to go to the Gentiles with the message of Christ (Galatians 1:1, 11, 12). On the first Pentecost after Christ's ascension, the apostles for the first time revealed to mankind the terms of eternal salvation. Divinely inspired by God's Holy Spirit, they continued to impart orally and in writing the teachings of Jesus to those whom they taught (1 Corinthians 2:13).

An examination of the New Testament reveals no hierarchy over which the apostles presided. On one occasion (Acts 15) they participated in a conference to settle a doctrinal controversy. Their decision was authoritative. Still they established no autocracy to run the universal church. Instead, after an initial period in which they remained in Jerusalem, they seemed to have spread in many directions as missionaries of Jesus Christ.

The apostolic office was temporary. Although Judas was replaced because he died before the day of Pentecost, there is no record of any other successors to these men. When James, the brother of John, was martyred (Acts 12:2), no one took his place. According to tradition all of the apostles, except John, died as martyrs for their faith. By the end of the first century all had died. The requirement that an apostle must have been a witness to the resurrection of Jesus could not longer be met (Acts 1:21, 22). The apostolic office was gone and with it the inspired authority which they had used in setting the church in order.

The Universal Church

Earlier we discovered that the word *church* is used both universally and congregationally. Universally it denotes all of the saved throughout the world. However, one searches the New Testament in vain for any kind of super-congregational structure. Nor does one find such in the writings of the second century church fathers. It is apparent that each congregation made its own decisions without direction from other human sources. *The local churches were united, however, by a common allegiance to Christ, a common doctrine, and a common love for one another.*

However, congregations cooperated with one another in a variety of ways. The Christians in Antioch sent relief during a famine to the church in Jerusalem (Acts 11:27-30). The church at Philippi sent funds to Paul to help him preach the word in Thessalonica (Philippians 4:15, 16). Several churches banded together to choose a messenger to carry money from Greece to Judea in time of need (2 Corinthians 8:18, 19). The Ephesian disciples sent a letter of endorsement of Apollos to the Christians in Achaia. All of these actions were voluntary and apparently determined at the congregational level. Although we might suppose that the cause of Christ would not spread without a super-organization, it is significant that during this period of strict congregational government Christianity enjoyed its greatest growth. Apparently the Lord knew best in instituting this kind of arrangement.

The Congregation

How the local church functioned is described by Paul in his letter to the Ephesians: "And his gifts were that some should be apostles, some prophets, some evangelists, some _pastors and teachers, to equip the saints for the work of ministry, for building up the body of Christ, until we all attain to the unity of the faith and of the knowledge of the Son of God, to mature manhood, to the measure of the stature of the fulness of Christ. . ." (Ephesians 4:11-13). Although the apostolic and prophetic offices were temporary, we can see from this passage that congregations operated with different individuals dividing a variety of duties. Their work was more functional than official. Some of these people were charged with responsibility to see that the work was done.
work was done.

112

Elders

On their first missionary journey Paul and Barnabas established several congregations in the interior provinces of what is now Turkey. After spending considerable time with each church, they retraced their steps. "And when they had appointed *elders* for them in every church, with prayer and fasting, they committed them to the Lord in whom they believed" (Acts 14:23).

Who were these elders and what was their function? *Elder* is often used in the Old Testament to designate those men who governed Israel. In the gospel we often read of the "elders of the people" (Matthew 26:47), usually in conjunction with the chief priests and other leaders of the Jewish community. The same word was later applied to the spiritual leaders of the Christian community. In the epistles it is used interchangeably with two other words—*bishop* (Titus 1:5-7), and *pastor* (Ephesians 4:11).

Elder (Greek—*presbuteros,*—from which *presbyter* is derived) implied an older man. The idea is more that of maturity than of chronological age. *Bishop* (Greek—*episcopos* from which *episcopal* comes) might better be translated *overseer*. In modern usage bishop often designates one in a high denominational position possessing great authority. This is not the New Testament concept. *Pastor* (Greek—*poimen*) was literally a feeder of the sheep or *shepherd*. In the biblical sense it denotes those who shepherd the spiritual flock or church.

From the definitions of these words we conclude that elders were mature men, who were responsible for overseeing the work of the congregation and looking after the flock. Several passages amplify this idea. Peter admonished elders, *"Tend the flock of God* that is in your charge, not by constraint but willingly, not for shameful gain but eagerly, not as domineering over those in your charge but being examples to the flock" (1 Peter 5:2, 3). Paul added, "Let the elders who *rule well* be considered worthy of double honor, especially those who labor in preaching and teaching" (1 Timothy 5:17). Elders were to be *able to teach* (1 Timothy 3:2) and to *care for the church of God* (Acts 20:28). Biblically speaking, then, the elders were responsible for pastoring the congregation which involved teaching, counseling, and decision making.

The qualifications of elders are given in two scriptures—1 Timothy 3:1-7 and Titus 1:5-9. Those who served in this capacity were to be men of high moral character who had previously demonstrated their capabilities in their own families. They were appointed by preachers of the gospel (Acts 14:23; Titus 1:5), but the manner of choosing the seven deacons in Jerusalem indicates that the will of the people was considered in the selection process (Acts 6:3).

Deacons

We are told less about deacons than about elders. Paul mentions the bishops and deacons together in Philippians 1:1, and gives the qualifications of both in his instructions to Timothy (1 Timothy 3:8-13). The qualifications were similar, the chief difference being that deacons are not required to be teachers.

The Greek word from which *deacon* is derived means *servant*. In some places it is translated *minister*. Sometimes it means a servant in the general sense while in other instances it designates a specific function in the church. In this sense seven men were appointed by the apostles to care for the widows in the Jerusalem church (Acts 6). Although the seven are not called deacons in this passage, the Greek verb used to describe their work has the same meaning as the noun from which *deacon* comes, indicating that this was the work they were performing. Their responsibility was to minister to the needs of the members while the apostles devoted themselves to the spiritual oversight of the flock. It appears, therefore, that the function of deacons is to carry out responsibilities which have been assigned to them by the church leaders.

Evangelists

When Paul visited Caesarea at the end of his third missionary journey he "entered the house of Philip the *evangelist*" (Acts 21:8). On one occasion Paul also instructed the young preacher Timothy to "do the work of an *evangelist*" (2 Timothy 4:5). The word *evangelist* literally means *a proclaimer of glad tidings* or a *gospel preacher*. Present day usage assigns it the meaning of a preacher who travels, but in New Testament times it simply meant one who preached the gospel whether he traveled or stayed in one locality. Paul, for example, often went from city to city, yet he also remained in Corinth for a year and a half (Acts 18:11) and in Ephesus for three years (Acts 20:31).

Paul outlines the work of a preacher in his instructions to two young men—Timothy and Titus. Timothy is charged, "Preach the word, be urgent in season and out of season, convince, rebuke, and exhort, be unfailing in patience and in teaching" (2 Timothy 4:2). Evangelists are to establish new churches, strengthen established congregations, and proclaim the word of God wherever opportunity affords itself. They may work with congregations having elders, as did Timothy at Ephesus (Acts 20:17; 1 Timothy 1:3). It should be remembered, however, that the responsibility of pastoring the flock is that of the elders rather than a gospel preacher, unless one serves in both capacities as did Peter (1 Peter 5:1). An evangelist is a minister of the gospel (Colossians 1:23) which means that his ministry is to preach the good news of Jesus. Still it is not biblically correct to speak of such a preacher as "the minister of the congregation" since every Christian has a ministry to perform.

If we are to fully reproduce the church of the New Testament, we must establish congregations organized as they were in the first century. We must remember that the church is a functioning body, not an ecclesiasticism. Those who serve as elders or deacons or preachers of the gospel are fulfilling their functions in the spiritual body rather than serving as executive officers in a corporation. Although in the church there are places of responsibility and authority that accompanies such, still there is equality in *the community of the redeemed.*

"For in Christ Jesus you are all sons of God, through faith. For as many of you as were baptized into Christ have put on Christ. There is neither Jew nor Greek, there is neither slave nor free, there is neither male nor female; for you are all one in Christ Jesus. And if you are Christ's then you are Abraham's offspring, heirs according to promise" (Galatians 3:26-29).

[1]James Hope Moulton and George Milligan, *The Vocabulary of the Greek Testament* (Grand Rapids: Wm. B. Eerdmans Publishing Co.), p. 195.

CHAPTER 11

The Priesthood of All Believers

The Protestant Reformation was founded on several great principles. These included: (1) the scriptures as the sole authority for faith and life, (2) justification by faith without respect to merits of good works, and (3) the priesthood of all believers. The first two have already been discussed. It is to the priesthood of all believers, as Martin Luther termed the biblical doctrine involved, that we now direct our attention.

Luther's View

In the midst of his struggle with the Roman Catholic Church, Luther in 1520 published a treatise entitled, *To the Christian Nobility of the German Nation.* In it he called upon the German rulers to unite against the Roman Church which he felt had oppressed the people. He then declared, "There has been a fiction by which the Pope, bishops, priests, and monks are called the 'spiritual estate'; princes, lords, artisans, and peasants are the 'temporal estate.' This is an artful lie and hypocritical invention, but let no one be made afraid by it, and that for this reason: that all Christians are truly of the spiritual estate, and there is no difference among them, save of office. As St. Paul says (1 Corinthians 12), we are all one body, though each member does its own work so as to serve the others. This is because we have one baptism, one Gospel, one faith, and are all Christians alike; for baptism, Gospel, and faith, these alone make spiritual and Christian people.

"As for the unction by a pope or a bishop, tonsure, ordination, consecration, and clothes differing from those of laymen—all this may make a hypocrite or an anointed puppet, but never a Christian or a spiritual man. *Thus we are all consecrated as priests by baptism, as St. Peter says: 'Ye are a royal priesthood, a holy nation' (1 Peter 2:9); and in the Book of Revelation: 'and hast made us unto our God (by Thy blood) kings and priests' (Revelation 5:10)."*[1]

Luther then concluded that a group of isolated Christians that found itself without a priest consecrated by a bishop had within itself the authority to choose one of its own number to perform the religious duties associated with the priesthood. His reasoning was that since each disciple of Christ is a priest anyway, the authorization of the church hierarchy is not necessary for one to perform these functions.

Our Great High Priest

Under the Mosaic dispensation there was a special order of priests. From the Israelite tribe of Levi all the priests were chosen of whom one, a descendant of Aaron, served as high priest.

The new covenant which Christians have with God has changed this. Our high priest is Jesus himself, who is called "the apostle and high priest of our confession" (Hebrews 3:1). The Jewish high priest was required to offer sacrifices for the sins of the people. Jesus offered himself, shedding his blood on the cross. "For it was fitting that we should have such a high priest, holy, blameless, unstained, separated from sinners, exalted above the heavens. He has no need, like those high priests, to offer sacrifices daily, first for his own sins and then for those of the people; he did this once for all when he offered up himself" (Hebrews 7:26, 27). No further sacrifice is necessary. Our high priest has made the supreme offering.

The old law required the high priest to interceed before God on behalf of the sins of the people. Since he ascended to heaven Jesus performs this function as our high priest. "For Christ has entered, not into a sanctuary made with hands, a copy of the true one, but into heaven itself, now to appear in the presence of God on our behalf" (Hebrews 9:24). He is able to identify with us in our struggles. "Since then we have a great high priest who has passed through the heavens, Jesus, the Son of God, let us hold fast our confession. For we have not a high priest who is unable to sympathize with our weaknesses, but one who in every respect has been tempted as we are, yet without sin" (Hebrews 4:14, 15). When we pray to the Father "in the name of Jesus Christ," we are invoking his aid as our high priest. He can serve as our intercessor because he knows our problems, having traveled the same road over which we journey.

If Jesus is our high priest, each of his disciples is also a priest. Peter speaks of Christians as constituting "a holy priesthood . . . a royal priesthood" (1 Peter 2:5, 9). Christ has "made us a kingdom, priests to his God and Father" (Revelation 1:6). Since this is true the Christian system does not make the distinction between clergy and laity usually found in the contemporary religious world.

The Clergy System

How did the denominational clerical system develop? As we have already observed, congregations in the first century were guided by spiritual pastors called elders or bishops (overseers). "Elder" and "bishop" were used interchangeably and there was a plurality of these men in the churches they served. By the next century this was being changed and a single bishop was elevated above his fellow elders and invested with authority not found in the New Testament.

This change is reflected in the early second century writings of Ignatius, bishop of Antioch. Ignatius seems to have had a fixation on the authority of bishops, and although his views do not seem to have been generally accepted at that time, they eventually came to represent the position of the church as a whole. Consider this comment in his letter to the church at Smyrna:

"Let no man do aught of things pertaining to the Church apart from the bishop. Let that be held a valid eucharist which is under the bishop or one to whom he shall have committed it. Wheresoever the bishop shall appear, there let the people be; even as where Jesus may be, there is the universal church. It is not lawful apart from the bishop either to baptize or hold a love-feast; but whatsoever he shall approve, this is well-pleasing also to God; that everything which ye do may be sure and valid.

"It is reasonable henceforth that we wake to soberness, while we have (still) time to repent and turn to God. It is good to recognize God and the bishop. He that honoreth the bishop is honored of God; he that doeth aught without the knowledge of the bishop rendereth service to the devil."[2]

In his exaltation of the bishop Ignatius clearly laid the basis for the clergy-laity relationship. Observe that Christians could do nothing without the prior approval of the bishop. The bishop was elevated to the position of God's representative, clearly standing between God and the people. Here also are the seeds of the doctrine

119

of apostolic succession, the theory which affirms that clerical authority is passed from bishop to bishop and that without the approval of the church, as represented by the clergy, certain religious functions cannot be performed.

The ideas of Ignatius were probably prompted by a fear that without some kind of churchly control the church would become the prey of false teachers which were beginning to pose a serious problem. However, his solution to the problem only created another. The holy priesthood was abandoned in favor of a clergy-laity distinction. Under this system the members of the clergy were elevated to a spiritual pedestal in which they were accorded the reverence due only to God.

What Jesus Teaches

The teaching of Jesus on this is quite clear. He explained, "Where two or three are gathered in my name, there am I in the midst of them" (Matthew 18:20). There is no requirement here for the presence of an ordained clergyman when Christians worship God. And in the very strongest language Jesus condemned all religious titles of distinction which are the mark of the clergy system: "But you are not to be called rabbi, for you have one teacher, and you are all brethren. And call no man your father on earth, for you have one Father, who is in heaven. Neither be called masters, for you have one master, the Christ. He who is greatest among you shall be your servant; whoever exalts himself will be humbled, and whoever humbles himself will be exalted" (Matthew 23:8-12). In condemning the use of rabbi, father, and other spiritual titles of distinction, Jesus also emphasized the equality of all of his disciples upon which the priesthood of all believers rests. For in Jesus Christ, "there is neither Jew nor Greek, there is neither slave nor free, there is neither male nor female; for you are all one in Christ Jesus" (Galatians 3:28). Christians have different functions, but in the family of God there are no ranks.

The Holy Priesthood

What does it mean to be a priest of God? Perhaps the most obvious implication is that one may commune directly with God through prayer. The Jewish priest had a direct relationship with God. Likewise, those who have accepted the service of Jesus may individually pray to the Father with only our high priest, Christ, as intercessor. It is not necessary to first confess one's sins to a human priest and then have this priest in turn invoke the Father on behalf of the penitent. Of course, it is our privilege to confess our sins to one another and to ask our fellow disciples to pray on our behalf. James wrote, "Therefore confess your sins to one another, and pray for one another, that you may be healed. The prayer of a righteous man has great power in its effects" (James 5:16). But this privilege of asking a "fellow priest" to assist one in approaching the divine majesty does not imply that the right of each individual Christian to the presence of God has in any way been diminished.

One of the prime functions of the Levitical priests was the offering of sacrifices on behalf of themselves and the people. The offerings of God's priests today are different in nature. Peter exhorted, "Like living stones be yourselves built into a spiritual house, to be a holy priesthood, to offer spiritual sacrifices acceptable to God through Jesus Christ" (1 Peter 2:5). No longer are priests of God to present animal offerings to God; their gifts are spiritual in character. For example, we are told, "Through him (Jesus) then let us continually offer up a sacrifice of praise to God, that is, the fruit of lips that acknowledge his name. Do not neglect to do good and to share what you have, for such sacrifices are pleasing to God" (Hebrews 13:15, 16). Thus, the praise to God which we offer with our lips in prayer and hymn, and even the good we extend in helping others are kinds of spiritual sacrifices offered in our priesthood.

Paul carries this idea even farther: "I appeal to you therefore, brethren, by the mercies of God, to present your bodies as *a living sacrifice,* holy and acceptable to God, which is your spiritual worship" (Romans 12:1). God is interested not just in what we have, but in us. The very lives we live constitute a sacrifice to God.

Responsibilities of Priesthood

The idea of a priesthood, in which each individual is his own priest and deals face to face with God, appeals to those raised in a democratic society and imbued with the philosophy of individual rights. However, Martin Luther's view of the priesthood of all believers did not include the concept that God's priest acts apart from others in doing his own thing. He believed that priestly functions should be carried out in the church. The idea of the individual reading the Bible and praying to God alone, without any effort to fuse his life with his fellow Christians, was the farthest thing from Luther's mind.

A simple definition of a priest is one who performs religious duties for other people. The Christian priesthood involves not only our personal confrontation with God, but also includes the responsibilities we discharge in service to others. Luther viewed the church not just as an ecclesiastical organization with clanking machinery, but as a communion of believers in which the people cared for and shared with one another. A Christian priest is a minister of God, that is, one whose function is to serve others in the divine family. The church, in the biblical sense, provides the fellowship in which this can be done. It is a place where we not only worship together and enjoy the association of those sharing our ideology, but also where we may truly serve others as priests of the Most High God. The role of God's priest in the lives of others is well summed up by Mark A. Noll:

"When we realize what it means to be a priest of God as Luther realized it, to have not only the right to stand before God but also the responsibility to act as his presence to others, we will come to value the Church as Luther did. For the Church is the place that God has ordained for his priests to be active in personal service to one another and to the world. The Church is simply God's living temple in which the priests of God are active in ministry to one another and to those whom God has ordained to bring into that communion.

"For this high view of our calling as priests in Christ Jesus, it would not be asking too much to relinquish our proud and self-serving concept of priesthood as a selfishly guarded 'right' pertaining only to our status before God. To be a priest is to be a servant; it is to act as Christ did in ministering the Gospel to others. And the Church must be the primary place fo this service. With great clarity Martin Luther stated the bedrock truth of Christianity that salvation is by grace through faith in Jesus Christ. With equal clarity he understood, and calls us today to understand, that the gift of faith also brings responsibility to believers. Chief among them is the necessity to exercise priestly functions in the church and thereby to restore the Church, the bride of Christ, to its rightful place of honor in the kingdom of God."[3]

[1]Martin Luther, "The Appeal to the German Nobility," Henry Bettenson, *Documents of the Christian Church* (London: Oxford University Press, 1967), pp. 193, 194.

[2]Ignatius, "Epistle to the Smyrnaeans," J. B. Lightfoot, *The Apostolic Fathers* (Grand Rapids, Michigan: Baker Book House, 1970), p. 84.

[3]Mark A. Noll, "Believer—Priests in the Church: Luther's View," *Christianity Today,* October 26, 1973, p. 8. Used by permission.

CHAPTER 12

Identifying God's People

One by one they entered the door of an inconspicuous building on a city side street. To the close observer it was apparent that a meeting was about to take place, but no sign was posted to show the purpose of the assembly, nothing, that is, except for a simple drawing of a fish next to the entry. Most people knew where they were going, but for the uncertain, the sign of the fish indicated that this was where the Christians met.

We actually know little about how the fish sign was used among the followers of Jesus in the post-apostolic period. Within a few centuries, however, it had become a common identifying mark of Jesus' disciples. Fish symbolism was found in Christian art and even on tombs. The origin of the practice seems to have been that the initial letters of the words, *"Jesus Christ, God's Son, Savior,"* form an acrostic spelling *ichthus,* the Greek word for fish.

Importance of Identification

All of us use identification in our daily activities. If you try to cash a check where you are unknown you may have to produce a driver's license and a major credit card. Your checks carry an identifying number. Your social security number must be attached to official documents. If you work in a factory where security is vital you probably have your picture on a badge which you show to the guard to prove that you are whom you claim to be.

Religious identification is also necessary. We need to be able to distinguish those who share our faith from those who do not. Christians travel from place to place for business and pleasure, and wish to locate congregations of the same persuasion. Many move to other communities and search for a group of like mind with whom they can cast their spiritual lot. In countries without religious liberty the ability to identify other Christians may spell the difference between freedom and imprisonment.

Examples of religious identification abound. The signs in front of places of worship and newspaper advertisements proclaim the desire to be known by those who may be influenced. Churches place their names on tracts, list themselves in telephone books, and communicate with the general public by radio and television. Most religious broadcasts try to identify a specific group with the message being taught.

The Apostolic Church

Among the early Christians identification was important for two reasons. *First, their faith needed to be distinguished from Judaism.* Since Christianity began among the Jews there was an initial tendency to consider the Christians another Jewish sect like the Pharisees and Sadducees. It was several decades before the Roman authorities understood the difference. In one sense this was a blessing because the Romans granted the Jews favored religious status which the Christians shared as long as they were considered to be a Jewish sect. Gallio, proconsul of Achaia, treated a dispute between Paul and the Jews as a family squabble (Acts 18:12-17). Only toward the end of the first century when the Romans awakened to the truth was Christianity regarded as illegal.

On the other hand, the Christians could not properly proclaim their message if they were not clearly identified. In fact, some of them viewed their own faith as an adjunct of Judaism. This was apparent when it was contended that one had to be circumcised before he could become a Christian. Circumcision was the distinguishing mark of Judaism. Paul vehemently opposed this view and his position prevailed in the Jerusalem council convened to consider the controversy (Acts. 15). In retrospect it is evident that Christianity would not have had worldwide success without separating from Judaism.

It was also necessary for Christians to distinguish themselves from pagans. In the first century there were many religions in the Roman Empire. Generally the Romans were quite tolerant. One could believe almost anything and not be molested so long as he complied with the outward forms of emperor worship and did not contend that his way was the only right one. But the Christians

126

would not acknowledge the emperor as a god nor admit that worship of pagan deities was acceptable. While this set them on a collision course with the government, it also clearly identified them as a distinct people and focused attention of the populace on their plea to follow Jesus.

Today's Need

Today we face a different problem. It is still important for the Christian to be distinguished from the non-Christian, whether he be Jew, Moslem, atheist, or just plain sinner. The greater difficulty is in separating nominal Christianity from the genuine article. The form of religion to which many have been exposed is so watered down as to mean little to the unbeliever. If one declares that he is a Christian it may mean little to the average man who views the typical churchgoer as a person with few real convictions. To be a Christian in Bible times meant to stand for one's beliefs; too often today it means to stand for nothing.

Moreover, our confused religious world presents such an array of ideologies that it is hard to promote the understanding of a return to original Christianity. Those seeking to be undenominational are hard pressed to explain the difference between being a Christian *only* and being part of a denomination. Many unacquainted with the non-sectarian plea have never considered that one might be a Christian without being in a denomination. When the name Christian is so loosely used, how can one urging others to be *just* Christians make this distinction?

Another current need for religious identification relates to false teaching, or heresy as it has been called historically. At the close of the apostolic period many heretical teachings began to surface. It was important to distinguish them from the true teachings of Jesus. Ecclesiastical power and human creeds developed, partially at least, from an effort to combat heresy. While we may disagree with these methods of opposing error, it is still true that such a distinction must be made. False teaching has always posed a problem and always will. Short of an absolute autocracy there is just no way of preventing heretics from promoting error. However, it is possible to define that error and to correctly identify the truth. In this way Christians can guard against false teaching.

Early Methods of Identification

Various means of identification were used in the first century church. The disciples used *letters of recommendation* as an aid when traveling. Paul alluded to this practice when he inquired, "Are we beginning to commend ourselves again? Or do we need, as some do, letters of recommendation to you, or from you?" (2 Corinthians 3:1). These letters served as credentials and were helpful in avoiding the acceptance of false teachers. The Ephesians used such a letter on behalf of Apollos when he went to Achaia (Acts 18:24-28). Such communications must have had their limitations just as they do today. Unless one knows the letter writer he cannot be sure of the truthfulness of the testimony.

The doctrinal test was also applied by the early Christians. John warned against accepting those who denied the deity of Jesus: "Beloved, do not believe every spirit, but test the spirits to see whether they are of God; . . . every spirit which confesses that Jesus Christ has come in the flesh is of God, and every spirit which does not confess Jesus is not of God. This is the spirit of antichrist, of which you heard that it was coming, and now it is in the world already" (1 John 4:1-3). Since the Gnostics, whom John opposed, denied that Christ had come in the flesh, he offered this simple confession as one means of marking the false teacher.

There are, of course, limits to how far doctrine can be used as a test of loyalty to Christ. The views of no two Christians are identical. I do not have the right to draw up a list of personal interpretations which I equate with the exact meaning of the scriptures and require you to agree in every particular as a condition of our fellowship. Still, there are great fundamental doctrines of the Christian faith which cannot be denied by one who claims the right to wear the name of Jesus. In this area the doctrinal test is valid.

The most important identification of the early Christians was by the *terms applied to them*. At first *disciple* was widely used. Since a disciple is a follower, this was appropriate for those who walked in the footsteps of Jesus. As we have previously noticed, they also were called *saints, brethren, priests,* and *heirs.* These are descriptive terms rather than proper names.

Soon, however, another term was applied to them. This was the name *Christian,* which from that time until now has been the word most frequently used to describe the followers of Jesus. It means "belonging to Christ." It was first used about the year 44. We are informed, "And in Antioch the disciples were for the first time called Christians" (Acts 11:26). The origin of the name is not explained, but it was not long before it was worn as a badge of honor. King Agrippa, before whom Paul appeared during his imprisonment, declared after listening to the apostle, "In a short time you think to make me a Christian!" (Acts 26:28). Peter admonished his persecuted brethren, "If one suffers as a Christian, let him not be ashamed, but under that name let him glorify God" (1 Peter 4:16). Certainly Peter regarded this name with approval. In the post-apostolic era it was applied to the disciples by Christians and their enemies alike.

In chapter two we examined in some detail the terms used to describe God's family in the first century. We noticed that the most frequent word found in the New Testament is *ekklesia,* usually rendered *church* in our English versions. We also observed that it is used both congregationally and universally. Moreover, the divine ownership of this spiritual body is expressed by such terms as "church of God" (1 Corinthians 1:2), "church of the Lord" (Acts 20:28), and "churches of Christ" (Galatians 1:22). We should understand that these were descriptive expressions rather than proper names and were the equivalent of saying, "God's church," "the Lord's church," and "Christ's congregations." In fact, no proper name is applied to the universal body of Christ in the New Testament. To unbelievers these people were simply "the Christians." As they had no buildings of their own at this early period, there was no need for an identifying sign in front of their places of worship. Later, as we observed, the sign of the fish was one means of identifying God's people.

How Shall We Be Known?

As already noted we face a different identification problem from that of the early disciples of Jesus. How should a non-sectarian Christian designate himself to others? Obviously he cannot use denominational names. One cannot be undenominational while still identifying himself denominationally. So far as possible he should speak in biblical terms. Any name worn by Jesus' followers is appropriate if it is used in the right context. *Christian* is always proper. However, if one is to avoid being sectarian, he should not prefix this name with a denominational expression. Paul deplored such grouping in the Corinthian church. He told these brethren that he had heard that they were saying, " 'I belong to Paul,' or 'I belong to Apollos,' or 'I belong to Cephas,' or 'I belong to Christ' " (1 Corinthians 1:12). Perhaps Paul's disciples would say, "We are Paulite Christians," while those following Peter would call themselves Peterite Christians. Paul said this was wrong and that we belong only to Jesus. It is just as improper today to blemish the name *Christian* by adding to it the name of a religious leader, a kind of church organization, or a religious doctrine.

You may respond, "When someone asks about my religion, won't he think I am presumptuous if I say, 'I'm a Christian'? After all, he claims to be a Christian, too." You may think he will believe you are condemning him if you do not "denominate" yourself in the usual way. However, what appears to be a hindrance may actually present an opportunity for the non-sectarian Christian to clarify his position. When you are asked to explain what you mean you can then respond, "I am a Christian only. I want to be just a Christian without being part of any denomination." This spells out your view without giving the other person a reason to believe that you are judgmental. This may be a new idea to him and you have given him a chance to reflect on what you have said.

Many people explain their religious persuasion in terms of church membership. Someone may say, "I'm a member of the _____ Church." This is the same as saying, "This is my denominational affiliation." The early disciples of Jesus did not express themselves this way. The biblical emphasis is on being saved from one's personal sins, not church membership, although it is true that one is added to the Lord's body when he is saved. However, it is preferable to follow the biblical example and to simply call oneself a Christian. This simplifies communicating the undenominational ideal.

Undenominational congregations must also determine how to identify themselves to the world. If they don't call themselves anything, you may be sure that others will come up with a name of their own. Some current denominational titles were originally nicknames given in derision by enemies. On the other hand, it would be a mistake for a congregation to deliberately choose a denominational name or one which would be used denominationally. This would only compromise its objectives.

We have already considered some descriptive terms applied to the family of God in the New Testament. Any of them may

130

appropriately be used to identify a congregation of Christians only. Thus a church meeting on Main Street might call itself the Main Street Church. This does not mean that other biblical phraseology is improper. There is, however, a danger of sectarianizing a biblical term if it is used exclusively. Paul spoke of the Corinthian congregation as the church of God in Corinth. It would be scriptural for a congregation to call itself a "church of God," but this should not imply that it is not also "Christ's church" or a "church of Christ." These terms are as biblical as "church of God." The problem in exclusively using a single biblical expression is that it soon takes on sectarian meaning.

Some fear that if all congregations do not designate themselves in precisely the same way it will be difficult for a person to find those of the same faith in another community. Identification problems will always exist, but the adoption of one invariable name, even a biblical one, will not remove all the difficulties. Just because a group labels itself a "church of God" or "church of the Lord" or "church of Christ" is no guarantee that it is following scriptural teaching. We must remember that as the early Christians used letters for identification purposes, so there are other available means that can be used in searching for those sharing one's faith.

Conforming to the World

Christians using non-sectarian language are confronted by the pressures of society which demand that they harmonize with denominational speech patterns. The world says, "Conform!" Believing that others may not understand language that does not fit the accepted mold, one may be tempted to take the easy way out and express himself denominationally rather than biblically.

Paul urges us to resist these pressures in order to comply with God's will. He writes, *"Do not conform any longer to the pattern of this world,* but be transformed by the renewing of your mind. Then you will be able to test and *approve what God's will* is—his good, pleasing and perfect will"* (Romans 12:2—N.I.V.). If we are to exalt the distinctive principles of apostolic Christianity, we must have the courage to free ourselves from the fetters of sectarian thought and to express ourselves to the world in such a way that the undenominational plea cannot be misunderstood.

The Ultimate Test

We have not yet mentioned the most important form of identification. Jesus said, "A new commandment I give to you, that you love one another. . . . *By this all men will know that you are my disciples,* if you have love for one another" (John 13:34, 35). When everything else has been said, the world still measures the people of God by their attitudes and lives. Nothing impresses it more than the love which Christians display to one another and also to those outside their circle. When people who profess to carry out God's will do not show love, they destroy everything for which they stand. The number of souls lost to the cause of the Master because Christians quarreled among themselves cannot be counted.

When a truthseeker considers his alternatives in his search for the true religion, he is less concerned with the sign over the door of the church building than the kind of people who worship there. Do their lives radiate the love of God. Do they love one another? This is what he is looking for. Too often it has been presumed that Christian identification is conveyed only by names and titles. We must not overlook that identification which measures God's children by their love.

CHAPTER 13

Unconditional Surrender

It was the year 155 A.D. In the Roman Empire a great persecution raged against the Christians whom the populace maligned as atheists. It was hard to be a disciple of Jesus, especially in the Asian city of Smyrna where the citizens were enjoying the games in the stadium. One by one the Christians were dragged into the arena to have their faith tested by the wild beasts who provided sport for the heathen populace. One young man bravely fought with the animals. Another turned coward when he saw them and denied his faith in Christ.

It was not these men, however, for whose blood the crowd lusted. "Away with the atheists; let search be made for Polycarp," they cried. The aged leader of the Christians was sought out. The soldiers found him in a farm house, and after granting his request to pray, took him to the stadium to be publicly arraigned. The Roman proconsul urged him to deny Christ. "Have respect to thine age. Swear by the genius of Ceasar; repent and say, 'Away with the atheists.' " Looking out on the heathen multitude, the real unbelievers who called for his death, Polycarp waved to them and said, "Away with the atheists." This was not what the proconsul wanted. He persisted, "Swear the oath, and I will release thee; revile the Christ." Polycarp's response was one of the most magnificent declarations of Christian faith ever spoken: *"Four-score and six years have I been his servant, and He hath done me no wrong. How then can I blaspheme my King who saved me?"*

Aware of Polycarp's influence upon his fellow believers, the proconsul still sought to persuade him to deny Christ. When Polycarp adamantly refused, he ordered that he be tied to the stake and burned to death for his faith in Jesus. By this courageous action Polycarp greatly inspired other Christians to stand up for their Lord, even in the face of death itself.[1]

Total Commitment

What motivated Polycarp to surrender his life in this way? We might reason that since he was eighty-six years old he didn't have much longer to live anyway. That is hardly the answer. It is no less painful to be burned at the stake at eighty-six than at twenty-six. The answer lies in his *total commitment* to Jesus Christ. This commitment was so complete that he was willing to die for his faith. While we cannot know without facing the same ordeal if we would die for Christ, we can be positive, as we previously observed—*no man will die for Jesus who will not first live for him.*

A great contrast between New Testament Christianity and contemporary religion is seen in commitment. In biblical times it was hard to live as a Christian. One who did so had to be committed. Today many nominal Christians possess little personal conviction. For them one religion is as good as another. The church is like a social club or parent-teacher organization—something it is fine to be a part of, but hardly essential. O yes! It is nice to have the church around when you get married, and certainly when you die, but in between you can pretty much take it or leave it. Christianity is something you can fall back on in time of trouble. If nothing else succeeds, try Christ; it might just work. Small wonder that the Christian faith provides little help for the average person. If you don't put something into your religion, you aren't going to get anything out of it.

Few of us will be asked to make the supreme sacrifice as was Polycarp. However, if we reproduce apostolic Christianity in our age we must make another kind of sacrifice. Paul mentioned it when he said, "I appeal to you therefore, brethren, by the mercies of God, to *present your bodies as a living sacrifice,* holy and acceptable to God, which is your spiritual worship. Do not be conformed to this world but be transformed by the renewal of your mind, that you may prove what is the will of God, what is good and acceptable and perfect" (Romans 12:1, 2). J. B. Philips renders part of this passage, "Don't let the world around you squeeze you into its own mould, but let God remould your minds from within." This sacrifice is expressed in our daily living for Jesus. By reshaping our lives to conform to the pattern he has given rather than letting them be governed by the standards of society or the pressures of friends we make a continual sacrifice to God. This is true commitment. Without it we cannot be disciples of Christ.

Once when Paul was gathering funds to help some poor Jewish disciples in Jerusalem, he used the example of poor Christians in Macedonia to motivate other Christians to give. He write, "We want you to know, brethren, about the grace of God which has been shown in the churches of Macedonia, for in a severe test of affliction, their abundance of joy and their extreme proverty have overflowed in a wealth of liberality on their part. For they gave according to their means, as I can testify, and beyond their means, of their own free will, begging us earnestly for the favor of taking part in the relief of the saints" (2 Corinthians 8:1-4). Imagine, a group of desperately poor people actually begging a missionary to accept their gift for other poor people whom they had never seen! What would possess them to give even beyond their ability? Paul explained their motivation: *"First they gave themselves to the Lord and to us by the will of God"* (2 Corinthians 8:5). Their giving of money came easy because they had first given themselves. When you give yourself that includes everything you own!

The implications of commitment are illustrated in a brief article written by a personal friend:

"We were in a canoe in a fast-moving Wisconsin stream. Often the stream would part for rocks, sand bars, logs, or some other obstacle. As we neared the place where the water split I would shout to my partner in the front of the canoe, 'Which side?' He would survey the situation, decide which passage was best and reply. We would both then maneuver the canoe in that direction. Once we rounded a bend, shot through some rapids and were faced immediately with an obstruction. Almost before I could shout, 'Which side?', we had quickly entered the passageway. My partner replied, 'Brother, we're committed.' What he meant was, the decision was made, we were on our way, there was no turning back, there was no stopping, there was no changing course.

"When one is committed to Jesus, the course is determined, the decision is made, there is no turning back. The song, 'I Have Decided to Follow Jesus' tells the story: 'The cross before me, the world behind me, no turning back, no turning back!' May God grant us the integrity of commitment!"[2]

It is much easier to mentally subscribe to commitment than to translate it into action. As with Polycarp the moment of truth comes when we must make a choice. Consider the practical implications of commitment to Christ.

A Decision Has Been Made

As with the two canoeists, when one chooses to follow Jesus, he has made a decision. Jesus was very popular in his early ministry. The people liked what he said, especially when he condemned other folks! But when it came to personal application some turned aside. Many said, "This is a hard saying; who can listen to it?" (John 6:60). They weren't prepared to accept all he had to say. Therefore, "many of his disciples drew back and no longer went about with him" (John 6:66). They had not yet made a decision to follow Jesus wherever he led them. But when Jesus asked the twelve, "Do you also wish to go away?" Simon Peter responded, "Lord, to whom shall we go? You have the words of eternal life" (John 6:67, 68). You see, they had made their decision. It was a deliberate, personal choice to follow Jesus.

No Turning Back

Luke tells us what once happened as Jesus and his disciples traveled toward Jerusalem. "As they were going along the road, a man said to them, 'I will follow you wherever you go.' And Jesus said to him, *'Foxes have holes, and birds of the air have nests; but the Son of man has nowhere to lay his head.'* To another he said, 'Follow me.' But he said, 'Lord, let me first go and bury my father.' But he said to him, *'Leave the dead to bury their own dead; but as for you, go and proclaim the kingdom of God.'* Another said, 'I will follow you, Lord; but let me first say farewell to those at my home.' Jesus said to him, *'No one who puts his hand to the plow and looks back is fit for the kingdom of God'* " (Luke 9:57-62).

That was pretty harsh, wasn't it? It almost sounds as if Jesus was trying to get rid of his disciples. We would have encouraged their interest instead of pointing out the problems. Actually he was stressing that once one has decided to follow Jesus there is no turning back. To the first man who wanted to follow him Jesus said, "Have you counted the cost?" To the second he declared, "I cannot take second place." And to the third he emphasized, "There is no turning back."

We cannot approach Christ's service on the basis that if it doesn't work out we'll give it up. That's the attitude many have when they marry. Small wonder that their marriages fail. If that is our attitude toward Jesus, he doesn't want us in the first place. To commit oneself to him is to go to the end of the way. This will discourage a lot of folks, but it will also make dedicated disciples of those who choose to follow him.

Divine Ownership

Those who life in free nations value private ownership. I speak of my home, my car, my job, my money. To commit myself to Jesus, however, is to acknowledge that he has first call on everything which I consider mine. Paul reminds us, "Do you not know that your body is a temple of the Holy Spirit within you, which you have from God? *You are not your own; you were bought with a price.* So glorify God in your body" (1 Corinthians 6:19, 20).

We don't even own our own bodies! We belong to God for two reasons. First, he created us and without him we wouldn't be here. Second, he gave his son to die for us and purchased our redemption with the blood of Jesus. As a sinner one is a slave of sin; when he becomes a Christian he becomes a slave of God. Paul writes that "you have been set free from sin and have become slaves of God" (Romans 6:22). Those who read Paul's letter understood what he meant. Some of them were slaves. They knew that when another bought their freedom they were under obligation to that person, just as we are obligated to Jesus because he purchased our freedom when he died for us. There is this difference between slavery to sin and service to Christ. The first is against our will. We don't really want to be controlled by evil. But the one who accepts Jesus does so voluntarily. He serves him because he loves him.

To commit oneself to Jesus is to acknowledge God's ownership of everything we possess—our bodies, our material resources, our talent, and even our time. He requires that as good stewards we manage them all in a proper way. While he expects us to use them for our personal benefit, the Christian should never say, "What I do is my own business and nobody else's. It isn't. It is God's business. We are simply caretakers of his things.

Complete Involvement

Have you ever heard someone say, "I don't want to get involved"? Perhaps you have said it yourself. You witness an automobile accident. Your testimony can insure that justice is served. However, to testify you must take your time to go to court and like the rest of us you are busy. Off the record you will state what happened, but you are unwilling to put forth that extra effort that involvement requires for justice to be done.

Many are like this with the religion of Jesus. They want their names on the church roll. They worship fairly regularly. They don't even mind giving their money for church projects. But when it comes to getting the work done they keep Jesus at arm's length. It just requires too much time and effort. What is lacking is commitment.

Jesus demands that we put him first. He said, "He who loves father or mother more than me is not worthy of me; and he who loves son or daughter more than me is not worthy of me; and he who does not take his cross and follow me is not worthy of me" (Matthew 10:37, 38). He does not ask that we love our dear ones less—putting Christ first will actually cause us to love them more. However, he does require as a condition of discipleship that we place him before our family and even ourselves.

To be involved with Jesus is to participate in his work. Since the church is his body, one must get involved with the activities of the local church of which he is a part. As a member of that body he will use his talents when and where he can for the advancement of Christ's spiritual kingdom. With other Christians he will avail himself of every opportunity to worship God and search out the meaning of the scriptures.

To be involved is to go the extra mile, even when others do not go the first. It is to pick up the load that another has laid down when you own burden seems too heavy. It is to do all of this without complaining because you love your brethren in Christ, and especially because you love your Lord and you know he wants you to do this.

Sharing One's Faith

The commitment of the early disciples prompted them to share their faith with others. Each one assumed as his personal responsibility the sharing of the good news. The gospel spread so rapidly that a generation later Paul could declare that it had been preached to every creature under heaven (Colossians 1:23). Of the Christians in Jerusalem dispersed by persecution it is said, "Now those who were scattered went about preaching the word" (Acts 8:4). They weren't all public teachers, but they believed in Jesus so much that they wanted to share their faith with others. Many years later Paul enjoined Philemon, "I pray that you may be active in sharing your faith, so that you will have a full understanding of every good thing we have in Christ" (Philemon 6—NIV).

If Jesus means anything to you, you will want others to know him too. The gospel is good news, and who doesn't like to tell good news? The key to world evangelism is for each Christian to share his knowledge of Jesus with others.

Unconditional Surrender

When the German nation sued for peace at the end of World War II its leaders were informed that the only acceptable terms were "unconditional surrender." Nothing else would be accepted. Neither will Jesus accept anything else of his disciples.

What does this imply? It means that I will consciously or unconsciously consider the will of Christ in making my decisions. It means that I will truly dedicate myself to him in my public and private devotion. It means that I will give him the first priority in all of my activities. It means that I will always try to live as Jesus wants me to live. All that we have said about commitment is summed up in the words—*unconditional surrender!*

[1]"Letter of the Smyrnaeans," J. B. Lightfoot, *The Apostolic Fathers* (Grand Rapids, Michigan: Baker Book House, 1970), pp. 109-117.

[2]Robert Fisk, "Committed," Church Bulletin, Central Church of Christ, Davenport, Iowa.

CHAPTER 14

The Ministry of Caring

She was a Samaritan woman drawing water from Jacob's well at Sychar. Though it was not considered proper for a Jewish man to talk to a strange woman, especially a Samaritan, Jesus struck up a conversation. Soon they were discussing her spiritual condition. You see, Jesus cared!

It was late in the day and the country was sparsely settled. Five thousand who had followed Jesus into the wilderness and had eagerly listened to his words were hungry. His disciples wanted to send them home. Instead, Jesus fed them. He cared!

A sinful woman entered the house of Simon the Pharisee where Jesus was a dinner guest. With her tears she wet Jesus' feet, kissed them, and then poured oil over them. "How disgusting!" Simon thought. But Jesus knew her depraved spiritual condition and how she longed for a better life. He lovingly accepted her acts of dedication. He cared!

Bartimaeus, the blind beggar of Jericho, cried out as Jesus passed by, "Jesus, Son of David, have mercy on me!" The crowd rebuked him because the Master was too important to hear a blind beggar. He persisted. Jesus listened and gave him his sight. He cared!

Jesus stood at the grave of Lazarus, his friend. The sisters, Mary and Martha, were weeping. Jesus knew he would soon restore Lazarus to life. He also knew how Mary and Martha were hurting. Because they hurt, he also hurt. "Jesus wept." He cared!

Why did Jesus make such an impact on the common people? Of course, he was the Son of God. He was also a great teacher. He healed the sick and gave sight to the blind. But beyond all these things, Jesus understood how they felt. He identified with them. By his attitudes and actions he showed that he cared, and for this they loved him.

Jesus has taught us how to live. Just as important, he has also showed us the way. "I have given you an example," he told his disciples, "that you should do as I have done to you" (John 13:15). No one can be a true follower of Jesus without seeking to capture that personal concern which characterized his ministry. Nor can we fully restore New Testament Christianity unless the church displays *the ministry of caring*.

The Alienation of Man

We live in an uncaring world. It is not unusual to hear these statements: "Everybody for himself;" "If you don't look out for number one, nobody will;" "Never give a sucker a break." Many people feel totally alienated. The average man is alienated from government. He believes that most politicians are interested only in padding their pocketbooks and getting reelected. He sees lifetime judges who cannot be replaced issuing mandates which do not reflect the will of the people. He feels totally helpless and wonders if the system has not failed.

This alienation extends to feelings about people. Francis Schaeffer, in his study of the rise and decline of Western thought and culture, *How Should We Then Live?*, concludes that most people are governed by two impoverished values—personal peace and affluence.[1] He defines personal peace as the wish to be left alone without regard to the interests of others or future generations. Affluence is the ever-present desire to get more and more of material things. All can be summed up by saying that society is largely governed by personal selfishness.

Those who are so motivated should understand that they cannot expect from others what they themselves will not give. Too often the one desiring other things than better clothes, a bigger car, and a finer home becomes convinced that most people really don't care. Strangely, the closer people live together, the less they know about one another. That is why the big city is the loneliest place in the world. How many apartment dwellers really know those who live in the same building? A neighbor could be seriously ill, or even die, without the others learning about it. The cooperative spirit which historians tell us existed in pioneer days is mostly gone; people don't help each other because they don't know each other.

Some are even alienated from the churches which ought to help them in coping with their problems. Of course, not all share this estrangement, but many honestly think that all that churches are interested in is their money. Whether or not the charge has a basis in truth, the fact that some feel this way focuses on the problem of human alienation.

Many social ills are rooted in this alienation. Since human beings are social creatures, they need the friendship and support of others. Where this is not present persistent loneliness results. Loneliness, in turn, compounds other problems such as depression and even occasionally leads to suicide.

Where does the alienated person go for help with his problems? Surely not to the government. And if you don't believe that other people care, you can't very well ask them for help. If you do not relate to the church where you hold membership, you will find it of little value. The result is total frustration, broken homes, and ruined lives.

The Christian's Concern

It is at this point that the troubled soul rejoices to discover people who share the genuine personal concern which was so much a part of the early Christian faith. Those who walked with Jesus must have radiated the feeling of concern which they learned from him. They in turn transmitted it to those whom they taught. Through the centuries, however, Christians have often forgotten how to care about people. Not until we rediscover that sense of caring can we truly affirm that we have restored New Testament Christianity.

The church must care. However, caring begins with the individual Christian. After all, the church is made up of individuals, and if the individuals do not care, neither will be church. One reason that citizens feel alienated from government is that the authorities have lost touch with the people. The same can happen in the church. Whether this occurs is not determined by the size of the congregation, but by the degree to which those who compose it genuinely care about others. Concern cannot be purchased with large donations of money. True concern proceeds only from within the person.

To care about people is to care about individuals. It is one thing to lament world hunger; it is another to know an individual who is hungry, feel for him, and try to help. Jesus' concern for people was personal and genuine. So must be that of the Christian. By attitudes and actions he must convey the message, "I care about you."

To care about people is to care about their friendship. It is to want to know how they think, and to share their fears and their aspirations. It is to get involved in their lives so that you can empathize with them when they are troubled, and rejoice with them when they are successful. Of course, friendship is a two-way street, and unless the extended hand is grasped there can be no meaningful relationship. However, some who find it hard to take the initiative in establishing a friendship will often eagerly respond to the overtures of another. Strange as it may seem, some have been so alienated that they find it hard to believe that others desire to form true friendships. A dear friend of mine once remarked after her visit to a congregation that she felt radiated genuine warmth, "I didn't know that people were friendly anymore—it almost made me afraid." She was not unfriendly herself, but she had found little genuine friendship in the circle of people in which she walked. For such a one the discovery of Christians who freely extend friendship is like finding an oasis in a desert.

To care about people is to care about their problems. You cannot separate your friendship with others from the negative factors which complicate their lives. All of us have problems, but some seem to have a superabundance. The Christian must first be concerned about the spiritual needs of his brothers and sisters in Christ. Paul wrote, "Bear one another's burdens, and so fulfill the law of Christ" (Galatians 6:2). While burden sharing involves helping those in physical want, the context of this passage relates to spiritual needs. It means assisting those about to succumb to temptation, or who may already have done so. Such a one needs encouragement to follow the right course, direction in making correct decisions, and if he has sinned, reassurance that through Jesus he can obtain forgiveness so that he will not be overwhelmed by despair.

Our caring about human problems is not limited to fellow Christians. It extends to involvement with others we may influence to follow Christ. It is not hard to be friendly with neighbors and associates if this only means talking about the weather or other trivialities. It is more difficult if it draws one into their daily problems and requires helping them find solutions.

Naturally we should not intrude ourselves when this will only worsen the situation. Good judgment is vital. It is important to develop sensitivity to the needs of others in order to know when to speak and when to remain silent.

To care about people is to care about their souls. This is the bottom line on all Christian concern. The disciple of Jesus must care enough to share with friends his knowledge of God's word and his experiences in following his Lord. If we are competent to share recipes or knowledge of how to fix a car, should we not be able to share Christ? We must care enough about human souls to display a positive example of Christian living. We must care enough to spend time with God in praying for their spiritual welfare. Genuine concern is the key to the spread of Christianity. One greeting card company has the motto, "You *cared* enough to send the very best." When Christians show the world that they care they will find that those searching for a better way will respond to their message.

Caring Means Action

To be of lasting value caring must be translated into action. James points out the practicality of the matter in saying, "What does it profit, my brethren, if a man says he has faith but has not works? Can his faith save him? If a brother or sister is ill-clad and in lack of daily food, and one of you says to them, 'Go in peace, be warmed and filled,' without giving them the things needed for the body, what does it profit? So faith by itself, if it has no works, is dead" (James 2:14-17). Words are not enough. They must lead to deeds. Someone has said, "It is fine to pray for the hungry, but don't forget the potatoes."

One cannot examine the ministry of Jesus and the actions of the first Christians without realizing that caring is at the heart of the Christian faith. When Paul and Barnabas visited Jerusalem to seek apostolic endorsement upon completing their first missionary journey, it was readily granted. There was, however, a condition which Paul and Barnabas eagerly accepted—they must remember the poor. (Galatians 2:10). This concern for the poor did not stem from a mere desire to alleviate the world's poverty. Rather it showed that Christianity involves concern—genuine caring involving action—for all people. This was undoubtedly one of the major factors in the rapid spread of the Christian faith in the first century. It can also be a powerful agent in the evangelization of today's world.

The discussion of the ministry of caring has not touched on that powerful motivation which ought to prompt every child of God to care. It is that of **love** which we will consider next.

[1]Francis A. Schaeffer, *How Should We Then Live?* (Old Tapan, New Jersey: Fleming H. Revell Company, 1976), p. 205.

CHAPTER 15

Controlled by the Love of Christ

How Jacob loved her! He had struck a bargain with his uncle Laban to work seven years for the hand of his daughter Rachel. The years passed quickly and "seemed to him but a few days because of the love he had for her" (Genesis 29:20). But at the end of the period Laban gave him Rachel's older sister, Leah, instead. It wasn't customary, he explained, for the younger daughter to marry before the older. Jacob wasn't happy about this, but there wasn't much he could do about it. So they reached another agreement. A week later he also married Rachel in return for his promise to serve Laban seven more years. It takes a lot of love to inspire a man to work fourteen years for a wife!

Love is the greatest motivator in the world. It may even prompt one to act unreasonably. It has often been said that love is blind. Loving parents bear with their children when no one else will put up with them. A mother dies in an effort to rescue her child from a burning building. Paul summed up love's power by saying, "So faith, hope, love abide, these three; but the greatest of these is love" (1 Corinthians 13:13).

The Meaning of Love

But what is love? To say that it is a feeling of affection which one has for another is woefully inadequate. The shades of meaning attached to the English word makes a definition even harder. The Greek language in New Testament times was more explicit. Several words were used to express related ideas. *Eros* (not used in the Bible) was sexual love. *Phileo,* found in several scriptures, meant to have tender affection or friendship. But the verb *agapao* (and its corresponding noun, *agape*) is the word most often used to describe the concept of love. It is this word which Jesus used when he said, "A new commandment I give to you, that you love one another;

147

even as I have loved you, that you also love one another" (John 13:34). It is of this kind of love that Paul writes, "But God shows his love for us in that while we were yet sinners Christ died for us" (Romans 5:8). Since the pagans did not use this word in the sense employed in the Bible, we must go to the New Testament to discover its meaning. There we learn that *agape love is an unselfish love which places the needs of others above its own best interests,* even as it motivated Jesus to surrender his life for sinful human beings.

The New Testament abounds in teaching about love. John's gospel and his first epistle especially stress this theme. For example, John writes, "Beloved, let us love one another; for love is of God, and he who loves is born of God and knows God. He who does not love does not know God; for God is love. In this the love of God was made manifest among us, that God sent his only Son into the world, so that we might live through him. In this is love, not that we loved God but that he loved us and sent his Son to be the expiation for our sins. Beloved, if God so loved us, we also ought to love one another. No man has ever seen God; if we love one another, God abides in us and his love is perfected in us" (1 John 4:7-12).

Notice that the reason we should love one another is that God has blessed us with his love in sending Jesus to die on our behalf. By observing the divine example we learn how to love.

The Love of Christ

We can best appreciate the love of God when we look at Jesus. After all, Jesus said, "He who has seen me has seen the Father" (John 14:9). When Jesus visited the grave of his dear friend Lazarus before raising him from the dead, he was greatly touched. As he stood beside the sisters Mary and Martha, "Jesus wept" (John 11:35). His tears were real and expressed his deep feeling for his friend. This prompted the Jews who observed to say, "See how he loved him!" (John 11:36).

In the gospels the love of Jesus for human beings is evident in both his life and death. The phrase—*the love of Christ*—is found just three times in the New Testament, all in Paul's writings. Collectively they tell us what the love of Christ (and hence the love of the Father) does in our lives.

In Ephesians Paul offers a prayer for Christians "that Christ may dwell in your hearts through faith; that you, being rooted and grounded in love, may have power to comprehend with all the saints what is the breadth and length and height and depth, and to *know the love of Christ which surpasses knowledge,* that you may be filled with all the fulness of God" (Ephesians 3:17-19). This is the *beckoning hand* by which Jesus, through his love, calls us to come to him for help. It was he who promised, "Come to me, all who labor and are heavy laden, and I will give you rest" (Matthew 11:28).

In Romans Paul poses the question, *"Who shall separate us from the love of Christ?* Shall tribulation, or distress, or persecution, or famine, or nakedness, or peril, or sword?" (Romans 8:35). This is the picture of the *clasping hand,* the hand that promises to protect us if we will only place ourselves under the shelter of divine love. When we allow Christ's love to reign in our hearts, nothing, absolutely nothing, can separate us from God.

Finally in Second Corinthians Paul writes what is probably the most important passage relating to the love of Christ in our lives. "For *the love of Christ controls us,* because we are convinced that one has died for all; therefore all have died. And he died for all, that those who live might live no longer for themselves but for him who for their sake died and was raised" (2 Corinthians 5:14). The love of Christ controls us! He rules our lives, not by fear or hate or duty, but by his love. The blind hymn writer, George Matheson, expressed the impact of Christ's *controlling hand* upon our lives in these words:

"O love that wilt not let me go,
I rest my weary soul in Thee:
I give Thee back the life I owe,
That in Thine ocean depths its flow
May richer, fuller be."

The control which Jesus exercises in our lives through his love is voluntary upon our part. He does not manipulate us to follow him. Each person decides to follow Jesus because he wants to. But once I make my decision to let him govern my life, his love reflected in my attitudes and actions becomes the dominant force in my behavior.

The love of Christ for us prompts us to love him. John says,

"We love, because he first loved us" (1 John 4:19). Experience teaches us that love begets love. Just as a mother's love for her child causes the child to love her, so we respond in love to that shown to us by Jesus.

Christ's love was expressed in his surrendering the joys of heaven for the sorrows of earth. Paul writes of this sacrifice, "Have this mind among yourselves, which is yours in Christ Jesus, who, though he was in the form of God, did not count equality with God a thing to be grasped, but emptied himself, taking the form of a servant, being born in the likeness of men. And being found in human form he humbled himself and became obedient unto death, even death on a cross" (Philippians 2:5-8). Jesus voluntarily divested himself of the blessings and rights which were his by virtue of being God. He assumed a human form and eventually suffered an excruciating death. He did this because he loved us. His sacrifice was not without purpose. It procured the forgiveness of our sins and life everlasting. Out of appreciation for this great love, we in turn love him.

Expressing Our Love for Christ

Our love for Christ transforms our lives. Obedience to his teachings is one of these changes. Jesus instructs, "If you love me, you will keep my commandments. . . . If a man loves me, he will keep my word, and my Father will love him, and we will come to him and make our home with him" (John 14:15, 23). A loving son will obey his father, not just out of duty or fear, but because of love. We ought not to obey Jesus simply because we are afraid not to, but because we deeply love him.

Our love for Jesus also elicits our devotion. Once when Jesus was a guest at a home in Bethany, Mary, the sister of Martha and Lazarus, poured a very expensive ointment over his head. This spontaneous act was criticized by Judas Iscariot who thought it an extravagant waste of money. But Jesus looked beyond the seemingly unwise action into the heart of the one who had done it. He knew that Mary's act of devotion was prompted by her love for him. Judas saw the waste; Jesus saw the love. He observed, "Wherever the gospel is preached in the whole world, what she has done will be told in memory of her" (Mark 14:9).

True devotion rendered in public or private worship does not stem from duty, but from love. When one communes with Christ and his fellow disciples in the Lord's supper, he is showing his love, not reacting from fear.

Perhaps the most obvious expression of our love for Christ is in the love which we show one another. John wrote, "Beloved, if God so loved us, we also ought to love one another. . . . And this commandment we have from him, that he who loves God should love his brother also" (1 John 4:11, 21). John even says that one cannot love God if he hates his brother. "If any one says, 'I love God,' and hates his brother, he is a liar; for he who does not love his brother whom he has seen, cannot love God whom he has not seen" (1 John 4:20).

Agape Love

But what is this *agape love* of which God's word says so much? It is, first of all, an *unselfish love*. It is the love one extends when he knows it will not be reciprocated. It is giving a gift when you will not receive one in return. It is caring for a person who has tried to harm you. But how can you love someone who is unlovable? Can you love a drunkard or a thief? To do so we must distinguish between one's actions, which we detest, and his person, which we must love because he is one of God's creatures. Surely, if God can love me in spite of all of my shortcomings and sins, I can learn to love others who also fall short of God's standards.

True agape love produces actions. John admonishes us, "Little children, let us not love in word or speech but in deed and in truth" (1 John 3:18). Jesus demonstrated this when he washed his disciples' feet and then said, "For I have given you an example, that you also should do as I have done to you" (John 13:15). His service proved his love.

The love among the early Christians was not lost on the world. It was one of the major factors in the rapid spread of the faith. Jesus had admonished his disciples, "A new commandment I give to you, that you love one another; even as I have loved you, that you also love one another. By this all men will know that you are my disciples, if you have love for one another" (John 13:34, 35). At the end of the second century Tertullian recorded the pagan comment, "See how they love one another." The unbelievers drew their conclusion by observing the conduct of the Christians.

Love in the Early Church

A study of love in the early church impresses us with the importance of restoring this element of the Christian faith. The Jerusalem congregation is a good example. On the first Pentecost after the resurrection of Jesus three thousand people became Christians. (Acts 2:41). Soon they numbered five thousand. (Acts 4:4). This growth explosion posed the problem of how to deal with poverty among the disciples. The solution was remarkably simple. "And all who believed were together and had all things in common; and they sold their possessions and goods and distributed them to all, as any had need" (Acts 2:44, 45). Now, such a generous act could probably not have resulted from an apostolic command. With so little grounding in their new-found faith, these converts would have resisted such an extreme order. Rather, their action was the natural response of love to a human need. This is shown by Luke's statement, "Now the company of those who believed were of one heart and soul, and no one said that any of the things which he possessed was his own, but they had everything in common" (Acts 4:32). They cared for one another because they loved one another. This emphasizes that the religion of Jesus is preeminently a religion of love. Too often this is forgotten in theological controversies.

The pure communism of the early Jerusalem church (for this is what it was) was apparently not practiced later. That was an extraordinary situation requiring a drastic solution. However, the same love which prompted these disciples to share their possessions motivated other acts of charity in the apostolic church. A few years later there was a great famine in the Roman Empire. "And the disciples (in Antioch) determined, every one according to his ability, to send relief to the brethren who lived in Judea; and they did so, sending it to the elders by the hand of Barnabas and Saul" (Acts 11:29, 30).

Still later, the Christians in Jerusalem were beset by chronic poverty. To help alleviate this condition Paul asked the Gentile congregations he had planted to aid these Jewish saints. By way of motivating the Corinthians to assist, he pointed to the example of the Macedonian churches which had contributed generously out of deep poverty. Paul asked them to give, not out of duty, but from love. "I say this not as a command, but to prove by the earnestness of others that your love also· is genuine" (2 Corinthians 8:8).

Toward the end of the first century, Clement of Rome explained how Christian love should be mutually expressed:

"Let not the strong neglect the weak; and let the weak respect the strong. Let the rich minister aid to the poor; and let the poor give thanks to God, because He hath given him one through whom his wants may be supplied. Let the wise display his wisdom, not in words, but in good works."[1]

In the same letter Clement also described the extremes to which some had gone in showing their love:

"We know that many among ourselves have delivered themselves to bondage, that they might ransom others. Many have sold themselves to slavery, and receiving the price paid for themselves have fed others."[2]

Imagine selling yourself into slavery in order to gain freedom for another Christian or to provide food for the hungry! Truly, this is love in action!

The early Christians cared for their own. Though travel in the Roman Empire was superior for its time, accomodations were greatly inferior to what we are accustomed. Traveling Christians depended on the hospitality of other disciples. A brother was granted free lodging for up to three nights if he demonstrated that he was a Christian. No other questions were asked. Naturally such generosity could be abused and probably was, but it was felt that it was better to extend mercy to an unworthy person than to take the chance of rejecting someone who was worthy.

An unknown author in the mid-second century explained how such acts of mercy proceeded from the love which Christians had learned from God:

"And loving Him thou wilt be an imitator of His goodness. And marvel not that a man can be an imitator of God. He can, if God willeth it. For happiness consisteth not in lordship over one's neighbours, nor in desiring to have more than weaker men, nor in possessing wealth and using force to inferiors; neither can any one imitate God in these matters; nay, these lie outside His greatness. But whosoever taketh upon himself the burden of his neibhbour, whosoever desireth to benefit one that is worse off in that in which he himself is superior, whosoever by supplying to those that are in want possessions which he received from God becomes a God to those who receive them from him, he is an imitator of God."[3]

Transforming Love

In few ways is there greater contrast between first century Christianity and contemporary religion than in the area of love. The spiritual dissatisfaction shared by many would be materially lessened by the practical demonstration of the agape love found in the early church. Consider the effect of the new convert in the first century.

First, the Christian family provided a sanctuary for the troubled. Human problems are universal. The new religion appealed to those of every social stratum. Here one found love to help him in his darkest hours.

The love in the church was the bond of social cohesiveness. One might be a slave in the world, but in Christ he was an equal. His proof was the love he saw in action. Among Christians he was a person of worth and dignity.

Christian love provided the new convert with an incentive to alter his lifestyle. He learned that true happiness was not in the debauchery of his former life, but in the moral purity of the religion of Jesus. When his faith was challenged, he could count on the love of his fellow disciples to sustain him.

Although all congregations had problems stemming from human imperfection, the great emphasis on mutual love provided a basis for true unity. Paul exhorted the Ephesians to be "forbearing with one another in love, eager to maintain the unity of the Spirit in the bond of peace" (Ephesians 4:2, 3). Such unity was essential for the spiritual tranquility of the babe in Christ. When churches today are beset by inner turmoil, it is almost invariably true that love for one another has not been sufficiently taught nor practiced.

Finally, although Christians were the major benefactors of their mutual love, they desired to share that love with others. The new convert whose life had been transformed by the love of Christ wanted others to know his joy. While persecution made the Christians a close-knit group, this was not a clique seeking to

154

exclude the unworthy. Rather, they sought to unite all men by the love of Christ. May that same objective motivate us as we search for a better way.

[1]Clement, "Epistle to the Corinthians," J. B. Lightfoot, *The Apostolic Fathers* (Grand Rapids, Michigan: Baker Book House, 1970), p. 29.

[2]*Ibid.,* p. 36.

[3]"The Epistle to Diognetus," J. B. Lightfoot, *The Apostolic Fathers,* p. 257.

CHAPTER 16

The Continuing Quest

The world has known many great people. A few have been remembered; most have been forgotten. The memories of some have been preserved only because of a single incident or saying attributed to them. So it is with Diogenes, the Greek philosopher. This Cynic thinker so disdained the comforts and values of society that he dressed in rags and resorted to begging. Nor was he awed by the mighty. When Alexander the Great found him basking in the sun by the roadside, the king introduced himself with the words, "I am Alexander the Great." To this the philosopher responded, "And I am Diogenes the Cynic." It is not for this, however, that Diogenes is known. Once he carried a lantern through the streets of Athens in the daytime. When asked what he was looking for, he responded, "I am seeking an honest man." Because his comment strikes so forcefully at a universal human frailty, Diogenes has been remembered. We must wonder if his search met with success.

In these chapters we have launched another quest—a search for the pure religion of Jesus. We have not found all of the answers. Many others have made the same search with varying degrees of success. Too often their efforts have been discontinued when the seekers concluded that they had restored the church of Jesus Christ in its totality. Restoration is a never-ending struggle to reproduce the original in contemporary society. We must never be so presumptuous as to conclude that we have discovered all of the truth. Though the Bible contains everything we need in this effort, our human limitations prevent us from completely understanding all of the message. Yet we must never stop trying to gain a fuller insight into the will of God. So to you, dear seeker of truth, I propose some approaches to restoration which I believe are essential if we are to capture the essence of New Testament Christianity.

A Humble Heart

Earlier we recounted the striving of King Josiah of Judah to bring his people back to Israel's true religion. An examination of his attitudes will assist us in our search. When Josiah learned that the Law of Moses had been found in a corner of the temple, he immediately set out to determine the implications of this discovery. He knew his people had been wrong. Accordingly he sent to Huldah the prophetess to determine the will of God. Through her, God informed the king, "Because your heart was penitent, and you humbled yourself before the Lord, . . . I also have heard you" (2 Kings 22:19). Josiah gained divine approval because his heart was right with God.

True restoration of the Christian faith can result only when proper attitudes, motivated by genuine humility, are displayed. Only the humble heart can produce the frame of mind that will accept the will of God, wherever it may lead. Only the humble person will recognize that he does not have all the answers, that he can be mistaken, and that he must ever be ready to revise his conclusions in the interest of eternal truth. Many religious leaders, having begun a search for genuine Christianity, have failed when they stumbled over their own pride.

Dedicated Study

When Josiah realized that his people did not know the recently discovered Law of Moses, he ordered that it be publicly read. "Then the king sent, and all the elders of Judah and Jerusalem were gathered to him. And the king went up to the house of the Lord, and with him all the men of Judah and all the inhabitants of Jerusalem, and the priests and the prophets, all the people, both small and great; and he read in their hearing all the words of the book of the covenant which had been found in the house of the Lord" (2 Kings 23:1, 2).

Since copies of the law were unavailable, the word of God had to be read to the people. Today we have a great advantage. The Bible is available to all for an insignificant cost. Most people can read. Though oral explanation by Bible teachers is most helpful, there is no substitute for personal study of the written word. Commentaries on the scriptures can help us determine the meaning, but they should never replace personal reading of God's message.

By examining the New Testament directly, each one can discover for himself the nature of the early church and the faith by which it lived.

Commitment to Truth

Once the law of God had been found, King Josiah had to make a decision. Would he comply with what he had learned? His attitude was clear. "And the king stood by the pillar and made a covenant before the Lord, to walk after the Lord and to keep his commandments and his testimonies and his statutes, with all his heart and all his soul, to perform the words of his covenant that were written in this book; and all the people joined in the covenant" (2 Kings 23:3).

Josiah was committed to truth! It is one thing to accept truth when it causes us no inconvenience, but another to pursue it when it requires changing our patterns of life. Am I willing to give up my friends, and even my family if necessary, rather than surrender what I know is right? This is the price we must be prepared to pay in following Christ. Some Jewish leaders in the time of Jesus faced this problem. "Nevertheless many even of the authorities believed in him, but for fear of the Pharisees they did not confess it, lest they should be put out of the synagogue: for they loved the praise of men more than the praise of God" (John 12:42, 43). Doubtless these rulers wanted to follow Jesus, but they lacked the commitment to truth which required that they pay the price of excommunication from the synagogue. So it is with us. Without such a commitment we will never succeed in recovering the substance of biblical Christianity.

An Open Mind

When Josiah learned that the Law of Moses had been found, he immediately wanted to know the implications of the discovery. He instructed his servants, "Go, inquire of the Lord for me, and for the people, and for all Judah, concerning the words of this book that has been found" (2 Kings 22:13).

Josiah had an open mind. He knew enough about the law to realize that a fuller investigation might not prove favorable to him and his people. He could have shut the book at that point, choosing not to learn what he knew might be disturbing. He might even have rationalized that since he had previously ordered the refurbishing of the temple, his restoration was complete and no further changes were necessary. He could have reasoned that since he had already done so much, God would not have held him accountable for his ignorance. But this was not Josiah's nature. He had a mind receptive to any new truth it might discover.

In searching for the right way we may find a position with which we are uncomfortable. When this occurs, there is a temptation to cease our quest and close our minds. We then become more concerned with defending the status quo than in probing more deeply into the meaning of the scriptures. At this point it is easy to develop a dogmatic spirit which will not allow questioning, or further examination of our conclusions. Many reformatory efforts have failed because men thought they had found all the truth. Often this occurs when a person acquires a thorough knowledge of God's will in a single area. He may overlook the fact that there remain other fields yet to be explored. If we succeed in reproducing the outward forms of the early church, it does not necessarily follow that we have also realized the implications of such other matters as commitment and holy living. Because restoration is a continuing process we must always be receptive to any new insights to which we may be exposed.

Reformation of Practice

After Josiah learned the will of God, he knew that idolatry could no longer be tolerated in the land. Even the temple was contaminated with vessels used in the worship of the god Baal. Idolatrous priests abounded in the kingdom. Josiah realized that his reformation would never be complete until he put into practice what he had already accepted in theory. He immediately instituted reforms designed to rid the country of every vestige of idolatry (2 Kings 23:4-25). Never before had the nation undergone so thorough a spiritual housecleaning.

It is not enough to accept, in principle only, the theory of restoring apostolic Christianity. Theory must be translated into practice. You can express platitudes about the importance of helping the poor, but it is valueless unless you do something to meet the need. We can also acknowledge the importance of restoring the original religion of Jesus, but such an admission has little meaning apart from an effort to make it a reality.

Finally . . .

The continuing quest for the true faith must be carried out on two levels—the congregational and the individual. The two are related because the congregation is a collective of individuals who have banded together to work for the Lord. No congregation can accomplish in unison what its members are unwilling to do individually. A congregation endeavoring to restore apostolic Christianity must commit itself to the principles we have considered. These include a recognition of the lordship of Jesus, the acceptance of the authority of the word of God in spiritual matters, the concept of the undenominational church, and the restoration of New Testament Christianity. If a congregation truly commits itself to these principles, in practice as well as in theory, it may justly profess to be a church of Jesus Christ.

And what of the individual Christian? He should associate with a congregation that is striving to be non-sectarian and to follow the apostolic pattern. However, he should also recognize that no congregation is perfect. Even among churches diligently seeking to copy the divine model, there will be sin and sectarianism. This is because congregations are composed of human beings subject to the frailties that all of us possess. These people are part of the body of Christ, not because they are perfect, but because they are imperfect and need the Lord. As such they will often fall short of the divine example. When one becomes aware of this fact, it is easy to become disenchanted and to conclude that he is associated with the wrong people. But Christians need to learn to bear with one another in their shortcomings. If a congregation is truly committed to New Testament Christianity, then the individual member of that body who is aware of these weaknesses will devote his efforts to helping that church more nearly conform to the will of God.

What if this congregation is not committed to the principles of undenominational Christianity? If there is no true commitment nor any hope that there will be, the non-sectarian Christian should cast his lot with those who do acknowledge these principles.

The faith of each Christian must first be rooted in Jesus Christ. Religious leaders make mistakes. Congregations depart from Christ. These things can shake the faith of the conscientious truthseeker. But if your eye is fixed on Jesus, you will not fall and your spiritual needs will be met. It was Jesus who promised, "Blessed are those who hunger and thirst for righteousness, for they shall be satisfied" (Matthew 5:6). Jesus keeps his promises.

Monroe E. Hawley